International studies in the history of sport
series editor J. A. Mangan

Sport and the working class in modern Britain

For Stephen Glyn Jones
1957–87

This collection of essays is dedicated to the memory of one of the contributors whose career was tragically cut short at an early age. His extensive published work will remain of enduring value; witness to an energy and intellect which will always be missed by those who knew him and all who work in the field.

Sport and the working class in modern Britain

edited by
Richard Holt

Manchester University Press
Manchester and New York

Distributed exclusively in the USA and Canada by St. Martin's Press

Copyright © Manchester University Press 1990

Whilst copyright in the volume as a whole is vested in
Manchester University Press, copyright in the individual
chapters belongs to their respective authors, and no chapter
may be reproduced wholly or in part without the express
permission in writing of both author and publishers.

Published by Manchester University Press
Oxford Road, Manchester M13 9PL, UK
and Room 400, 175 Fifth Avenue,
New York, NY 10010, USA

Distributed exclusively in the USA and Canada
by St. Martin's Press, Inc.,
175 Fifth Avenue, New York, NY 10010, USA

British Library cataloguing in publication data

Sport and the working class in modern Britain.-
  (International studies in the history of sport; ISSN
  0955–8284).
  1. Great Britain. Working classes. Leisure activies,
  history
  I. Holt, Richard, *1948 Apr. 19-* II. Series
  306.48'0880623

Library of Congress cataloging in publication data

Sport and the working class in modern Britain/edited by
  Richard Holt.
      p. cm. -- (International studies in the history of
      sport
    ISBN 0–7190–2650–4.
    1. Sports—Great Britain—History. 2. Working class—
    Great
  Britain—Recreation—History. I. Holt, Richard. 1948-
  II. Series.
  GV605.S725   1990
  796'.0941—dc20   89-49177

ISBN 0 7190 2650 4

Printed in Great Britain
by Billing & Sons Ltd., Worcester

Contents

Contents

Figures and tables

Series editor's foreword

In my introduction to the Series in the first volume – Stephen Jones's *Sport, politics and the working class: organised labour and sport in inter-war Britain*, I suggested that the contributors to the Series would prove to be 'historiens–sociologues' rather than 'historiens–historisants' due, among other things, to their interest in change within specific cultural contexts. This collection of essays focused on the British working class, edited by Richard Holt, serves attractively to prove my point.

In addition, with its concentration on the relationship between British working-class culture and sport, it sits well with Stephen Jones's consideration of the role of the British labour movement in the development of British sport between 1918 and 1940, and Nicholas Fishwick's study of the impact of soccer on the lives of English working-class men and women between 1910 and 1950; the second volume of the Series entitled *English football and society, 1910 – 1950*. These three early volumes in the Series offer interestingly complementary perspectives to the reader, but more importantly, they provide a great deal of new material about the close relationship of the working class with modern organised sport, a subject hitherto largely neglected by historians.

Holt's Introduction is typically stimulating and raises important questions which will occupy and indeed preoccupy social historians for some time to come. He is certainly right to draw attention to popular sport's lack of, in his own elegant phrase, 'graceful essays and handsome books' and to urge, in lieu, close scrutiny of newspaper sources and the promotion of the oral historical method.

He is perhaps just a little too romantic in his moralistic view of an upper-class 'amateur elite with its Olympian priorities and self-imposed code of fair play'. It has yet to be widely recognised that the concept of 'fair play' was initially a self-serving and practical device promoting cohesion and reducing anarchy in the late nineteenth-century public school system.

His essayists, for their part, with a range of contributions covering the role of individual 'stars' (and clubs) in creating a sense of communal and even national identity, 'submerged traditions' and their resilience, obsessions and their potency, and the determined longevity of attempts at moral improvement through the leisure movement, provide both theoretical and empirical riches for social historians.

G.M. Trevelyan once wrote that if the French aristocracy had played cricket there would have been no French Revolution. Clearly fanciful nonsense, however it does hint at the power of sport to act at times as a cement bonding the social classes, and the evidence of this process at work in the case of league cricket is an especially interesting element in this volume. Even more attractive perhaps is the subtlety of analysis these studies offer in their collective emphasis on the heterogeneity rather than the homogeneity of working-class culture. This stress of divergence rather than convergence is pleasing not only within the framework of social class but in its wider relationship to nation, region and district.

This volume blazes several exploratory trails but, as Holt makes clear, there remains a 'large forest' for academic adventurers to explore before these trails make any sizeable impression on the 'landscape' of popular sport. Arguably the most valuable contribution these essays could make to social history would be to stimulate other trail-blazers.

J.A. Mangan

Acknowledgements

I would first of all like to thank the general editor, J. A. Mangan, for suggesting I contribute to this significant and innovatory series. Without his invitation this collection would probably not have seen the light of day. Then, odd though it may seem, I must thank the contributors themselves for responding so politely and constructively to intermittent requests for work or revisions from an editor whose own creative input was limited to commenting upon the hard work of others.

My chief debt is to Neil Tranter, the perfect colleague and collaborator. The original idea of commissioning essays on neglected aspects of popular sports arose in conversation with him. He read and commented on a number of these essays with speed, good sense and good humour. Finally, Margaret Dickson has been very helpful, typing, and retyping material quickly and competently in her usual cheerful manner. Margaret Hendry also helped in the final preparation of the typescript.

Introduction

There is nothing like attempting a synthesis to show up the gaps in a subject. This, at least, was what I found when I tried to write a social history of sport in modern Britain.[1] Inevitably and at times embarrassingly reliant upon the work of others, the generalist soon becomes aware of those areas where there is already a rich vein of original research. More gradually, areas of patchy coverage and unexplored topics come to light, which make up a kind of hidden agenda of work to be done. It was with this in mind that I put out feelers to a number of established scholars in the field of the history of British sport and working-class culture asking if they could help either by writing an essay themselves or putting me in touch with others doing relevant research. I had been particularly impressed by three collections of original essays on the social history of popular recreation edited by Walton and Walvin, Storch, and by Eileen and Stephen Yeo; hence editing a collection of a similar kind, partly linking popular sports with major themes in recent social history but also striking out in new directions, seemed a good idea.[2]

For, despite the remarkable upsurge in good-quality writing on the economic and social history of British sport in recent years, the world of popular sport remains in many ways less well understood than that of the gentleman amateur and public-school athleticism. Consider for a moment the paucity of writing on league rugby and cricket as opposed to the dominant 'national' forms. There is an entire dimension of sport in the industrial communities of Britain which, though vigorous and successful, has been largely ignored by the amateur elite with its Olympian priorities and self-imposed code of fair play; nor has popular sport been celebrated by its followers with graceful essays and handsome books. Much of the lore of popular

1

sport has been passed on by word of mouth from father to son. Hence the enormous importance of the rise of the local newspaper in the mid nineteenth century. Such papers, more responsive to the rising literacy of the working class than national newspapers or even the official sporting press, supplemented where possible by oral evidence, are the main source for the serious study of this 'submerged' tradition of popular recreation.

All of the contributors to this volume have made use of the pronounced interest of the press at all levels for sport and several have searched systematically through long runs of relatively little known newspapers. Even Douglas Reid's work, which unlike the other contributions has to fall back upon the 'stamped' press of the first half of the nineteenth century, demonstrates the value of exhaustive searching of the relevant newspapers. Painstaking scrutiny of the local press is most remarkably illustrated in Tranter's use of the *Stirling Journal* to trace references to quoiters and the checking of their names against census data to provide a precise social breakdown of participants. Similarly, Metcalfe's study of the Newcastle press permits a surprisingly vivid and detailed reconstruction of bowling amongst the miners of East Northumberland. He has been able to calculate the number of matches held and the shift towards longer-run handicap tournaments primarily through searching the *Newcastle Journal* and the *Newcastle Daily Chronicle*. What would historians of earlier periods give for such sources for all their partialities and imperfections?

Of course, it is not merely the fate of traditional sports that can be studied in this way. Neglected aspects of modern sports also come to light. For example, Bowker's careful examination of the *Ashton-under-Lyne Reporter* allows us to glimpse for the first time something of the process by which an inter-war local authority moved towards wider provision of sporting facilities. Williams uses the Saturday 'specials', in his case the *Buff* (*Bolton Evening News, Saturday sports edition*), alongside even smaller papers such as the *Radcliffe Times* and the *Farnworth Weekly Journal* to bring back to life the dense network of local cricket clubs with their fierce rivalries and ties of sociability. Jeff Hill's study is of the larger league cricket clubs and so he has been able to use club records alongside the local press.

Both Hill and Williams were able to supplement the written sources with interviews and this trend to oral history will surely open more locked doors. For the unit upon which so much of working-class sporting life was built – the private club – remains in some respects a kind of secret society with its informal social network, ties of family and friendship, and even perhaps its own patterns of courtship and marriage. Anyone who could crack the 'social code' of a single club could produce a fascinating piece of historical anthropology. But those who consider this should be warned by my own failure. Time is short, as I found when several of the informants for a projected essay on an inter-war athletics club on Tyneside died before I could talk to them. Korr too makes good use of interviewing individuals involved with West Ham and Dai Smith's fulsome tribute to his informants on Welsh boxing give a measure of the importance which oral evidence used alongside and checked against conventional sources can provide.

Making 'submerged' traditions and cultural identities more visible is the purpose behind this volume, but of what do they really consist? The contributions here were not collected at random from work in progress but with particular questions in mind. First, how popular and persistent were certain 'traditional' sports in nineteenth-century Britain? It may be that rumours of their sudden demise as a result of the 'modernization' of sport have been greatly exaggerated. Second, how much do we know about the actual patterns and structure of participation either in older or for that matter newer forms of sport? How working men took part in sport, who they were and what, if any, facilities were provided for them comprise a vast question which engages several of the contributors and adds a few more building blocks to what is going to be a long task of ethnographic construction. Thirdly, what can we say that is new about the world of professional sport? Despite the endless journalistic discussion of great moments and great men, we really know very little about the kinds of meaning that have been attached to professional sporting performance either through the veneration of a particular club or individual. 'Stars in their courses', as Moorhouse says, 'send complex signals'. It may sound odd to ask 'what did Stanley Matthews *mean* to millions of football fans' but it is a fair question and one to which Tony Mason provides a thoughtful answer here.

Despite the remarkable growth in the social and cultural history of the nineteenth century in recent years, there remain a group of popular activities whose appeal is still obscure. Of these, cruel sports like cockfighting or bull-baiting are perhaps best known through pioneering works like Malcomson's *Popular Recreations in English Society* or the researches of Brian Harrison on moral reform movements like the RSPCA.[3] The view of popular sports, especially animal ones, which comes across is the one 'from above'. But what of the view 'from below'? This is what draws Douglas Reid 'with a certain fascinated distaste' to bull-baiting and cock-fighting. These sports fought long and hard against the attempts at suppression by the outraged conscience of middle-class evangelicals and radical, improving artisans. Even after the introduction of the 'new model' police forces – the key instruments of prohibition – and the banning of cockfighting altogether in 1849, a covert tradition continued around 'fighting' pubs until the activities of the licensing authorities finally stamped out the sport in all but more remote rural areas. This, then, was a tale not so much of gradual decline as of active suppression. Had cock-fighting not been banned, it would presumably have continued to thrive as it did in northern France into the twentieth century.

The vigour of customary sports generally is even more evident in other activities less repugnant to the Victorian conscience and in consequence even more obscure, such as bowling and quoits. The articles by Tranter and Metcalfe try within the limits of the surviving evidence to resurrect the vitality and meaning of these forgotten pleasures, placing them in their local and regional context, uncovering their habitual forms and the values that shaped them. The undimmed popularity of both these sports in the late nineteenth century despite the advent of football is most striking. Metcalfe estimates that the combined support for fives, quoits and bowling among the Northumbrian miners around the turn of the century was as great as their love of football. Tranter similarly points to the success of quoits in certain communities around Stirling where, according to the *Stirling Journal* in 1897, 'nearly every village has it club and the game has almost entirely supplanted football'. Journalistic licence notwithstanding, this is an important claim which has somehow been overlooked in the rush to establish the dominance of the People's Game.

There are other arresting features of such sports apart from the simple fact of their survival and success. They drew, for example, not only on younger but also on older men. Metcalfe's Davy Bell of Benton started bowling at fifteen and carried on into his fifties. Over a quarter of the quoiters whose ages Tranter can trace were over forty. The middle aged have been unreasonably excluded from the history of sport through our obsession with activities which require exceptional energy as opposed to great experience and stamina. Of the major sports, only cricket has kept a place for the ordinary ageing sportsman as Williams shows in his study of Bolton.

Another distinctive feature of traditional sports has been their obsession with gambling. The frenzied betting which took place at cockfights is well known but less familiar is the extent to which other customary sports were largely organised around creating opportunities for gambling. Tranter has even been able to tabulate the amounts involved and Metcalfe provides details of the wagers of 'match' contestants – eighty-two matches in 1906 with sums ranging from £5 to £100 – and the extensive side-betting that accompanied them. Small wonder the Victorian amateur elite with their cultivation of games for 'character-building' either ignored or denounced these survivals from a time when all sportsmen – gentleman and commoner – were happy to stake money on the outcome of a sporting event. The persistent fascination with gambling and its newer as well as older forms emerges from Steve Jones's wide-ranging survey of popular sports in Manchester. Boxing had always attracted punters and its popular success was enormous as Jones indicates and Smith reveals in greater detail in setting the scene for his Welsh fighting heroes. Greyhound racing provided the single most important new outlet for gambling and profit-seeking proprietors of tracks were even known to provide makeshift baby-minding facilities to attract young mothers.

All this was in sharp conflict with the tradition of moral improvement through leisure ('rational recreation') which has been extensively analysed for the nineteenth century.[4] The current verdict that it failed or died out needs some revision in the light of the contributions of both Jones and Bowker, or for that matter the evidence of Williams, who found that the bulk of cricket clubs had Church affiliations. Much of Steve Jones's extensive published work on sport and leisure in inter-war Britain revolved around the conflict between moral reformers, frequently on the left but also of the right, and commercial influences seeking to provide amusement for the masses. However, as Bowker reveals, there were serious obstacles to large-scale participation in sport because of the lack of facilities and the reluctance of councillors to spend the rate-payers money to provide them. Significantly, the largest items of recreational expenditure in Ashton-under-Lyne were on swimming baths – tremendously successful in the 1920s – and public parks, both harking back to a

Victorian ideal of improvement through cleanliness, health and the family contemplation of a carefully sculptured 'nature'. Spending money on football and cricket pitches was slow despite the efforts of pressures groups like the National Playing Fields Association. Space forever lagged behind demand and pitches were often of atrocious quality – a fact attested by many of the 'wickets' in the Bolton area according to Williams.

There are, of course, many books about cricket, some of them elegantly written and well-researched, but relatively little has been written about the working-class professional and even less about the enormously popular 'league' form of cricket in Lancashire and Yorkshire. Devotees of the 'first-class' game maintained almost a conspiracy of silence about alternatives to county cricket. It took a West Indian Marxist intellectual, C.L.R. James, a companion of Learie Constantine in the great days of his Lancashire League appearances in the 1930s, to state the obvious. Until Jeff Hill's recent work, a further instalment of which is included here, the subject of a competitive one-day cricket as a working-class spectator sport had hardly been even recognised let alone explored.[5]

League cricket was not simply important because it provided paid entertainment for a specific market. It is interesting in the way it mobilised not just working men but also business people below the rank of the prestigious liberal professions and gentry who shared a public-school background and controlled the county game. Although the larger league cricket clubs could be quite exclusive – a useful discovery in its own right which qualifies its cloth cap image – league cricket as a whole provides useful evidence of inter-class contact and co-operation, especially at the recreational level examined by Williams. The solidarity of British society in the 1930s, which exasperated Orwell and satisfied men like Baldwin, perhaps owed at least something to the vigour with which voluntary associations continued to be a force within the dense network of popular leisure activities; however, it must be stressed that neither Jones or Williams give much importance to the rather limited provision of recreational facilities by employers. Crude domination by the lure of sporting and other perks was not seriously considered. The affirmation of social authority – 'hegemony' in neo-Marxist terms – was the more or less unintended product of religious and social contact outside the workplace or arose from the willingness of local worthies to continue long-standing family traditions by agreeing to be club 'patrons' – a topic worthy of further investigation.

The subtlety of class division and interpenetration emerging here accords well the wider emphasis on continuity, resilience and adaptation, which has been a feature of some of the best recent work on working-class experience under industrialisation. Crude economic determinism and the idea of homogenous class formation and consciousness are being replaced by more complex accounts which give due weight to the continuing strength of pre-industrial traditions, of persistence of certain forms of paternalistic behaviour as well as the profound importance of local and regional identities. The 'labour history' approach to the life of urban industrial society has tended to talk the language of class solidarity within an emerging national framework. Not until a few of the bohemian bourgeoisie ventured out in the late 1930s under the name 'Mass Observation' to record the cultural as opposed to the economic characteristics of the working class was there much intellectual interest in what working people actually did in pubs, at the seaside, in the cinema or elsewhere.[6] Richard Hoggart picked up this thread in *The Uses of Literacy* in the late 1950s but confined himself to the conflict between 'real' experience – lived, rooted in habits of language and thought – and the growth of mass journalism. Hoggart said relatively little about sport, but the emergence and increasing appeal of popular culture as a subject for serious study owe much to his work as well as that of Edward Thompson's emphasis on the self-creating powers of working-class culture in *The Making of the English Working Class*. The more literary and conceptually orientated work of Raymond Williams, which along with Thompson helped to move Marxism away from a crude determination of culture by economics, completes what is now a familiar trinty of influences. Unfortunately for the historian the work of Hoggart and Williams has been more important in stimulating conceptual rather than ethnographic research.[7] Moreover with the notable exception of Williams, whose own Welshness was of real importance to him, Hoggart and Thompson in their different ways have, quite reasonably, rather English priorities. However, the diversity of Britain, let alone the United Kingdom, requires greater awareness of the differing national cultures within the union.[8]

This brief excursion into the historiography of popular culture serves as an introduction to the final set of essays in the collection. These examine the ways in which solidarities of class are mediated through, or even overshadowed, by powerful loyalties of locality and nationality. Sport has been an exceptionally important vehicle in creating and sustaining a sense of place. Charles Korr uses West Ham's annus mirabilis of 1923 to explain the creation of a new kind of East End sporting community, an invented local tradition which grew up around the identity of the club. Winning promotion to the First Division and a place in the first Wembley Cup Final coincided with a shift in the nature of the East End economy towards recession in the midst of outer-London affluence. This, in turn, fostered a belief in the distinctiveness of West Ham with its friendly, 'family' style and traditions, attractive if ineffective method of play, its locally produced players and resistance to the flashiness and extravagance of its larger London rivals. How much of the image was based on fact is quite another matter. But, as Korr argues, this is less important than the fact that large numbers of supporters wanted to believe in 'the West Ham way of doing things'.

Enormous local pride could focus on a single player who might be held to embody the essence of an entire region. This, as Mason shows, was the fate of Stanley Matthews, at least in his earlier years, as he rose to become the most famous son of the Potteries. When there was speculation about his transfer from Stoke in 1938 an extraordinary committee of leading employers demanded his retention in the name of their area and their employees. Subsequent events conspired to loosen the grip of his legend on the area without ever breaking it. Meanwhile the quiet barber's son had moved on and greater symbolic responsibilities were thrust upon him. He became no less than a popular embodiment of decent 'Englishness' rather like Jack Hobbs had been in the 1920s. His modesty, craftsmanship, good conduct, cool nerve and 'unassailable commonsense' were rewarded in the Wembley final of 1953 where he engineered a late victory for Blackpool against Bolton and crowned his career with a cup winners's medal. This made him the first English footballer to become a truly national celebrity in the sense of being admired not only in the north and the south but throughout the social hierarchy as well.

This modest kind of hero was not the sort with which the public of either Scotland or Wales could really identify. They produced their own kind of stars with their own distinctive cultural meanings. For great players may represent different and even conflicting elements of a composite national culture. As Moorhouse shows, beneath the unifying Scottish working-class devotion to football as a form of national expression, there are fissures both in terms of the antagonistic relationship to England and in their attitudes to each other. Scottish football stars have rarely escaped the controversies surrounding the steady drain of good players to England (the 'Anglo' problem) or the bitter rivalry of Catholic and Protestant. The kind of stars the Scots have most appreciated often dramatise some or all of these ambiguities; 'partial and unpredictable, proud and put-upon', the erratic genius rather than the stable artisan, Jim Baxter casually juggling the ball from foot to chest against the England team that had won the World Cup the year before – such is the true Scottish hero.

Moorhouse's 'emblematic figures' find an echo in Dai Smith's 'focal heroes'. His boxers too have a heavy burden of national expectation upon them but Wilde, Welsh and Driscoll were far from a uniform crew of patriots in their Edwardian heyday. Jim Driscoll, for example, with his Irish roots and charitable Catholic work in Cardiff cuts a very different figure from Freddie Welsh whose Yankee glamour and internationalism struck a different note in the hearts of those who had stayed at home but yearned in some part of themselves to wander and seek their fortune. Then later there was Tommy Farr, the supreme expression of the heroic loser, the honest battler from Tonypandy, who stayed the course with the great Joe Louis, epitomising the spirit of a people defeated by the Depression but still clinging to their dignity and belief in themselves.

All sorts of other important issues are raised in these essays and deserve further study. The social participation of women in working-class sport, for example, could be explored in a host of activities from cricket to athletics, swimming and even football. The role of women as participants needs to be taken further than the history of middle-class schoolgirls.[9] Flat and crown green bowling is another place to look for female involvement – and how, to follow another lead, was bowls integrated into the holiday calendar, especially in Blackpool? Precious little is known about the playing of darts, billiards or snooker beyond a few great names; similarly the extraordinary world of pigeon racing still needs a proper study. Bowker's data on the use of swimming baths is suggestive but this most popular of sporting recreations remains something of a mystery. Much the same could be said for the many athletics clubs which might never have had a AAA's champion but met, ran and drank as a group, going off to dances and on country walks together. Walking as a sport and a recreation also needs further work – race-walking would make an excellent topic – and further clarification of status of the 'hiker' as opposed to the

Introduction

more exclusive 'rambler' would be welcome. Whilst new research has
begun to unravel the strange regional patterns of Rugby League
more needs to be done and the Scottish Borders surely deserve the
kind of enduring tribute which Dai Smith and Gareth Williams gave
to Wales in *Fields of Praise*.[10]

And so it goes on, the itinerary is almost endless. In short, the
history of popular sports in Britain is still wide open. It ranges from
economics to sociology to anthropology, from profits and professionalism, to social structure and patterns of culture. Perhaps future
studies will try to integrate all these elements. Certainly it is to be
hoped that the essays collected here point the way to a more complete
account of the complexity and richness of the relationship between
sport and the British working class than we have at present.

Richard Holt

Notes

1 R. Holt, *Sport and the British: a Modern History* (Oxford, 1989).
2 J. Walton and J. Walvin, *Leisure in Britain 1780–1939* (Manchester, 1983);
 R.D. Storch, *Popular Culture and Custom in Nineteenth Century England* (London,
 1982); E. and S. Yeo, *Popular Culture and Class Conflict 1590–1914: Explorations
 in the History of Labour and Leisure* (Brighton, 1981); see also the useful theme-
 based collections on middle-class sport and gender edited by J.A. Mangan
 and R.J. Park, *From Fair Sex to Feminism* (London, 1987); and J.A. Mangan and
 J. Walvin, *Manliness and Morality* (Manchester, 1987).
3 R.W.L Malcolmson, *Popular Recreation in English Society 1700–1850* (Cambridge, 1979 edn); B. Harrison, 'Animals and the state in nineteenth
 century England', *English Historical Review*, vol 88, (October 1973).
4 The most recent and reliable survey of what is now a large literature is
 F.M.L. Thompson, *The Rise of Respectable Society: a social history of Victorian
 Britain 1830–1900* (London, 1988), esp. chs 6 and 7.
5 C.L.R. James, *Beyond a Boundary* (London, 1963); the issue and the
 'invisibility' of the League form is raised explicitly by J. Hill in ' "First class"
 cricket and the leagues', *International Journal of the History of Sport*, 4, (May
 1987).
6 T. Harrison and C. Madge, *Britain by 'Mass Observation'* (London, 1986 edn).
7 The whole debate over the historiography of leisure is admirably summar-
 ised with full references by P. Bailey, 'Leisure, culture and the historian:
 reviewing the first generation of leisure historiography in Britain', *Leisure
 Studies*, 8, (1989).
8 K. Robbins, *Nineteenth Century Britain: Integration and Diversity* (Oxford, 1988),
 esp. ch. 6.
9 The early history of female sport has recently been thoroughly examined
 by K.E. McCrone, *Sport and the Physical Emancipation of English Women 1870–*

1914 (London, 1988); significantly there is no entry in the index for 'working class'.

10 D. Smith and G. Williams, *Fields of Praise: the Official History of the Welsh Rugby Union 1881–1981* (Cardiff, 1981).

1

Beasts and brutes: popular blood sports c. 1780–1860

Douglas A. Reid

In this essay I explore the history of bull-baiting and cock-fighting, both because of the intrinsic interest in investigating an unrespectable part of the past, and because it may shed further light on the propensity of men to indulge in brutal sport. So, with a certain fascinated distaste, I have tried to see these sports from the point of view of their supporters, in a case study focused on Birmingham, and, to a lesser extent, on the wider West Midlands. Birmingham and Wednesbury were great centres of cock-fighting, and bull-baiting was 'particularly prevalent' in the West Midlands as a whole.[1] Several questions need to be posed. To what extent was bull-baiting declining already by 1800, as some contemporaries asserted? When did it take place in the calendar of festivity? How was it organised? Why was it enjoyed? How far was it a matter of 'sport', how far one of tradition? In what ways was cruelty inflicted on the bull? How was this defended? How and why did the sport finally decline? Similar questions are raised about cock-fighting. Broadly, while the evidence points to a substantial plebeian following for brutal sports, we can distinguish between bull-baiting, which was more of a plebeian festivity, and cock-fighting, in which a commercialised and aristocratically patronised sector heavily influenced the sport, particularly in Birmingham, the metropolis of the region. Despite legislative prohibitions a pub-centred sub-culture of brutal sports was sustained well into the second half of the nineteenth century, though by then they had begun to lose their cultural centrality as they were forced underground and as other diversions beckoned to the working-class population.

I

How far – as William Windham paradoxically asserted in its defence –

was bull-baiting in decline by 1800?[2] To judge from West Midlands accounts the sport was still thriving well into the 1820s, at least. Thus, in 1851 a bourgeois witness remembered that 'the popular sports in Birmingham . . . were, till within about twenty-five years ago, bull-baiting, cock-fighting, badger-baiting, and bear-baiting. These were the great favourites of the working men'.[3] In the town itself the last bull-baiting apparently took place in 1811, but it had only migrated to the suburbs away from the parish constables, where it survived, with crowds more than a thousand strong, until 1840.[4] Moreover, Birmingham men were 'greatly implicated in the evils of the practice' in the Black Country, 'not only by resorting in great numbers to the scenes of action, but also by feeding and training the dogs which are employed on such occasions'.[5] Although there were offensives against the Tipton and Bilston Wakes in the mid 1820s, at Oldbury the later 1820s saw 'more bulls brought to the stake' than had been known 'for several years past', and the sport was flourishing at Wednesbury.[6] Thus bull-baiting did not simply fade away – it had to be suppressed.

Who were the chief supporters of bull baiting? It was undoubtedly a thoroughly popular sport: the 'working population', 'our labouring classes', the 'operative classes', were the terms used to describe its aficionados. However, 'some portion of their employers', especially 'small manufacturers' were also said to be involved.[7] The chief actors were men – they trained the dogs, and handled them and the bull, but there is also clear evidence that women and children were present in the crowds.[8] For example, it was recalled in the 1870s that 'ladies . . . went in crowds to see a bull bait or a prize fight as they now go to see a race'.[9]

A witness recalled that 'for weeks before a Bull-baiting was arranged to take place in any of the Black Country towns excitement ran high in joyful anticipation of the day's sport'.[10] It usually took place during the summer 'wake' holidays, especially on the Mondays and Tuesdays.

At the country wakes it was quite common to have three or four bulls to bait, and on one occasion, in the year 1798 . . . no less than seven bulls [were] placed in a row to be baited on a level piece of ground close to a church in the neighbourhood of the town. The ground was about 150 yards long by about 40 yards wide. Generally, when a bull was baited at a country wake near the town . . . it was brought into Birmingham on the Wednesday afternoon and baited again. These were chance baitings, however. The regular matches were got up during the holidays or wakes in town.

Such was the frequency of the wakes that one bull 'was often baited on three or four successive Mondays'.

> The first baiting took place early in the morning, and lasted for about an hour; after breakfast the bull was again brought out and baited for about the same time, and in the afternoon and evening the scene was repeated, so that the bull was generally baited for about four hours a day. The intervals were filled up with cock-fighting, badger-baiting, or bear-baiting.[11]

How was the bull paid for? At Burslem Wake, in North Stafford-shire, the 'bull-ward' – a farmer or a butcher perhaps – would visit publicans and offer, for a fee, to have his bull baited next to their pubs to attract people. Publicans undoubtedly solicited such visits.[12] Dog owners themselves were charged anything between 6d and 2s for a four or five minutes assault on the bull, and if they ran out of money then they passed the hat round the crowd for more. In addition the bull-ward might give a prize – a tea kettle or warming pan was mentioned – to the owner of the dog which pinned the bull's nose most often.[13] It is worth noting a certain measure of prosperous assistance – viz. the payment of fines for arrested bullards.[14] On the other hand, there is also evidence of that prominent feature of working men's culture – collective self-help – in connection with bull-baiting:

> it was customary for the workmen to club together a sufficient sum to purchase [a bull]. . . . The animal was brought forward early on the Monday of the wake, and whoever had a dog paid 6d or 1s to let it have a fly at the bull. The proceeds went to pay for the bull, which was sold after the baiting.[15]

After the baiting the animal sometimes lived to fight another day, as we shall see; sometimes it went for slaughter, and its meat was sold cheaply. At Bilston, for example, in the 1820s, a baited bull which had escaped and terrorised the town was shot and its carcase 'sold to the poor people at twopence a pound'.[16]

Why were bulls baited? In the first place, it was customary. As Bob Bushaway has stressed, custom had a peculiar force in eighteenth- and nineteenth-century society.[17] Secondly, the common people lived rough lives, and enjoyed rough, unrefined pleasures. To them it was simply an amusement utilising resources at hand. Thus when the vicar of Darlaston tried to suppress the sport – acting as a magistrate presumably – their response was: 'I say it's a nation shame to stop our sport; he has his fun in sorm [psalm] singing, and whoy don't he let us have our fun.'[18] Above all, bull-baiting was probably regarded by the common people as a matter of good 'sport' – that is, as a matter of spectacle, uncertainty and excitement, in a period when there were few alternative traditions. In the recollection of a nonagenarian buckle-maker in 1851 bull-baiting was classed alongside 'cock-fighting. . . skittle-playing, quoits, foot-ball, leapfrog, etc.' as a 'manly amusement' – 'manly' because it was associated with other outdoor sports, and because it contrasted with sedentary indoor activities of the 1840s.[19] In the popular ballad of 'Darlaston Wake Bull-Baiting' the dominant impression is given that a bull-bait was memorable when it offered 'rare good game' – that is to say, when it was exciting because the bull was lively, and because it was not a one-sided contest, as, for example, when a dog 'pin'd him fast by the groin/ which caused them rare good fun'.[20] Gambling also played its part in creating excitement – one man is recorded as betting 'two gallons o' . . . ale, as how my pup pinned the bull by the nose first run'; another one bet 'tankards round, that the bull would toss his bitch'.[21] Finally, there was the prevalent legitimating belief – based on no-longer enforced bye-laws – that the sale of bull beef was illegal unless the animal had been baited, in order to tenderise the meat.[22] Thus the common people were at the tail-end of a tradition which dated back centuries. However, by 1800 many influential contemporaries had come to regard animal baiting as abhorrent and disgraceful, for both humanitarian and socio-economic reasons.[23]

In what did the cruelty consist in bull-baiting? If one reads its opponents, the bull was said to be by no means naturally aggressive, and had to be goaded into action.[24] However, judging from the testimony of those who referred to the sport's passing in something of a nostalgic tone, it was the dog which suffered. If it did not succeed in fastening itself upon the bull the chances were it would be wounded by the horns, or by the fall after being tossed in the air – unless, that is, it was caught in the working apron of its owner, a gun-smith or a lock-filer perhaps.[25] Another, very unpleasant, recollection spoke of dogs with 'their sides torn open and their entrails protruding'.[26]

Indeed:

> By practice some of the bulls became so conversant with baiting, that
> when in the fields or passing through a town, the boys had only to cry out
> 'A lane! A lane!' to make them immediately assume a posture of defence
> and paw the ground impatient for the attack. These were well known in
> the neighbourhood, and I remember at least five noted 'game' bulls. They
> became so expert in defending themselves that even two dogs at once had
> no chance of success with them. I have seen such a bull toss a couple of
> dogs as lightly as a man might play with a couple of balls. A premium was
> frequently offered to the man who could produce a dog able to touch one
> of these game bulls.

Hence, it was argued, 'there was real sport' in bull-baiting, 'and it was
much less cruel than hunting a fox with a pack of hounds, or spurring
horses almost to death at a race'.[27]

Nevertheless, the dogs did not always come off worst. 'Sometimes
the dog seized the bull by the nose and "pinned" him to the earth, so
that the beast roared and bellowed again, and was brought down
upon its knees.' But, reported this sympathetic witness, 'the people
then shouted out 'Wind, wind!' that is, to let the bull have breath, and
the parties rushed forward to take off the dog' – a difficult
endeavour.[28] However, bulls were sometimes pinned 'between the
hind legs, causing . . . [them] to roar and rave about in great agony'.
By the end of the day 'blood would be dropping from the nose and
other parts of the bull'.[29] Thus, while bull-baiting did have real
sporting merits, such considerations were vastly outweighed by the
sympathy for the sufferings of animals which developed in the early
modern period.[30]

Contemporaries explained the decline of bull-baiting on the one
hand in terms of the Cruelty to Animals Act (1835) and on the other
by 'the growth of a taste for music and for reading' and 'rational
amusements'; only the 'uneducated portion of the workmen and small
manufacturers' were said to be still 'of the old school' by mid
century.[31] Gradual developments were certainly an important source
of popular cultural change in this period.[32] In fact, however, bull-
baiting in Birmingham had been under legal attack since 1773, when
the Street Commissioners had made it a fineable offence 'in any part
of the town', and 1777, when the Magistrates appointed additional
constables in order to enforce the prohibition of bull-baiting and races
at the Wakes, because of their concern to preserve 'the Publick
Peace'.[33] Similarly, in 1798, when a bull was baited in a field behind
the Salutation Inn, Snow Hill, 'in conformity with the wishes of the
respectable inhabitants (who desired to put down the nuisance) the

Birmingham Association – a body of militia voluntary, formed by the trading classes – undertook the formidable task of capturing the bull and dispersing his tormenters'.[34] In 1811 *Aris's Birmingham Gazette* gave publicity to the Attorney-General's opinion that bull-baiting 'in the public highway to the hindrance of business' was an indictable offence. It hoped this decision, would check 'this barbarous and brutal sport'.[35] And indeed 1811 was also the last year when bull-baiting was tolerated in Birmingham itself.[36] Clearly, it is an oversimplication to assert that gradual, voluntary, cultural change was mainly responsible for the decline of the sport. The distribution of political and legal authority formed a crucial context to cultural change, for it informed the perceptions of those who voluntarily gave up bull-baiting.[37]

This is illustrated by the following account of the temporary reprieve of the Darlaston bull-baiting. Jack Probin, a Birmingham gun-maker, who regularly visited Darlaston in pursuit of gun locks, was there for its Wake one year, and he 'found the people stood about in much perplexity; consternation and gloom . . . depicted on every countenance':

'My lads,' said Jack Probin, 'what is the matter? . . . Who's dead, and who is going to be buried?' 'Ah, you may well say who's jid,' said old Muncher. '. . . here's the parson come and stopt the baiting'. . . . 'What's a wake good for I should like to know, if there is no bull.' 'It's a shame' said one, 'A nation shame,' said another; 'Dem the parson,' said one, 'for two pins I'd go and brake his windows.' 'And I'd go and pull him out on it,' said another. 'No, no,' said Probin, 'let us have no disturbance. If Muncher, and old Mo, and Whistling Dick, will join me, we'll go and see the parson. I know we can persuade him to let us have the bull.'. . . They went to the parson. Probin represented that the sudden determination to stop the bull-baiting had given general dissatisfaction, and that if it were intended to put down the sport, in justice to the people they should have sufficient notice, so that some other sports might have been substituted; that if the prohibition were persevered in, some outbreak might reasonably be expected. 'Allow them to have the bull this time,' said he, 'and in a few days let notice be given that no more baiting will be allowed; the object his reverence had in view would be accomplished more mildly, and quite as effectually.'[38]

And this, apparently, was what happened. By the later 1830s bull-baiting was curtailed in places like Darlaston and Wednesbury by magistrates, parsons acting as magistrates, and parish constables, and in the Birmingham suburbs it was finished off by new-model police forces, which effectively eradicated it from the entire region.[39]

II

Clearly, bull-baiting was a spectacular, relatively costly, and out-of-the-ordinary sport. Cock-fighting was much more prevalent, and survived much later. Thus, in 1851, it was asserted that it was 'indulged in almost every day in some part of [Birmingham]', particularly on winter Monday afternoons.[40]

Unlike what seems to have been the overwhelmingly plebeian support for bull-baiting, cock-fighting was a sport which attracted socially superior participation and support – most notoriously from Parson Moreton of Willenhall (1759–1834) – and in Birmingham, in particular, it developed a significant level of commercialisation.[41] In the 1740s regular contests had begun to be held at Duddeston Hall, 'a gentleman's seat, about a mile from Birmingham, fitted up for the reception of company, in imitation of Vauxhall Gardens'.[42] Between the 1790s and the 1810s at least three new cock-pits were created in the town itself.[43] One, in Coleshill Street, was probably that referred to in the following quotation:

> A sort of arena was fitted up for . . . sports [of about half-an-acre in extent, where] . . . the workmen and other young men of the town used very frequently to assemble . . . for playing at foot ball, leap-frog, and other games of the sort; but cock-fighting and more brutal amusements were more popular than healthy games. . . . There was a covered part of the inclosure set aside for cock-fighting, in which a pit was dug for the cocks, and seats were ranged round, so that the fight could be seen by all.

Cock-fights held here often lasted two or three days and 'were attended by thousands of people':

> Contests were got up between two counties, as for instance between Warwickshire and Worcestershire, each side being presided over by some gentleman or nobleman of the respective counties. There were generally two or three grand 'bouts' in the course of a year, and parties came from London, and greater distances, to witness the contest. The number of cocks brought forward on these occasions . . . varied considerably, but generally, on grand occasions, about ten pairs of cocks were pitted against each other before dinner, and ten pairs in the afternoon, with a little badger-baiting or other sport by way of varying the entertainment.

Apart from the spectacle created by flying feathers and gory blows, the other chief attraction of the sport lay in its potential for gambling, because of the uncertainty of the contests. Thus, in 'several instances . . . a cock had apparently killed or utterly subdued its antagonist, and stood crowing over it, when the vanquished suddenly started up and struck the other such a blow as proved fatal'. With 'noblemen and gentlemen' the stakes were high, depending on how many cocks were fighting: 'frequently forty or fifty guineas, and on a grand occasion, as much as 100 guineas were staked upon the result of the fight'.[44]

Working men were also keen on the excitement and potential gains of gambling 'whatever money they could spare'. For particularly important matches in the Black Country towns, it was recalled, 'people sold their fat pigs, their kits of pigeons, pledged their clothes, and even stripped their houses of the greater part of the furniture, in fact, they would sell or pawn anything they could lay their hands on . . . to raise the cash wherewith to back their respective favourites'.[45]

Some workmen who were fond of 'cocking' bred fowl themselves.[46] As G.R. Scott has pointed out, however, many cocks were bred by professional 'feeders'.[47] One of the most famous names in this profession was that of Gilliver of Polesworth near Tamworth, who 'was nearly always retained by the gentry of Birmingham and district when a big main was to be fought with a neighbouring county or with London'. Another noted Midland name was Wilkinson of Oldbury in Staffordshire. These 'feeders' put out their birds in twos or threes to publicans. Then 'a couple of weeks before an impending battle the "master" would have the cocks returned to him and subject them to his own special feeding process – a secret . . . never . . . divulged – and prepare them for the fight'.[48] This involved trimming the tail feathers and fitting and adjusting the deadly artificial spur.[49] In addition the birds might be set before a mirror and allowed 'to punish vigorously the image of himself', or be put into conflict with a cock whose spurs were muffled or with an old bird whose stamina was gone, 'with the result that the young one obtained the mastery and killed his rival. This gave him pluck'.[50]

In assessing the popularity of the sport we may also witness the great popularity of 'sporting ballads' with workmen – of which the most famous was the 'Wednesbury Cocking' – a song 'once as popular and effective as 'Lillibulero', or as 'Shall Trelawny Die?' among the workmen of Birmingham'.

> Six battles were fought on each side,
>   And the next was to decide the main.
> For they were two famous cocks,
>   As ever this country bred;
> Scroggin's a duck-winged black,
>   And Newton's a shift-winged red.

The conflict was hard on both sides,
  Till brassy wing'd black was choaked,
The colliers were nationly vexed,
  And the nailors were sorely provoked;
Peter Stevens he swore a great oath
  That Scroggins had play'd his cock foul;
Scroggins gave him a kick on the head.
  And cried, yea G-- d--n thy soul.

The company then fell in discord,
  And a bold fight ensued,
Kick, --, and bite was the word,
  Till the Walsall men were subdued.
Ralph Moody bit off a man's nose,
  And wish'd that he could have him slain,
So they trampled both cocks to death,
  And they made a draw of the main.

Some people may think this is strange,
  Who Wednesbury never knew,
But those who have ever been there
  Won't have the least doubt that it's true;
For they are savage by nature,
  And guilty of deeds the most shocking;
Jack Baker whack'd his own father,
  And so ended Wednesbury cocking.[51]

Although there is undoubtedly an element of hyperbole in these verses they do emphasise the physicality which characterised unrefined popular culture, much of which can undoubtedly be traced to the tough conditions of work in trades like nailing and mining, and in virtually any kind of labouring.[52] It is not surprising then, that prize fighting was so often an accompaniment of animal baiting sports; such sports were also encouraged by local rivalries, and it is in this context also that we should see the sneering at Wednesbury in a song written by a Brummie.[53] Just as the gentry banded together to fight mains against the gentry of another county, so the working men of the Black Country towns, or at least the substantial number who made up the cock-fighting fraternity thereof, would band together to test their birds' skills against their local rivals: Willenhall v Wednesfield for example. On other occasions, however, these two allied themselves and 'pitted the best birds of each place against the pick of Wednesbury, Darlaston, or any other town for miles around'. Such rivalries were not easily contained in the cock-pit, and the result was often 'bitter strife springing up between the respective partisans' and 'many severe battles . . . between the human bipeds after the close of the struggle between the feathered crowers'.[54]

In the context of this culture it is unlikely that most aficionados of cock-fighting (or other baiting sports) felt a need to justify the sports. However, in the face of the attacks made upon this sport in the nineteenth century, justifications were evolved – along the following lines:

> It was intended by nature that cocks should fight. Look at two cocks brought up in one brood; they will not fight so long as they belong to that brood, but separate them for some time, and then bring them together, and they will fly at each other's eyes the moment they meet. Now, in hunting, it is not enough that the horse strains itself to the utmost, with a good will, but the rider must keep digging his spurs into the poor beast's side to make him go faster, till at last he falls down quite brokenhearted. But two game cocks will by themselves fight till one or the other is killed, and nature has given them 'pluck', strength, and activity for fighting.

It is true that this is not quite consistent with the training process which we have seen was employed, but the riposte to that was also cogent: 'So long as fox-hunting, coursing, and horse-racing are allowed by law, I do not see why cock-fighting should be forbidden'.[55]

Nevertheless, keeping a cock-pit was forbidden by the Cruelty to Animals Act of 1835, and cock-fighting itself was made illegal in 1849.[56] In Willenhall the initial campaign against cock-fighting relied on the device of paying informers a portion of the penalty incurred by the offenders; in Birmingham the magistrates tried public ridicule. A worker recalled:

> I was one of forty taken into custody by the police. . . . We were all tied together with ropes round the body or arms, two by two, and were marched in procession through the principal streets of the town as an example, and then brought before the magistrates. The ringleaders, who actually got up the cock-fight, were fined, and the rest of us, who were spectators only, were discharged.[57]

This policy clearly recognised that heavy-handedness would be counter-productive, and tried to discourage the organisers. However, whereas bull-baiting had become extinct, cock-fighting survived behind closed doors – usually, but not always, public-house doors.[58]

Details of these pubs, and of their landlords, have come down to us through late nineteenth-century century reminiscences. 'Honourable' John Tailby, of the Jim Crow, Hill Street and 'Solid' John Coates, of the Three Crowns, Tower Street, were two of the most important impresarios of the sport in Birmingham – their soubriquets indicated their reputation as reliable stake holders. Implicitly, there were others who were less renowned for their straight-dealing. Thus 'Hines the cockfighter' was remembered by one who had 'been paid by him when a youth, with other youths, to get up a "jolly" – i.e., to do the rough business when the bird Hines fought was not well up in form and could not win; these "jollies" always meant a free fight all round'. This kind of cheating was also accompanied by fight-fixing between the principals. Once Hines 'fought a cock against a favourite one of Ben Terry's. . . . Ben's was backed heavily, and being the better of the two, there was an arrangement made between Ben and Hines to adjust the spurs of Ben's cock negligently, the result being that Ben's bird was struck down by his opponent and killed'.[59] Presumably Terry got a share of Hines's winnings from his long-odds bets.

Terry was well known as a pugilist, and his houses – the Green Dragon, Lichfield Street and Gunmaker's Arms, Moor Street – were centres of cock and dog fighting and ratting.[60] 'Solid' Coates had also been a pugilist – 'one of the quietest lads out; but only let a quarrel begin – and low, there was "blood for supper", as one of them once said in describing a shindy'. At least five other public houses were specifically remembered in 1905 as centres of such sports. Terry was born in a public house – known as 'Terry's Castle'; two other notable pugilists – John and Harry Broome – were gun-barrel makers.[61] The popularity of the sports with working men is also attested by the status of the witnesses who were called when Tailby, Terry, and other landlords were prosecuted for cock- and dog-fighting in 1854: John Mangon, labourer; Robert Wicks, shoemaker; Edward McGrane, silk dyer.[62]

Shrove Tuesday continued to be a particularly important occasion for plebeian cock-fighting, it 'being the first holiday after Christmas'.[63] Sports involving cocks had been associated for centuries with Shrove Tuesday, and the notorious 'cock-shying' also survived into the mid-nineteenth century:[64]

a lot of men would club together and purchase a cock, taking him to a neighbouring 'pub', and . . . [the] skittle alley . . . was converted into an arena. . . . The cock was secured to a post, or log of wood, by a string tied to his leg, a foot or two of which was allowed for freedom in jumping from the missile thrown at him, for the sum of threepence. A short thick stick, or cudgel, was handed to the thrower, who, standing some distance away, aimed at the bird, which of course leaped up to evade the blow; if the stick hit him, and the thrower could run up to, and catch hold of the cock before he recovered from the effects of the blow he claimed it as his own; but if the bird was up first, as in most instances he was after being knocked over, others paid their money and shyed at him.

Another version of this was shooting at the cock! It was given the same amount of tether as in shying, but the man with the gun stood at a greater distance. 'In this manner many birds were tortured and killed during the day, and at night were cooked and eaten at the "pub" and washed down with gallons of fourpenny'.[65]

III

Police action against such sports was undoubtedly a key factor in their eventual suppression.[66] Perhaps more significant in the long run, however, was the disappearance of their numerous indoor venues; by the 1880s it was said that 'most of the fighting "pubs" are gone'.[67] As the landlords retired or died the new generation must have felt that the risks were too great, especially from the 1870s, as beerhouse licences were not renewed, and the industrial brewers, with respectable names to lose, began to take over the Birmingham pub scene.[68] With the passing of these pubs cock-fighting as a significant element of popular culture in Birmingham also passed away. But that is not the only reason; there were also wider changes in metropolitan popular culture and leisure which diminished the importance of these sports. Space does not permit a full exposition here, but the future clearly lay with music halls, railway excursions and football matches, rather than with furtive meetings in public house back rooms, in urban pleasures rather than those which referred back to the rural past, in mechanical amusements rather than animal amusements.[69] In the Black Country, however, with its waste land and rural enclaves, the long tradition of cock-fighting was never entirely eradicated, and dog-fighting still went on 'to a considerable extent' in the 1870s. Moreover, at tavern grounds other sports substituted for the illicit baiting and fighting: pigeon and sparrow shooting, dog-racing, rabbit coursing, and pedestrianism.[70] Despite this, some observers felt that the last decades of the nineteenth century had witnessed fundamental changes in the tone of popular leisure. By the later 1870s free public libraries and board school education were in place in Wednesbury and Willenhall. They may not have contrived a revolution of manners by themselves, but they symbolised the changed cultural milieu. It was similarly significant that by 1900 'the better class . . . of artisans' now spent 'a week . . . in North Wales or breezy Blackpool' as their diversion during Willenhall Wake week'.[71] The reference to a 'better class' of artisans is also a pointer to the factor of long-term improvements in brutal working conditions, which may be supposed to have diminished the tendency to indulge in brutal play.

Therefore, the curtailment of bull-baiting and cock-fighting as popular sports resulted from a combination of repression, cultural and economic change, and the emergence of alternatives. Their suppression notably contributed towards the reduction of brutality in popular culture. Unfortunately, however, the tendency by members of all social classes to maltreat animals for excitement or gain is by no means dead even today.[72]

Notes

1 G.R. Scott, *The History of Cockfighting* (London, 1957), p. 114; F.W. Hackwood, *Old English Sports* (London, 1907), pp. 254–6, 284; R.W. Malcolmson, *Popular Recreations in English Society 1700–1850* (Cambridge, 1973), see esp. p. 123. My chief sources will be reminiscences which appeared in the provincial 'Labour and the poor' articles in the London *Morning Chronicle* (hereafter *M.Chron.*) in 1850–51, and in Birmingham newspapers, particularly in their Notes & Queries columns – hitherto largely unexplored by professional historians, though see J.H. Porter, 'Cockfighting in the eighteenth and nineteenth centuries: from popularity to suppression', *Report of the Transactions of the Devonshire Association*, 118 (1986), pp. 63–71. The Birmingham Notes and Queries (hereafter 'N. & Q.') are in bound volumes with the following location numbers in Birmingham Reference Library (hereafter BRL): A (1856–65) – 144951; C (1871–80) – 144953; D (1881–4) – 144954; E (1885–8) – 144955; F (1889–92) – 144956; G (1893–6) – 144957; R (1894) 122437. Curiously, the *Manchester Notes & Queries*, 6 vols (Manchester, 1878–84), have very few references to bull-baiting or cock-fighting, though see J.K. Walton and R. Poole, 'The Lancashire wakes in the nineteenth century', in Robert D. Storch (ed.), *Popular Culture and Custom in Nineteenth Century England* (London, 1982), pp. 105–6.

2 *Parliamentary History* (XXV), c. 208 (2 April 1800).

3 This account is based on the following: *M.Chron.*, 3 Mar. 1851 – the testimony being from a 'man of much experience and of excellent memory for local facts', one of 'two gentlemen holding official situations' in Birmingham, 'whose duties brought, and still bring them into contact with assemblages of the people, and with offenders against the laws'. The other

is cited later. In 1777 Matthew Boulton stated that 'barbarous amusements', including bull-baiting, had 'prevailed in the neighbourhood' in the *seventeenth* century, however 'the scene is now much changed; the people are more polite and civilised'. Yet Boulton's statement cannot be taken as disinterested. The context was an attempt to achieve a Royal Patent for the New Street Theatre. Boulton's aim was to persuade Lord Dartmouth that the playhouse had already contributed to the elevation of popular taste. To deny the patent, and put the future of the theatre in jeopardy, would also be to put the progress of civilising the populace into jeopardy: Historical Manuscripts Commission, *Fifteenth Report, Appendix, Part I. The Manuscripts of the Earl of Dartmouth*, vol. 3 (1896), pp. 234–5. Thus, while Boulton was perhaps registering a real decline in the popularity of bull-baiting since the seventeenth century, his statement certainly exaggerated the extent of decline which had taken place by 1777.

4 *M.Chron.*, 3 March 1851; *Birmingham Chronicle*, 11 September 1823; *Aris's Birmingham Gazette* [hereafter *A.B.G.*.], 24 March, 13 October 1828 (cf. *ibid.*, 1 November 1824); *Birmingham Journal* (hereafter *B.Jo.*), 13 September 1828; D.A. Reid, 'Interpreting the Festival Calendar: Wakes and Fairs as Carnivals', in Storch, *op. cit.*, pp. 133–5.

5 *A.B.G.*, 24 March 1828.

6 *A.B.G.*, 4 August 1823, 9 August 1824; 13 October 1828; *B.Jo.*, 12 September 1829; see also 'N. & Q.' D, p. 244, F, p. 78 (Sambourne and Claverdon in Warwickshire in the 1820s), and Malcolmson, *op. cit.*, pp. 122–3.

7 *A.B.G.*, 9 August, 1824, 10 January 1825; *M.Chron.*, 3 March 1851.

8 'N. & Q.', C, p. 80 – Handsworth, witness refers to 1818–22; 'N. & Q.', G, p. 99 – witness born 1797, probably referring to the 1820s, at Bilston; 'N. &. Q.', E, p. 129 – Gosty Hill, Halesowen; witness born in 1830.

9 'N. & Q.', C, p. 220.

10 'N. & Q.', G, p. 99. Hackwood, *op. cit.*, contains a vivid, though often undocumented account of bull-baiting, particularly in the West Midlands; on pp. 306–7 he seems to show that the ribbons and garlands with which the bull was often festooned were actually a direct imitation of Spanish bull-fighting practice, transmitted to England by an eighteenth-century soldier.

11 *M.Chron.*, 3 March 1851; see also the statement of a nonagenarian bucklemaker in *ibid.*, 27 January 1851, and Hackwood, *op. cit.*, pp. 309.

12 *A.B.G.*, 10 July 1777; 8 October 1792; 'N. & Q.', A, p. 94, citing 'an aged amateur of the sport'.

13 'N. & Q', D, p. 236; G, p. 99.

14 *A.B.G.* 10 January 1825.

15 *M. Chron.*, 3 March 1851; in 1828 a certain John Hoyland hired a bull in order to bait it at Edgbaston Wake, William Field was 'keeper of the ring': *A.B.G.*, 15 September 1828. Hackwood claims that there were 'individuals of the loafer type' who promoted the baiting of bulls 'almost as a profession', and cites the case of John Field, 'a man of respectable appearance', and his ragged lieutenants from Wednesbury, at Lichfield Greenhill Wakes in 1828: *op. cit.*, pp. 314–5. Cf. Malcolmson's contention

that bull-baiting was 'particularly dependent on some form of outside assistance – patronage, sponsorship or promotion'; Malcolmson, *Popular Recreations*, p. 123.

16 'N. & Q.', G, p. 99; see also Hackwood, *The Wednesbury Papers* (Wednesbury, 1884), p. 20.
17 Bob Bushaway, *By Rite. Custom, Ceremony and Community in England 1700–1880* (London, 1982), pp. 5–6.
18. Cited in *Birmingham Daily Post* [hereafter *B.D. Post*], 24 August 1859.
19 *M.Chron.*, 27 January 1851.
20 *M.Chron.*, 3 March 1851.
21 *B.D. Post*, 24 August 1859. For a £5 wager (undated) see Hackwood, *Old English Sports*, pp. 303.
22 'N. & Q.', A, p. 94; according to K.V. Thomas, *Man and the Natural World* (London, 1983), pp. 93–4, 'most towns' in early modern England had had such bye-laws to this effect.
23 *Ibid.*, chap. IV; Malcolmson, *op. cit.*, pp. 118–9, 122–6, 152–7; James Turner, *Reckoning with the Beast. Animals, Pain, and Humanity in the Victorian Mind* (Baltimore, 1980), pp. 20–29.
24 *Parliamentary History* (XXVI), cc. 829–30, 845, 854 (24 May 1802); E.S. Turner, *All Heaven in a Rage* (London, 1964), pp. 106, 114.
25 *M.Chron.*, 3 March 1851; Hackwood, *op. cit.*, pp. 318–9.
26 'N. & Q.', G, p. 99.
27 *M.Chron.*, 3 March 1851.
28 *Ibid.*
29 'N. & Q.', E, p. 129.
30 In addition to references at n. 23 see also Thomas Young, *An Essay on Humanity to Animals* (London, 1798; Birmingham, abridged edn, 1804); Thomas Moore, *The Sin and Folley of Cruelty to Brute Animals: A Sermon* (Birmingham, 1810); Abraham Smith, *A Scriptural and Moral Catechism* (Birmingham, 2nd edn, 1833).
31 *M.Chron.*, 3 March 1851.
32 D.A. Reid, 'Labour, leisure and politics in Birmingham c. 1800–1875' (University of Birmingham PhD, 1985), pp. 36–7, 60–1, 168–70.
33 Reid, in Storch, *Popular Culture*, pp. 130.
34 *B.Jo.*, 10 March 1856.
35 *A.B.G.*, 4 February 1811; see also *ibid.*, 6 February 1809 for similar publicity for Lord Erskine's unsuccessful Bill of that year.
36 See references cited at note 4 above. Bull-baiting was also suppressed at Wolverhampton in 1815 under a local bye-law, and in Lichfield in 1828 under the 1823 Turnpike Act: Jon Raven, *The Urban and Industrial Songs of the Black Country and Birmingham* (Wolverhampton, 1977), pp. 120–1; Hackwood, *Old English Sports* pp. 314–5.
37 For local religious influences on popular attitudes see: Scott K. Phillips, 'Primitive Methodist confrontation with popular sports; case study of early nineteenth century Staffordshire', in R. Cashman and M. McKernan (eds), *Sport: Money, Morality and the Media* (Kensington, NSW, 1981), pp. 289–303.
38 *B.D. Post*, 24 August 1859.

39 Malcolmson, *Popular Recreations*, pp. 119, 125–6; 'N. & Q.', E, p. 133 (Willenhall); Samuel Lloyd, *The Lloyds of Birmingham* (Birmingham, 1907), p. 196 re. Wednesbury; Reid, in Storch, *Popular Culture*, p. 134.

40 *M. Chron.*, 3 March 1851. For the significance of Mondays see D.A. Reid, 'The decline of Saint Monday, 1766–1876', *Past and Present*, 71 (1976), pp. 76–101; and Denis Brailsford, 'Sporting days in eighteenth century England', *Journal of Sports History*, 9 (1982), pp. 41–54.

41 For Moreton see: 'N. & Q.', R, pp. 17–17a; Newspaper Cuttings – in BRL 302129, p. 52; Norman W. Tildesley, 'William Moreton of Willenhall' in M.W. Greenslade (ed.), *Essays in Staffordshire History Presented to S.A.H. Burne* (Stafford, 1970), pp. 171–85.

42 *Gentleman's Magazine*, VXII (1747), p. 292. See also *A.B.G.*, 2 June 1746, 22 January 1750.

43 J.A. Langford, *A Century of Birmingham Life*, 2 vols (Birmingham, 1868) I, p. 135, II, pp. 268, 402. There is an interesting parallel to be drawn here with the development of cock-fighting as a spectator sport, on a commer-icialised basis, in northern French towns: see Richard Holt, *Sport and Society in Modern France* (London, 1981), pp. 106–7, 113.

44 *M.Chron.*, 3 March 1851. See 'N. & Q.', F, p. 138 for the cock-pit at the Racquet Court Tavern, Bath Street, one of 'the most noted' in Birmingham, where matches 'involving hundreds of pounds were fought weekly': 'The "pit" was situated in an upper room . . . low ceilinged, of considerable size, and practically bare of furniture . . . the cocks used to fight on a piece of turf, about eight feet square, flattened down with a ram-rod, and edged round with wood. The 'setters' or men who were going to set the cocks down to fight, took opposite corners of the square of turf, whilst the privileged spectators, for prices of admission ran high, stood all round.'

45 *M.Chron.*, 3 March 1951: *Birmingham Weekly Post* (hereafter *Wkly Post*) 12 May 1894.

46 *M.Chron.*, 3 March 1851.

47 See, for example, *A.B.G.*, 26 February 1750; Scott, *History of Cockfighting*, pp. 111–12.

48 *Ibid.*, 'Bygone Birmingham' (BRL 302135), pp. 118–20 (December 1905).

49 *M.Chron.*, 3 March 1851; *Wkly Post*, 12 June 1886.

50 'N. & Q.', F, p. 138.

51 *M.Chron.*, 3 March 1851. According to a writer in *B.D. Post*, 24 August 1859, the song was written by Jack Probin, the nineteenth-century Birmingham gunmaker cited at n. 38 above. See also Raven, *Urban and Industrial Songs*, pp. 110–13, 116, 128–9.

52 See Will Thorne, *My Life's Battles* (London, ?1925), ch. 1 for strong evidence of links between brutality at work and brutality at play, including cock- and dog-fighting during the 1870s.

53 Thus a coach guard who played the air of the song on his bugle was attacked by the infuriated cockers: cited by Lloyd, *op. cit.*, p. 195. For prize fighting see *Wkly Post*, 12 June 1886; 'N. & Q.', F, p. 138; also text attached to notes 60–1 below.

54 *Wkly Post*, 12 May 1894. A similar rivalry lay behind the Black Country

practice of stealing the bull from an adjacent parish on the eve of the baiting: Hackwood, *Old English Sports*, pp. 316–17.

55 *M.Chron.*, 3 March 1851.

56 Malcolmson, *op. cit.*, p. 124.

57 'N. & Q.', E, p. 133; *M.Chron.*, 3 March 1851. See also *B.Jo.*, 7 December 1839, 9 May 1840, 27 March, 3 April 1841, 4, 18 March 1843.

58 See (a) the autobiography of a newspaper editor, H.J. Jennings, *Chestnuts and Small Beer* (London, 1920), p. 139, for cock-fights in the leafy suburbs, (b) the report in the *Birmingham Daily Mail*, 17 April 1874, of a main fought at Lichfield at which 'Noble lords were present, county families were well represented, and the elite of the "fancy" mustered in force', and (c) the account of the 'select' cock-fighting circle around George Kynoch MP for Aston Manor, in the 1880s, in BRL 302127, p. 180. See also Scott, *op. cit.*, pp. 168–72, for survivals elsewhere.

59 'N. & Q.', F, p. 138; for Hines see *A.B.G.*, 5 April 1824.

60 *Wkly Post*, 12 June 1886.

61 'N. & Q.', C. p. 220.

62 *B.Jo.*, 9 April 1853.

63 *M.Chron.*, 3 March 1851; 'N. & Q.', E, p. 94.

64 Peter Burke, *Popular Culture in Early Modern Europe* (London, 1978), pp. 182–91.

65 *Wkly Post*, 12 June 1886.

66 See, for example, *Birmingham Gazette & Express*, 9 October 1908, for the suppression in the 1860s of outdoor shooting-at-cocks in suburban fields, which had attracted 'hundreds of people at a time'. See also *A.B.G.*, 22 August 1868, and Hackwood, *Old English Sports*, p. 241, for the suppression of cock-fighting at the Globe Tavern, Great Hampton Street, Birmingham. Slum parsons were also active in the 1850s and 1860s in seeking the suppression of dog-fights, boxing matches, and the gambling gangs which were part of the same milieu: J.M. Brindley, *Church Work in Birmingham* (Birmingham, 1880), pp. 103, 181, 211.

67 *Wkly Post*, 12 June 1886.

68 Alan Crawford & Robert Thorne, *Birmingham Pubs 1890–1939* (Birmingham, 1975), pp. vi–xiii.

69 Badger-baiting was said to have been 'almost as common as cock-fighting' in the 1820s and 1830s (*M.Chron.*, 3 March 1851), but badgers must have been harder to procure in the mid-nineteenth-century city, of course, and references to them in the press are conspicuous by their absence by then.

70 'Black Country sports', *The Lion* (Birmingham), 25 January 1877; Hackwood, *Odd Chapters in the History of Wednesbury* (Wednesbury, 1920), p. 88; 'Mrs Thatcher's Poor', *New Society*, 26 January 1984, p. 124.

71 BRL 302129 (Newspaper Cuttings) p. 52; Norman W. Tildesley, *A History of Willenhall* (Willenhall, 1951, pp. 92–3; J.F. Ede, *History of Wednesbury* (Wednesbury, 1962), p. 295. See also *M.Chron.*, 3 March 1851 & Hackwood, *Old English Sports*, p. 318, on the significance of popular education in changing ideas about brutal sports.

72 Whether covert badger-baiting and dog-fighting, or overt fox-hunting, hare-coursing, and stag-hunting.

2

'Potshare bowling' in the mining communities of east Northumberland, 1800–1914

Alan Metcalfe

Despite a significant increase in research into working-class sport, little has been done to examine what happened to traditional working-class games during the massive changes of the second half of the nineteenth century. The growth of professional football as the sport of the working class has been well documented, but what happened to other less celebrated sports?[1] Cunningham suggests that traditional sports survived and adapted better than many imagined.[2] Such was certainly the case with the miners' sports of bowling, quoits and fives. Indeed it is arguable that at the outbreak of the war in 1914 bowling and quoits combined still attracted as many participants and spectators as the all-pervasive football. Although quoits and fives also shared the same relationship to inns, lack of formal organisation and written rules, and stressed the centrality of money prizes and gambling, 'potshare bowling' – a sport that was unique to the miners – will be used here as a case study to illustrate the wider history of these traditional sports. The term 'potshare' refers to the custom whereby each player put his stake into a purse which was the property of the winner.

On 8 July 1906 'Sitter On', the *Newcastle Daily Chronicle* reporter on 'potshare bowling', suggested the postponement of the much-awaited match between the two great protagonists Tommy Thompson of Newbiggin and James Nicholson of Burradon. The reason was that it would conflict with a 'great' football match to be played at St James Park, Newcastle. This epitomised the changes at work within the sporting activities in the mining communities of east Northumberland and, in particular, the emergence of association football to challenge the popularity of the deeply rooted traditional sports. Throughout the nineteenth century 'potshare bowling' was played

29

nearly exclusively by miners of Northumberland and Durham. Its history reflects the power of tradition; its persistence and eventual decline illustrate the interplay of social forces at the very roots of mining society. At the same time the history of 'potshare bowling' also reveals much about the ways in which the miners created their own culture and resisted the efforts of school, church, and colliery to effect change.

The colliery districts of east Northumberland comprised approximately sixty-six mining villages and towns located in an area twenty miles by seven miles from the River Tyne to just north of the River Wansbeck. During the nineteenth century the collieries expanded in geographical area, in the number of villages, and the size of the population. By 1881 the district contained a population of 92,031. It was amongst the miners of east Northumberland and their compatriots in the adjacent Durham coalfield that 'potshare bowling' reigned supreme.

In July 1900 a reporter for the *Newcastle Daily Chronicle* paid a visit to the Town Moor, Newcastle, to observe the miners' sport of bowling. 'The fact that it is still followed shows that it has a strong hold upon a minority', he noted. 'Most of the old time sports have been superseded by modern developments – have succumbed before the bicycle and football. But with several bowling still holds the field.'[3] In fact, the reporter understated the hold the game had in the mining communities. Perhaps its structure and continuing appeal to the community can best be illustrated by examining a typical year.[4] During 1906 eighty-two matches were held for sums ranging between £5 and £100. Fifteen handicaps promoted by local innkeepers attracted, on average, over 100 competitors per event. Two championship sweeps involving four of the premier bowlers competed in front of crowds of up to 10,000 spectators. The mecca of bowling which attracted bowlers from both Durham and Northumberland coalfields was the Town Moor, Newcastle. During 1906 competitors and spectators trekked to the Moor on sixty-nine separate occasions, mainly Saturdays, to watch the matches and handicaps which took place on the 'mile' (875 yards) located along the eastern edge of the Moor. Neither cold nor heat discouraged the bowling fraternity. It was played throughout the year despite snow, rain or sun. On 1 September the temperature reached 91°F but bowling went on. At the end of the year, when the great snowstorms caused the cancellation of all the football matches, the miners still travelled to the Moor in the hope of watching a contest. Crowds ranged from a handful to over ten thousand and on at least twenty-six occasions crowds estimated at over a thousand were present.

Much of the season was filled with handicaps promoted by innkeepers, and these will be examined later to explain the continued success of bowling as a participant sport. However, it was the matches between the leading bowlers that traditionally attracted the largest crowds, the biggest purses, and the greatest amount of wagering. James Nicholson of Burradon, Jack Cordner of The Mount, Tommy Thompson of Newbiggin and George Armstrong of Newbiggin competed in front of crowds of between four thousand and ten thousand on six different occasions. The match itself was the culmination of several weeks of activity during which the competing parties met at various inns to arrange the event. On the day of the match the protagonists and their supporters met at the sponsoring inn for the weigh-in. During 1906 both the weigh-in and post-game celebrations were frequently held at the Chancellor's Head Inn, Newgate Street, or the Blue Post Inn, Pilgrim Street, in Newcastle itself. On some occasions darkness stopped play, and there were numerous complaints of the late starts and spectators encroaching upon the track. Central to all aspects of the matches were the miners, who were the pre-eminent players, acted as officials, and provided the handicappers.

While the Newcastle Town Moor, a large area of common land on the northern edge of the inner city, was the undisputed centre of the game, there was a secondary centre on Newbiggin Moor located in the north-east corner of the coalfield. During 1906 twenty-nine matches were played and three handicaps sponsored by the Newbiggin innkeepers. Matches and/or handicaps were held on thirty-six days. The greatest crowds attended matches involving the two Newbiggin bowlers, Tommy Thompson and George Armstrong. By far the majority of participants were drawn from the immediate vicinity, few travelling from the southern edge of the coalfield to hazard the wilds of Newbiggin Moor. Although the moors at Newcastle and Newbiggin were the home of about nine out of ten matches throughout the nineteenth century, other sites were used on an irregular basis, in particular the sand beaches at Seaton Sluice, Blyth, North Blyth, Cambois and North Seaton. Additionally a number of inns hosted contests in fields adjoining the inns or on the disused waggonways that ran through the district. In fact over fifty sites were used infrequently throughout the century.

What then was this game that so dominated the miners' sporting lives during the nineteenth century? Basically it was a simple game that pitted two men with potshare bowls weighing between five and fifty ounces against each other over a predetermined course usually called the 'mile'. The miner who got to the end of the course first was the winner. The character of the game is captured most accurately in an account in the *Newcastle Daily Chronicle* of a match on the Town Moor on 21 July 1906:

> The bowl came grandly away from the hand and having been propelled with immense power it fairly flew over the ground. There was an avenue of spectators stretching away for fully three hundred yards, but fortunately the bowl was never impeded. It kept low all the way, and rarely jumped more than a foot. It was felt that Cordner had a severe task before him to come up to it. The crowd surged about in great excitement, all being desirous to see Cordner deliver. After careful preparations the bowl was placed in his hand, and, taking a lengthy run to the trig, he put the bowl exactly on the spot desired by the setter on. It bounded away from its beat very fast and true, taking also a grand course.[5]

In fact the game as played in the Edwardian years was little different from the one played a hundred years before. Its hold on the miners was related to the power of tradition and custom in mining life. Bowling more than any other sport reflected the traditions of the miners – their independence from outside influences, their love of gambling and sociability. It was played only by the miners of the north-east coalfield and this represented something that was uniquely their own.

Prior to the 1860s we can only get glimpses of 'potshare bowling' through indigenous poetry, prosecutions in court, and evidence given before the Commissioner of Mines in 1842. Several pitmen poets alluded to the popularity of the game and as early as 1805 the Council of Newcastle attempted to ban bowling on the Town Moor. It was during the 1820s that the first recognised champion emerged, Davy Bell of Benton. One of the first records to provide a deeper insight into the nature of 'potshare bowling' was given by John Elliott, Chief Justice for the West Division of Castle Ward in 1842, when he stated with regard to bowling:

> That it is very often pursued on the public roads in the country, to the great danger and annoyance of travellers, that generally a considerable number are engaged in the game, and that sometimes what are called

'matches' are made, upon which occasion a great concourse of people are assembled, and pitmen belonging to different collieries are brought together, disorder and breaches of the peace are likely and indeed have occasionally occurred.[6]

Little changed during the next seventy years. Bowling continued to be played on public ground; it attracted large numbers of spectators; challenge matches remained the most popular forms of competition; it was played nearly exclusively by miners; and it faced intermittent opposition from the authorities. Its role in mining life was illustrated in October 1891 when William Wardle, a prominent bowler of the 1860s, was killed by a fall of stone at Dinnington Pit. His funeral attracted over a thousand mourners, who travelled from the mining villages of Northumberland and Durham to pay their respects to a man whose reputation had lived on in the cultural traditions of the colliers.

Throughout the century bowling provided many of the sporting heroes of mining society. Early in the twentieth century champions of the past were used as benchmarks against which to measure the heroes of the present. James Nicholson and Tommy Thompson, the main contenders for the championship in the 1890s and 1900s, were regularly measured against champions from the past such as Davy Bell (1820s), Harry Brown (1830s and 1840s), Thomas Saint (1850s and 1860s) and John Gibson and Robert Gledson (1870s). These great names and their deeds were transmitted from generation to generation by word of mouth and formed a living part of the culture of the miners. The status of bowling champions is nicely illustrated by the formal nature of the representations made to them. On 20 December 1873 a massive gold watch valued at twenty guineas was presented to Robert Gledson, the champion bowler of England, at the Clayton Arms, Dudley. Two years later John Gibson, of Pegswood, was presented with a handsome gold stop lever watch with gold Albert and appendage at a dinner chaired by the Mayor of Morpeth. In 1895 a gold Albert and a gold brooch for his wife were presented to James Nicholson, 'Champion of the World' at a ceremony at the Lord Byron Inn, Choppington. The chair was assumed by Wm Johnson, under-manager at Choppington Colliery and the vice-chair by Robt H. Wheatley, a butcher and farmer of Choppington.[7]

There were certain elements of bowling that remained unchanged during the nineteenth century. In the first place bowling was practised throughout the year; unlike cricket and football and other sports it had no particular season. Additionally there were no clearly defined age limits. Many bowlers' careers spanned thirty years; the great Harry Brown, for instance, was active between 1835 and 1868. Another champion, James Nicholson, first graced the bowling track in 1886 and did not retire until 1909. These individuals were not exceptional, with several bowlers playing in top-class competition into their fifties. For many men it was the dominant free-time activity, starting at the age of fifteen and retiring from active competition around fifty-four but continuing in various roles for the rest of their lives. Such was the case with James Sample, who was active until six weeks before his death in 1901 at the age of 80.[8]

Though bowling matches were played throughout the year, there was no uniformity in their progamming either from month to month or year to year. The only predictable feature was the fact that the majority of matches were held on Saturdays. Unlike the sports that developed in the later part of the century bowling did not have regular schedules. In fact it was characterised by its irregularity both in a general and individual sense. In 1876 201 challenge matches were played on either the Newcastle Town Moor or Newbiggin Moor. Every Saturday and some weekdays witnessed matches at either or both locations. Twenty years later in 1896 only sixty matches were held throughout the year. Cycles of activity were followed by periods of inactivity. Perhaps the pattern is illustrated best during the 1890s by the number of days when contests were held on Newbiggin Moor. The number of matches per year varied from a high of eighty in 1890 to a low of six in 1899. Consecutive years often witnessed significant drops, for example, from forty-four in 1895 to eleven in 1896. In 1894 the first match was not held until 20 February. Between then and the beginning of November rarely a Saturday passed without at least one competition on the moor. This same pattern was reflected in the histories of individual players. In 1863 the young Lance Mordue played six matches in four months. Robert Ward of Bebside played fourteen matches during 1876. As late as 1913 Pringle Rutherford, an up-and-coming star, played twelve matches in seven months. These were unusual. The irregularity of individual competition is reflected in the records of various champions. For example, Harry Brown, the second recognised champion, competed in ninety-two matches during his career which stretched from 1835 to 1868, an average of less than three matches a year. Tommy Thompson of Newbiggin, the last of the pre-war champions, played only thirty-two matches between 1891 and 1911. On several years, 1891–93, 1895–6, Thompson played no matches. His great years, 1906–8, averaged four per year. There was no regularity both in terms of matches and individual participation from year to year, although the long-term trend seems to have been toward fewer major matches.

One of the most significant differences between bowling and the sports that emerged late in the century was the lack of written rules or formal organisations. The rules of bowling were customary, passed from one generation of miners to the next by word of mouth. Matches were made by following generally recognised communal procedures. A challenge was issued by placing an advertisement in the *Newcastle Daily Chronicle*. The challenger met his opponent, backers and supporters at a designated inn or public house. At the meeting various issues were discussed: handicaps, location, referee, stake-holder, stakes, and date were negotiated. The dates from the depositing of stakes were agreed and the location for the weigh-in finalised. One can well imagine the build up of excitement in Choppington that surrounded any of James Nicholson's matches in the 1890s. The negotiations and the ensuing training were part of the daily lives of the miners in the district. The actual match was the end point of a complex set of negotiations involving relatively large groups of people – a neglected aspect of the history of traditional sports.

From the 1850s miners and their families frequently travelled from the colliery villages to Newcastle on Saturdays; the wives to shop in the city, the men to watch bowling matches on the Town Moor. Throughout the century crowds varying from a few hundred to 20,000 attended the bowling matches. Since the Moor was common land it could hardly be fenced or roped off to passers-by. Bowling was always played over public land without charging spectators. There were further features of bowling that also differentiated it from other sports. First, and most important, was the fact that it was rarely played for anything but money. From the 1850s until 1914 there were few instances in which money was not at stake. In fact, the stakes were often very high. During the 1850s Thomas Saint competed in sixty events with stakes of between £1 and £50. During 1876 Robert Ward of Bebside competed for £670. During his career, Tommy Thompson played for over £1,000. Additionally, betting frequently accompanied the matches. For example, at a Championship match in 1894 it was estimated that three 'pencillers' took £408 in bets. In 1906, when James Nicholson played George Armstrong for the championship, no less than £1,000 was wagered. Betting was central to the sport. Although the miners were universally recognised as good 'sports' there was little pretence that the object of the competition was anything other than victory. Frequently, even in championship matches, a competitor 'picked up' when it was evident that the match was lost.

Surprisingly there was little concern over the weather conditions under which the game was played; uncertainty was a basic element of life and of sport. Rarely were games cancelled because of inclement weather. 'Awful conditions', 'miserable weather', and 'wretched conditions' discouraged neither spectator nor participant. Changeable weather posed new problems to test the true skill of the contestant. Snow, thunder and lightning and torrential rain failed to dampen their ardour. On 10 February 1902 the local derby between Newcastle United and Sunderland was postponed because of snow.[9] Less than two miles away bowling continued as usual. While strength and skill were important elements of bowling, uncertainty was also an essential part of the sport. Many championship matches were won and lost as a result of a chance occurrence. On 14 July 1873 the great match between Thomas Saint and Robert Gledson for a £100 stake was declared a draw after Saint's winning throw struck a post and rebounded back to where Gledson lay. Such examples of luck were common and formed part of the living history of the sport recited time and again by enthusiasts. Finally, both the starting times of the matches and their length varied greatly. Although specific starting times were often negotiated in advance, few contests started on time. In part this was related to the number of matches competing for the 'mile'. It appears that it was first come first served no matter how important the match. Thus some championship matches started at ten in the morning while others started at four in the afternoon. The actual length of a contest might vary from one to eight hours.

On the surface it appears that bowling remained unaltered for over one hundred years. Yet changes that attacked the very foundation of the sport and presaged its demise after the First World War were underway. The expansion of the coalfield itself in terms of numbers of collieries and miners served to increase the number of participants and spectators. The establishment of the railway network in the 1850s and 60s simplified the access to the two main bowling venues. One consequence of these changes was an increased presence of the miners both on the highways of east Northumberland and in

Newcastle. It was this increased visibility that evoked a response from the authorities. From early in the century there had been infrequent complaints about 'the reprehensible practice of bowling on or near the public roads'.[10] However, it was not until the early 1850s that a series of prosecutions against Seghill miners removed bowling from the public highways.[11]

The 1870s witnessed a greatly increased number of miners and their families coming to Newcastle to shop and watch the sport on the Moor, which in turn provoked a hostile reaction from the local authorities. From 4 February 1874 efforts were made in the Newcastle Town Council to have bowling on the Town Moor stopped. These efforts culminated in the magistrates issuing a total ban on bowling in January 1880. This, however, was not the end of the story and the history of the battle between pro- and anti-bowling factions reveals the complexity of the economic, social and cultural forces surrounding the sport. While the majority of councillors resented the presence of so many bowlers, there was no unanimity as to the approach to be taken. Some were concerned over public rights of property and passage; other fretted about damage to the Moor; while still others were concerned about the moral consequences of contact with the miners. Yet in the final analysis the council could not impose its will. This was not simply because the opponents of bowling were disunited. Significantly, the main reason for their failure was a deputation of businessmen representing nearly twelve hundred large ratepayers. They complained about the loss of business which resulted from the absence of the miners and their families. Retail capitalism came to the rescue of traditional recreation. The subsequent return of bowling in 1881 revealed the powerlessness of the council to change established customs. For bowling returned not to the site, which the council had constructed at a cost of £400 on the north-west edge of the Moor, but rather to the traditional 'mile'. Further attempts were made to ban bowling on both Newcastle and Newbiggin Moors, though none succeeded.

In many respects the game appeared to sail along immune to interference and alteration. However, the seeds of change had already been sown with Henry Wardle's first Newcastle Handicap in 1867.[12] Figures 2.1 and 2.2 provide an overall view of the history of bowling during the second half of the nineteenth century.[13] These figures represent two contradictory patterns. Figure 2.1 illustrates the great rise in the popularity of matches during the 1860s reaching

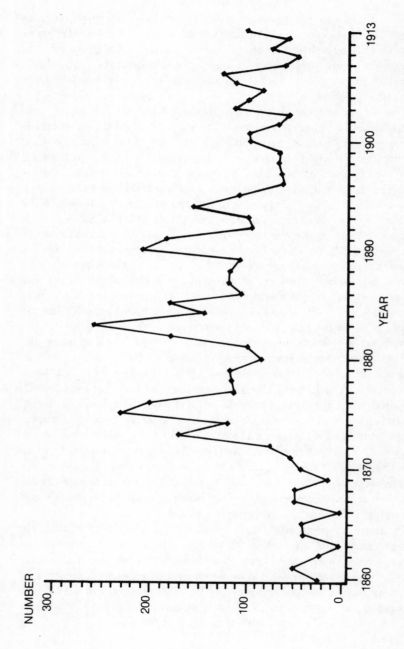

Figure 2.1 Bowling matches in east Northumberland, 1860–1913

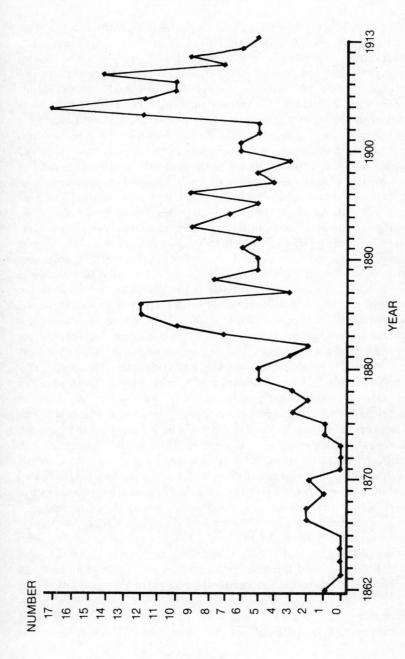

Figure 2.2 Bowling handicaps in east Northumberland, 1860–1913

a high point during the 1870s and 1880s before commencing a slow but steady decline. A different pattern is illustrated in Figure 2.2, which charts the number of handicaps that were promoted during any given year. The handicaps followed the opposite pattern to the matches, a slow but steady increase until the early 1900s before commencing a decline. These two opposing trends illustrate basic changes in the sport and its place in the mining communities.

What then is the significance of the histories of matches and handicaps to our understanding of sport in the mining communities? First, bowling was directly linked to the material conditions of mining life, in particular the availability of 'ready' money to provide stakes for the participants and wagers for the host of spectators. This was especially true in the case of the matches which were the most prestigious form of competition. It was economic conditions that determined the yearly variations in the number of matches. In fact Figure 2.1 is a reasonably accurate reflection of shifting economic conditions within the coalfield.[14] The increased number of matches in the early 1870s was directly related to the gaining of the eleven-day fortnight in 1872 and the increasing prosperity that spread throughout the coalfield during the period 1868 to 1874. Rapidly falling wages and the coalfieldwide strike of 1877 precipitated the decline in matches of 1878 and 1879. Returning prosperity in the 1880s brought an immediate response from the bowling fraternity. This prosperity was short-lived and was followed by declining wages which resulted in a bitter seventeen-week strike in 1887. Once again the return of good times in 1890 brought a resurgence of interest in the game. The decline of 1892 and 1893 was a result of a lengthy strike in the adjacent Durham coalfield. Unrest in the northern part of the coalfield culminated in the 1897 strike at the large Ashington Colliery which resulted in the near extinction of bowling on Newbiggin Moor. The cultural resilience of the mining communities is illustrated in the early 1900s when returning good times brought an increase in matches on both the Town Moor and Newbiggin Moor, although they were never to regain the peaks that were reached during the heyday of the 1870s and 1880s. Unsettled conditions returned to the coalfield in 1909 and terminated in the strike of 1912 when bowling reached an all-time low to rebound with returning good times in 1913.

If matches had been the only form of competition the decline of bowling would be indisputable. However the history of matches provides a misleading view of the popularity of the game. What, in fact, happened was a shift from matches to handicaps which attracted large numbers of participants and spectators over a number of days or evenings. In 1876 only three handicaps were promoted and these were relatively short events which were completed in four or five days. In the ensuing years both the number and length of the handicaps increased. By 1886 sixteen inns were sponsoring handicaps which, on average, stretched over two months. During the next twenty years there was a gradual increase in the number of handicaps and participants. In 1905 thirty different inns promoted handicaps. The rising popularity of handicaps is illustrated by the fact that an average of around forty entrants per handicap in the 1870s and 1880s had doubled by the Edwardian years. This in turn led to events of a longer duration with the ten-week average of 1880 rising to between twenty and thirty weeks after 1900.

This shift in focus from matches to commercially sponsored handicaps represents a fundamental change in bowling and its place in the mining communities, especially in relation to the role of the inn. It is impossible to understand sport or the mining communities without recognising the centrality of the inns to the social life of the community and to bowling. They served as the meeting place for preliminary negotiations, the location of the pre-game weigh-in, and provided the venue for post-match settlement of accounts and celebrations. It is the changing role of the inn that lies at the heart of the changes in bowling and its role in mining life.

It was the innkeepers of Newcastle who first became involved in promoting the miners' sport. Although evidence suggests that inns were involved earlier in the century, the first recorded promotion was in 1860 when Henry Wardle of the Cock and Anchor Inn, Newcastle, sponsored a championship competition for five leading bowlers. This was won by Thomas Saint who was awarded £50 and the Championship Belt, which incidentally is still in the possession of the Saint family. It was not until the late 1870s that any innkeepers became involved in a systematic manner. From 1876 until his death in 1901, Christopher Barrass, who lived in Seghill in the heart of the coalfield, used his inn in the centre of Newcastle to run his annual handicap which was held on the Town Moor. Over the years other innkeepers sponsored handicaps but none on a permanent basis. From 1868 until his death in 1895 Williams Shanks promoted several handicaps on Newbiggin Moor. Frequently he was joined by six or seven other innkeepers. The expansion of bowling in the 1870s was accompanied by an increased interest by innkeepers within the coalfield. Between 1886 and 1913 thirty-eight different inns within the mining district sponsored handicaps but only seven of these on a relatively permanent basis. The high point of their involvement was in the 1880s and 1890s. From 1886 to 1897 the Halfway House, Camperdown, sponsored events on its own track at the back of the inn. The Miners Arms at Seaton Burn, the Astley Arms at Seaton Delaval, and the Beehive Inn at Seghill also sponsored handicaps on tracks adjacent to their hostelries.

The late 1890s and 1900s witnessed a decline in the handicaps within the coalfield and an increased interest in both Newcastle and Blyth. The inns of Blyth and Seaton Sluice promoted handicaps on the sands near their inns. However, it was in Newcastle that real changes took place in the early years of the century. Prior to his death in 1901, Chrisopher Barrass was the primary sponsor of bowling. His death appeared to stimulate a new interest on the part of the Newcastle innkeepers. In 1904 the innkeepers of Newcastle decided to reduce entrance fees from five shillings to two shillings per person. This was the beginning of a concerted effort to promote bowling as a widespread participant competitive activity. They undertook initiatives to expand the base beyond the mining community. Novice handicaps, and handicaps for glassmakers and other working-class groups were played on the Moor. Events were promoted on week nights and at the weekends. The length of the handicaps ran to as much as eight months which sustained custom over an extended period. During the period 1904 to 1908 when good times reached Tyneside, twenty-four different inns promoted handicaps. There was more activity on the Moor than there had ever been, though the miners were no longer the sole participating group. Whereas prior to 1900 over 95 per cent of the bowlers came from recognised mining villages, by 1913 this had declined to 60 per cent. Bowling was no longer purely a miners' sport. In response, some miners began to exclude outsiders by organising competitions from within their own institutions; for example, Sunday morning competitions between miners representing their respective social clubs in Ashington took place on Newbiggin Moor.[15]

What then is the significance of the role of the innkeepers to our understanding of what happened to bowling and mining life in general? Matches, the most important form of competition, never fell under their jurisdiction. The miners simply made use of the inns as a location to organise their own matches. While some of the innkeepers were ex-bowlers and others such as Christoper Barrass became involved as stakeholders and officials, they were never central to matchmaking itself. This remained firmly in the hands of the miners. Handicaps, on the other hand, were used by the innkeepers to generate revenue. They used the miners to make a profit by organising events *for* them rather than providing facilities for miners to run their own events. Hence publicans brought above changes in the early 1900s which meant that the sport no longer belonged unquestionably to the miners alone.

Of course, the gradual decline of bowling, especially match bowling, cannot simply be explained by the activities of Newcastle innkeepers. More fundamental changes were taking place within the mining communities. From the early 1880s the miners were eager participants in soccer. In fact, in the 1880s and 1890s Shankhouse Black Watch, a team comprised of miners, was one of the most successful teams in the north east. As football became institutionalised in mining life it provided an alternative for both participants and spectators.[16] However, the most important change probably took place within the schools in the late 1890s when young boys were formally introduced to football. No longer did they go straight down the mine and thus become imbued with the sports of their fathers. The intrusion of teachers from outside the community implied a gradual erosion of deeply rooted traditions. Then there was the emergence of a national Football League as the pinnacle of popular commercial sport. No longer did miners look only to James Nicholson and Tommy Thompson as local heroes; they now turned to Newcastle United as another symbol of the pride of the north-east. The rise of United to become one of the most successful teams in Edwardian England graphically illustrates the changing focus of the mining communities. Instead of remaining inward-looking industrial villagers were gradually 'modernised'; they became 'north easterners' and joined the shipyard workers, factory workers and others as ardent supporters of United. The world of the miners was being transformed and it was this complex process that insidiously changed and finally undermined 'potshare bowling' in the mining communities of east Northumberland.

Notes

I wish to recognise the support given by the Social Sciences and Humanities Research Council of Canada through research grants in 1979 and 1986.

1 Although there are many books and articles which address the relationship of professional football to working-class life there are two that raise the debate to a higher level, T. Mason, *Association Football and English Society, 1863-1915* (Brighton, 1980) and C. Korr, *West Ham United: the Making of a Football Club* (New York, 1987).

2 The discussion on the decline of traditional sports is encapsulated by R.W. Malcolmson, *Popular Recreations in English Society, 1700-1850* (Cambridge, 1973) and H. Cunningham, *Leisure and the Industrial Revolution* (London, 1980); see also A. Metcalfe, 'Organised sport in the mining communities of south Northumberland', *Victorian Studies*, summer (1982).

3 *Newcastle Daily Chronicle (NDC)*, 18 July 1900.

4 Data compiled from all issues of the NDC, *Newcastle Journal, Newcastle Sporting Chronicle, Newcastle Weekly Chronicle, Blyth News and Weekly Transcript*, 1906.

5 *NDC*, 23 July 1906.

6 *Royal Commission on Mines* (1842). Evidence of John Elliot, p. 673.

7 *NDC*, 26 October 1891.

8 *NDC*, 11 April 1901.

9 *NDC*, 10 February 1902.

10 *Newcastle Magazine*, July 1822, p. 385.

11 *Newcastle Weekly Chronicle*, 8 August, 22 September, 3 October 1851.

12 *NDC*, 28 September 1867.

13 Database created from *NDC*, 1858-1913.

14 Profile of economic conditions derived from B.R. Mitchell, *Economic Development of the British Coal Industry, 1800-1914* (Cambridge, 1984).

15 Jack Dorgan, Life before the 1914-1918 War in Ashington, 'Bowling on Newbiggin Moor', Northumberland Records Office, 2520/78.

16 For the growth of football see A. Metcalfe, 'Football in the mining communities of east Northumberland, 1882-1914', *International Journal of the History of Sport* (December 1988).

3

Organised sport and the working classes of central Scotland, 1820-1900: the neglected sport of quoiting[1]

N.L. Tranter

By the second half of the nineteenth century, in that part of central Scotland which is the focus of this study, as elsewhere, many of the sports traditionally practised by working-class sections of the population – among them, bullet throwing, cock-fighting and cock-shooting, dog-fighting, prize-fighting and wrestling – had either wholly or very largely disappeared. Their place was taken by a host of more organised and codified, less violent and barbaric sporting activities, some of them, like archery, athletics, bowling, cricket, curling, golf, soccer and rugby, revised and more extensively practised versions of much older recreations, others, like boatracing, croquet and tennis, entirely new. In some of these sports – archery, croquet, golf, rugby and tennis, for example, the number of working-class participants was negligible or, at best, very limited. In others – angling, bowling, curling and cricket – working-class representation was more substantial.[2] In a few it was very substantial indeed. One of these, undoubtedly, was soccer, the game most usually held responsible for integrating the labouring populations into the habit of organised and codified methods of sporting activity. Another was quoiting. The purpose of the present paper is to suggest that quoiting too, played an important part in transforming working class sport from its traditional association with cruelty, violence and casual, ill-regulated involvement towards more ordered, codified, humane and less tempestuous modes of play.[3]

Although its earliest origins are obscure, the game of quoiting dates back to at least medieval times. According to one authority it originated in Britain in the late fifteenth century. According to another it was already widespread by the fourteenth. During the Tudor period, we are told, it was played by all classes of society.

Subsequently, however, it became predominantly a pastime of the peasantry.[4] That quoiting was still being practised in central Scotland in the late eighteenth and early nineteenth century is evident from the existence of a quoiting alley at the Bencleuch Inn, Tillicoultry in the 1790s, and from references in the local press to matches between teams of eighteen players a side drawn from the inhabitants of Doune, Dunblane, Falkirk and Stirling in 1830.[5]

During the 1830s, described by the *Stirling Observer* as a 'quoit playing age',[6] the popularity of the game within the region increased dramatically. 'The ancient national game seems to be gaining much ground of late', the *Observer* noted in 1836.[7] In some parts of the region the enthusiasm evident in the 1830s was maintained in subsequent years. 'Alva is prolific of good quoiters', it was reported in 1850.[8] Around Falkirk ten years later 'interest in the ancient and favourite game of quoiting (was) undiminished' while, at Auchterarder, it continued 'to occupy great attention among the working classes'.[9] But this was not the case everywhere. 'A number of years ago quoiting was a favourite game with manly youth of the neighbourhood of Doune . . . subsequently quoiting as a public game became almost unknown', the *Stirling Journal* wrote in the early 1860s.[10] As late as 1888 the management committee of the Doune Moray Park was urging 'young men to form clubs for the revival of games like quoits, for which the district was once, but is not now, famous'.[11] At Bonnybridge in 1879 a quoits club was formed in the hope of stimulating interest in a 'once favourite pastime in the village'.[12] At Kilsyth an interest in quoiting was not rekindled until 1890, after an interval of sixteen years.[13] By the closing years of the century, however, quoiting was as popular with the inhabitants of central Scotland as it had ever been. 'The old game . . . has made a great revival in west Perthshire and western Stirlingshire . . . nearly every village has its club and the game has almost entirely supplanted football', the *Stirling Journal* claimed in 1897.[14] 'I don't think quoiting was ever more popular than at present', Alexander Blackwood informed members of the Milngavie Craigton Quoits Club.[15]

Accompanying the growth of interest in quoiting in the nineteenth century were two novel developments: organisation and commercialisation. The first was exemplified by the emergence of properly constituted quoiting clubs: the second by the inauguration of money matches between the game's leading exponents, usually on a one to one basis, occasionally involving two players a side.

Table 3.1 Number of quoits clubs and average number of inhabitants and males aged 15–44 per club, 1830–1900: by decade

Decade	Number of clubs	Inhabitants per club	Males (15–44) per club
1831–40	21	6,383	1,371
1841–50	13	11,479	2,570
1851–60	10	16,203	3,584
1861–70	21	7,813	1,720
1871–80	24	7,055	1,547
1881–90	28	6,694	1,492
1891–1900	45	4,593	1,007

Decade by decade totals of the number of quoits clubs known to have existed, together with estimates of the average number of inhabitants and males aged 15–44 per club, are given in Table 3.1. In the 1830s, measured in terms of total population and male population 'at risk' per club, only curling of all club-based sports rivalled quoiting in popularity. Following a temporary slump in the number of quoits clubs during the 1840s and 1850s, recovery began in the 1860s, proceeding slowly through the next two decades and more rapidly in the 1890s. By the last decade of the century the number of quoits clubs was more than twice that of the 1830s and ratios of total population and male population 'at risk' per club lower than ever before.

Part of the explanation for the relatively early development of a club format in quoiting lies in the existence of an established tradition of competitive matches between neighbouring communities and districts. How frequent these were prior to the 1830s is impossible to say. During the 1830s, however, contests of this type were by no means uncommon and the feelings they aroused must have helped generate an interest in competition between more formally constituted bodies.[16]

In view of the early origins of club formation, the initiation of inter-club league and knock-out cup competitions was surprisingly late in emerging. A Scottish Central Quoits League was not established until April 1899 and a Stirlingshire Quoiting Association not until November of the same year.[17] One reason for this may have been the fact that only a minority of club members participated in inter-club matches. The eight players representing the Doune Quoits Club against the Thornhill club in 1865 were drawn from a total membership of forty-three: and the teams of six or eight players representing the Dunblane Quoits Club in the mid 1880s from a membership of twenty three. During the 1890s the Milngavie Quoits Club drew its eight or ten representative players from a total membership of between thirty-five and thirty-seven: the Milngavie Craigton club and its teams of eight from a total active membership of between nineteen and twenty-two. The majority of club members competed only amongst themselves and this may have lessened whatever pressures there were to develop inter-club contests on anything other than a friendly basis. For most of the century inter-club games were designed more to promote the honour of the community and relieve the monotony of intra-club competition than to compete for money stakes, cups or league points.[18]

One indication of the relatively muted interest in inter-club competition was the small number of such matches played in the course of a season. Although the quoiting season lasted rather longer than that for other summer sports, extending from April to October and sometimes from March to November, few clubs were involved in more than a handful of competitive fixtures. In 1834 the Falkirk Quoits Club played a total of six; in 1894 and 1896 the Deanston club five and seven respectively; in 1895, 1896 and 1899 the Stirling club ten, eight and seven; in 1896, its first season, the Milngavie club just four; and in 1896 and 1899 the Craigton club just three.

Most of the matches were played between clubs from within a very narrow catchment area. Only the larger clubs like Falkirk and Stirling more than occasionally competed against clubs from further afield. Among the opponents of the Stirling Quoits Club in the 1880s and 1890s, for example, were Auchterarder (sixteen miles), Perth (twenty-eight miles) and Dundee and Dundee Cleppington (sixteen miles). But even in the case of the Stirling club the bulk of fixtures were against clubs lying within a radius of a dozen or so miles of the town – Causewayhead (three-quarters of a mile), Bannockburn and Bridge of Allan (two miles), Dunblane and Menstrie (four miles), Alloa, Deanston and Kinbuck (six miles), Fishcross, Stenhousemuir, Denny and Thornhill (seven or eight miles), Longcroft (nine miles), Dollar (eleven miles), Redding and Buchlyvie (twelve or thirteen miles). Apart from an occasional fixture against the Rumbling Well and Dunfermline clubs, played on the Stirling Kings Park, and the

Edinburgh and Falkirk clubs, the Doune Quoits Club of the 1830s and 1840s cast its net no wider than Blairdrummond (three-quarters of a mile), Dunblane (two miles), Bannockburn (eight miles) and Alva (ten miles). In the 1860s it played competitive matches only with the Dunblane and Thornhill (four miles) clubs and, throughout the last thirty years of the century, only with the neighbouring Deanston Club (half a mile). During the 1830s the Dunblane Quoits Club competed only against the nearby Doune club. By the 1850s it was playing clubs at Blackford (nine miles) and Crieff (twenty miles) and by the 1860s clubs at Doune, Buttergask (played at Greenloaning, a distance of five miles), Blackford and Braco (seven miles). In the 1880s its fixtures were restricted to clubs at Dunblane Ashfield, Dunblane Barbush, Bridge of Allan and Kinbuck (two miles), Braco and Stirling. The Muthill Quoits Club looked no further for its opponents than the adjacent communities of Braco, Comrie, Crieff and Strathallan: the Auchterarder club no further than Blackford, Braco, Crieff and, in the 1890s, Stirling.

The format within which inter-club quoiting matches were conducted varied considerably. Matches between clubs competing in the Scottish Central Quoits League were standardised at eight players a side. Otherwise teams might comprise anywhere between two and twenty-four players. Until the 1860s there was little regularity in team size, the number of players varying from two to four, five, six, eight, nine, ten, twelve, sixteen, twenty, twenty-one and twenty-four. Normally these were divided into rinks of two players each though rinks of one, three, four and even six players a side were not uncommon. Beginning in the 1870s, however, the size and arrangement of teams became more standardised and by the final quarter of the century teams of four, six or eight, split into two, three or four rinks of two players a side, were the norm.

Victory in inter-club matches went to the team with the greater aggregate number of shots scored over all rinks.[19] Since, prior to the mid 1880s, the number of shots required to win each rink was usually as high as forty-one, forty-five, fifty-one or even sixty-one, matches often took a considerable time to complete. With a duration of two hours, the ten-a-side, five-rink contest between the Braco Ardoch and Blackford clubs in July 1860 was probably one of the shortest. By contrast, a one-rink, two-a-side match between Auchterarder and Blackford in August of the same year lasted four hours and a twenty-a-side match between Auchterarder and Crieff in September 1859 five hours. Beginning around the mid 1880s the number of shots required for game on each rink was reduced to twenty-five or thirty-one and the duration of matches accordingly shortened.

Regrettably, there is little evidence on the extent to which inter-club quoiting contests attracted spectators. At least during the period between the 1830s and mid 1860s scattered press comments on crowd size suggest that substantial attendances were not unusual. In September 1833 a crowd of between two and three hundred watched a game between the Denny and Falkirk clubs. Two years later a twenty-four-a-side match between the same two clubs attracted four hundred spectators. In 1836 matches between the Doune Quoits Club and a combined team from the Denny and Stirling clubs attracted 'many spectators'; the Doune and Dunblane clubs a 'large crowd'; and the Bannockburn Muir and Milton clubs an 'exceedingly large number of onlookers'.[20] In August 1840 the crowd at a game between the Doune and Bannockburn clubs was recorded as 'very numerous' while two matches between the same clubs in September both drew a 'vast concourse of spectators'.[21] When the Doune and Alva clubs met at Bridge of Allan in 1841 the 'overflow of spectators' was so great that 'the players, being unguarded by ropes or police, were much incommoded by the crushing and crowding'.[22] How typical such crowds were we have no way of knowing. But the fact that 'the crowd did not muster so great as we have seen on former occasions' for a match between Falkirk and Linlithgow at Polmont in 1834, and that the explanation was believed to be that 'it was not until Saturday evening before the game was generally known', implies that they were far from uncommon.[23]

Compared with the size of crowds attracted to championship and money matches between the game's leading, individual players, however, those attending inter-club fixtures were modest. 'Monster' attendances like the two thousand or so which watched Peter McLachlan of Bannockburn and Thomas Osprey of Carron at the Falkirk Tryst in 1853 and Osprey against John Rennie of Alva at Larbert in 1855 were, of course, exceptional, even at Glasgow venues where the major championship matches were played and the size of the stakes involved particularly large.[24] More typically, on the evidence of the few cases in which numerical estimates of crowd size are recorded, attendances ranged from four or five hundred to around a thousand.[25]

How regular attendances of this magnitude were is difficult to

Table 3.2 Description of attendance at matches between individual quoiters, central Scotland, 1859–1900: number and per cent of total

Description	Number	Per cent
Immense, great, big	4	7.4
Very large, large	33	61.1
Good, good many	6	11.1
Numerous, considerable	10	18.5
Not large	1	1.9
Total	54	100.0

judge. For most of the contests between the game's leading exponents the newspapers offer no comment on crowd size. And when they do the comment is invariably descriptive rather than numerical. Where descriptions of attendance are given, however, they indicate consistently substantial numbers. Table 3.2 summarises descriptions of crowd size at matches played between individual quoiters at twenty-two different venues in central Scotland during the second half of the nineteenth century. As the table shows, on only one occasion was the attendance described as other than considerable.[26] Given that indications of crowd size are not available for the majority of matches and that newspapers have a preference for reporting what was unusual rather than usual this conclusion must be treated with some caution. It is tempting, nonetheless, to suppose that sizeable audiences were the norm. Even players of moderate skill and strictly local reputation, competing for the smallest stakes, seem to have attracted large numbers of spectators.[27]

A summary of the amount of stake money involved in local quoiting matches is given in Table 3.3. In almost half of all matches for which we have information the stakes risked by each competitor and his backers were less than £10. In only a quarter of all contests did individual players and their backers hazard £15 or more on the result and in just one in ten £25 or more. Only players whose skill and reputation transcended the region and who were among the best in the country – like Rennie, Osprey, Clarkston Rae of Carronshore, John Kirkwood of Haggs, William Murray of Grahamstown, Andrew Hunter of Alva and Robert Kirkwood of Banknock – were able regularly to raise and compete for stakes of £15 or £20 and above, and

Table 3.3 Total stake money involved in matches between individual quoiters, central Scotland, 1845–1900

Total stake (£)	Number	Per cent
Under 10	34	24.1
10–19	33	23.4
20–29	37	26.2
30–49	19	13.5
50	15	10.6
Over 50	3	2.1
Total	141	99.9

even then only for matches against players of similar prowess from other parts of Scotland. With the sole exception of the £50-a-side match between William Murray and Andrew Gourlay of Glasgow at Stenhousemuir in July 1874, the stakes involved in local quoiting matches never approached the large sum sometimes risked at the most prestigious Glasgow contests.[28]

Any explanation for the enduring, if variable, popularity of quoiting must take account of a variety of factors. Among these was the approval and support it received from 'respectable' upper- and middle-class society. In contrast to traditional working-class sports like bullet-throwing, cock-fighting and prize-fighting and even more acceptable activities like highland games, horse-racing, pedestrianism and soccer, quoiting, whether practised on a club or an individual basis, was rarely criticised for its association with gambling or for the potential threat its spectators posed to public order.[29] On the contrary, the game was widely commended by 'respectable' opinion as a 'harmless', 'innocent' recreation conducive to the moral and, above all, physical improvement of all who played it. Quoiting is 'particularly conducive to health', the Stirling Journal claimed in 1833.[30] 'Of all athletic games, none offers so fine a scope as quoiting for bringing into full prominence the qualities of body and eye', insisted Alexander Blackwood, chairman of the Milngavie Craigton Quoits Club in 1898.[31]

One consequence of this favourable response was that quoiting had little difficulty in persuading middle-class sponsors to supply it with the facilities and resources it required in order to thrive. True, much of the land needed for quoiting pitches and many of the prizes provided for club competitions came from tradesmen, most of them hotel- or inn-keepers, who saw quoits clubs and quoiting events as useful sources of additional income.[32] But upper- and middle-class men with no such commercial motivation also figured prominently among the ranks of prize-givers and donors of land. Of twenty-seven donors of land of known occupation 40.7 per cent were farmers or farm tenants, 7.4 per cent manufacturing employers and 7.4 per cent members of the nobility and property-owning classes. Of nineteen prizegivers whose occupations are known 26.3 per cent were manufacturing employers, 15.8 per cent men in public service or professional occupations, 10.5 per cent nobility or substantial property owners and the remaining 15.9 per cent builders, farmers or employees in the transport sector of the economy. In the case of at least one quoits club, the Milngavie Craigton, the patronage received from 'prominent local gentlemen' was accorded a vital role.[33] Commercial gain was clearly a significant motive for many of the game's patrons. But the not inconsiderable amount of sponsorship provided by the propertied, professional and employing classes, together with what their representatives said about the sport in the press, indicates that quoiting was often valued for less materialistic reasons too.

Certainly, quoiting was a highly physically demanding recreation. Money matches between individual players were normally won by the first player to reach sixty-one shots and invariably lasted several hours or more.[34] In 1842 a sixty-one-up game between Rennie and James Forbes of Doune took two hours to complete. Usually, however, games lasted much longer: three hours in the case of Paterson of Alloa and Cook of Sauchie in 1862; almost four hours in the case of John Thompson of Alva and William Fleming of Longcroft in 1877; four and three-quarter hours for Rennie versus Marshall of Edinburgh in 1852; and five hours in the cases of Rennie versus Woodburn of Ayrshire in 1858 and James Armour versus John Kirkwood in 1883. In 1870 an eighty-one-up British championship match between Robert Walkinshaw and George Graham of London was reported to have taken six and a half hours to complete.

Bearing in mind the time required to complete matches and the distance over which the quoits had to be thrown (usually eighteen or twenty-one yards), the size and weight of the quoit is startling. Among the game's chief exponents the lightest quoit used, 6lb, was that of John Wilson of Townhill, a champion of Fifeshire. William

Whittacker and John McGibbon, a man of 'lesser muscle power', threw a 9½-lb or 10-lb quoit; Rennie, who weighed between nine and ten stone and stood five feet six or seven inches in height, a 12½-lb or 13-lb quoit, 8 inches in diameter; the 'big and powerful' George Graham a 12¼-lb quoit; Robert Walkinshaw a quoit of between 12-lb and 12¾-lb with a diameter of 8½ inches; James Armour a 12¾-lb quoit 8⅝ inches in diameter; Alex. Smith, a five feet nine inch man of 'rather unhealthy' appearance, a 13-lb 8-inch quoit; and John Kirkwood a 14-lb quoit, 8⅞ inches in diameter. None, however, compared with David Weir, the 'rather powerful', six feet tall champion, who 'regularly' threw 19-lb 9 inch quoits and, sometimes, 10-inch quoits as heavy as a barely credible 23 lb. As the *Stirling Journal* commented, 'to throw heavy quoits for four hours with unerring accuracy requires great strength and . . . indominitable nerve'.[35] Little wonder that in April 1870 Walkinshaw and Graham were reported to be 'hard in training' for their match the following June.[36]

That quoiting was not a game for the physically frail and therefore understandably appealing to those anxious to promote the health, strength and stamina of the labouring populations is evident from the age structure of its players (Table 3.4). The vast majority of quoiters were young, fully mature males aged between twenty and forty-nine. Few were younger than twenty and none older than fifty.[37] The careers of players competing at the highest levels rarely extended beyond the mid forties. Rennie became Scottish champion in 1847 at the age of twenty-five and four years later was being described as 'the first player in England and Scotland'.[38] In 1854 he lost his British championship but remained Scottish champion for at least another several years. The last reference to his participation in a match of any significance was in 1858 when he contested the championship of Scotland with William Lindsay of Glasgow. He was then thirty-six years old. By 1864 Rennie was a spectator, described in the press as the 'ex-champion player'.[39] At his death in 1888, aged sixty-six, it was noted that he had not 'much indulged in his favourite pastime for the last twenty years'.[40] David Weir, who did not take up the game until his mid thirties, was still one of the country's leading players at the age of forty-three. Thereafter, he too disappeared from the scene. In contrast to less physically demanding activities like bowling and curling, quoiting was not a sport which was usually continued into later middle age.

For those who played and watched it, quoiting had several major

Table 3.4 The age composition of quoits players, 1880–83: per cent of total

Age	Per cent
15–19	5.6
20–24	33.3
25–29	16.7
30–34	11.1
35–39	5.6
40–44	16.7
45–49	11.1
All ages	100.0 (N = 18)

attractions. Firstly, its rules were simple to understand and difficult to flout. The quoit, itself little more than an iron ring, was thrown alternately towards two 'ends', usually eighteen or twenty-one yards apart, at each of which a metal spike (variously known as a 'hob', 'peg', or 'pin') had been driven into the centre of a circle of stiff, sticking clay approximately three feet in diameter. Sometimes the spike was exposed an inch or so above the ground; sometimes it was left flat with the surface. Each player threw two quoits per 'end', the object being to land the quoit nearer the spike than one's opponent. Ringing the spike scored two points, with one point awarded for each quoit other than the ringer nearer to the spike than that of the other player.[41] It was permissible to attempt to dislodge an opponent's quoits. On balance, the heavier and wider the quoit thrown, the greater the chance of doing so.[42] At times this gave rise to complaints and attempts to standardise the size and weight of the quoit thrown.[43] Generally, however, attempts at standardisation failed and players continued to use the size and weight of quoit which best suited them.

A second factor in the attractiveness of quoiting to working-men was that it was a relatively inexpensive game to play. The only piece of playing equipment required, the quoit, was cheap and easily available. Unlike soccer and cricket, moreover, the amount of land needed for a pitch was small and, unlike bowling greens, quoiting pitches needed little preparation or maintenance. Accordingly, the financial requirements of quoits clubs were minimal. In the first season of its existence, for example, the Milngavie Craigton club had a total expenditure of just £5 18s 7½d, of which £3 13s went on players' expenses and refreshments for visiting teams, £1 15s 7½d on the upkeep of the pitch and 10s on prizes. In 1899 the club spent even less, £3 3s 3d. From what few data exist, it seems that quoits clubs had no difficulty in raising the revenue required to meet these modest outlays. In 1896 the Craigton club reported an income of £5 19s 5d (£3 7s 7d from members' subscriptions and £2 11s 10d from monthly collections) and a surplus income over expenditure of 1s; in 1899 an income of £3 17s 3d and a surplus of 14s.[44] The result was that the annual subscriptions imposed by quoits clubs on their members were distinctly lower than in most other sports.[45] Of course, by no means all working-class quoiters participated in the game as members of clubs.[46] But the relatively low cost of membership certainly made it easier to do so if they wished. In this context an observation made by the *Stirling Journal* in 1885 on the formation of a quoits club 'by some of the younger men' of Doune is instructive. The club, the newspaper noted, 'from its inexpensiveness, will probably be joined by others who find our excellent bowling club rather too heavy for their finances'.[47]

Thirdly, at least for those of exceptional talent, quoiting offered working class men a chance not only of fame but also of useful, additional income. At a time when skilled workers earned between £50 and £75 a year, and many semi-skilled and unskilled workers much less, professional quoiting, like professional cricket and soccer, could prove a lucrative pastime for the most talented. Even men involved in matches for stakes of £1 or £2 a side were playing for a sum the equivalent of a skilled worker's weekly wage. Half the money matches played in central Scotland during the second half of the nineteenth century were for stakes of between £5 and £14 per player, a considerable amount for an ordinary working man. And where stakes were as high as £25 or £50 and more a side, the amount involved was very substantial indeed. Admittedly, much, perhaps most, of the stake money wagered was put up not by the player himself but by his backers, all of whom would require a share of any winnings. But quoiters who played sufficiently regularly and successfully could also expect to profit. By December 1844, in the course of a competitive career which had then lasted little more than five years, David Weir was reported to have earned over £900 for himself and his supporters.[48] Between the early 1840s and August 1851 John Rennie competed in a total of thirty major money matches in England

and Scotland, losing only once.[49] It is impossible to estimate how much this long run of success won for himself and his backers, but the amount must have been considerable since at the height of his fame he normally played for stakes of £25 or £50 a side. Between 1861, when he became British champion, and 1868 Robert Walkinsaw successfully defended his title on six occasions, for total stakes of £800.[50] James Armour, first recorded as champion of the Lothians in April 1873, by July of that year had already 'won several hundred pounds for his supporters'.[51] By the beginning of September 1875 David Haddow had achieved his 'seventh great success' of the year and in October was also to defeat George Graham of London in the best of two games for stakes of £100 a side.[52] A match between Andrew Hunter of Alva and J. Hunter of Oakley for £10 a side at Beveridge's quoiting ground, Rumbling Well, in November 1875 was recorded as the fifth meeting between the two players that season.[53] Clearly, for the Hunters and the many other quoiters who regularly and successfully participated in head-to-head money-match contests quoiting was a profitable activity. Together with the prize-money that could be earned at open handicap tournaments and at tournaments sometimes held at highland games' gatherings,[54] these matches made it an attractive sport for working-class men looking to improve the quality of their lives.

For the working-class spectator, apart from the excitement and camaraderie it engendered, quoiting was attractive, above all, for the opportunities it provided for gambling. Irrespective of the reputations of the competing players or the amount of prize- and stake-money involved, gambling was both normal and extensive among the crowds at quoiting matches and remained so throughout the century.[55] How much money was wagered is impossible to say with any precision. But there can be no doubt that it was often substantial. 'Considerable betting' occurred among the crowd at a £10-a-side contest between Rae and Wilson at Carron's Inn in 1861 and 'much betting' among spectators at a £1 a side match between Wardrope and Gowans at Bannockburn ten years later.[56] Large amounts of money 'changed hands' among spectators at matches between William Murray and John Kirkwood in August 1865 and Adam Hunter and Andrew Rae in July 1900.[57] In 1851 an Edinburgh innkeeper reputedly pocketed over £300 from wagering that Rennie would defeat Ewing of Pollokshaws by at least twenty shots in their match on the Bruntsfield Links.[58] When James Armour met John Wilson at

Rumbling Well in April 1873 for a total stake of £20 it was claimed that 'ten times that sum depended on the match'.[59]

Even at the peak of its popularity quoiting was never as popular with working-class men as soccer was to become.[60] In this respect its relative contribution to the spread of organised forms of sporting activity among the working classes was limited. In other respects however, its contribution was of equal, if not greater, significance.

To begin with, in sharp contrast to most other sports, quoiting, like soccer and probably athletics, was dominated by players of working-class background. Among the game's leading exponents, David Weir was originally an agricultural labourer, Alex. Smith worked in a snuff box factory, John Rennie was a woollen weaver, William Hodgson a miner, William Stewart a railway luggage guard and Thomas Osprey a moulder at the Carron ironworks. The great majority of its more humble players were craftsmen of relatively modest status, miners and skilled or at least semi-skilled industrial workers. 'Mechanics' and tradesmen's hours of relaxation cannot be better employed than in spending an hour or two in the open air playing this exhilarating game', it was noted of the general revival of quoiting in the 1830s.[61] At Bannockburn in October 1837 six rug weavers played six tartan weavers. 'These creeshy cotton spinners continue to lick all and sundry', it was remarked of a victory by the Doune Quoits over the Alva Quoits Club in 1838.[62] At Blackford in the early 1870s there was an annual match between a team representing local boot and shoe makers and a team of masons. At the Gowanbank quoits ground, Stirling, in 1895 a team of warders from the Perth Penitentiary played a team of warders from Barlinnie Prison, Glasgow. 'Quoiting is a favourite game among miners', the *Stirling Observer* reported in 1898.[63]

A more precise assessment of the occupational and social composition of quoits players is given in Tables 3.5, 3.6, and 3.7.[64] Table 3.5 is based solely on statements of occupation contained in the newspapers. More than half of all quoiters were employed in manufacturing occupations of one kind or another, a quarter in the building trades and just over one in ten in mining. By comparison, agriculture, trade and transport occupations together supplied less than one in ten and other occupations none.

Tables 3.6 and 3.7, which relate only to the period 1880–3, are based on a comparison of names of quoits players given in newspapers with data on their occupations and other indications of

Table 3.5 The occupations of quoits players, 1820–1900: per cent of total

Agriculture and fishing	2.3
Building	25.6
Dealing	2.3
Domestic service	–
Manufacturing	55.8
Mining	11.6
Property owning	–
Public service and professional	–
Transport	2.3
Other	–
Total	99.9
N	43

Table 3.6 The occupations of quoits players, 1880–83: per cent of total

Agriculture and fishing	–
Building	11.1
Dealing	–
Domestic service	–
Manufacturing	50.0
Mining	27.8
Property owning	–
Public service and professional	–
Transport	–
Other	11.1
Total	100.0
N	18

social status derived from the unpublished, manuscript census enumerators' books of 1881.[65] Table 3.6 confirms the dominance of manufacturing, mining and building employments as the principal occupational sources of the game's active participants. Table 3.7 shows that almost three-quarters of all quoiters came from social class C and, within that class, primarily from among skilled industrial workers and miners. Classes D and E, the semi-skilled and unskilled, and B, the middle class, made only a modest contribution. Interest-

Table 3.7 The social composition of quoits players, 1880–3: per cent of total

Social class	Per cent
A	–
B	11.1
i	–
ii	–
iii	11.1
C	72.2
i	5.6
ii	66.7
iii	–
D	–
E	16.7
Total	100.0
N	18

ingly, the representation of unskilled workers (class E) among quoits players was larger than that for any other sport except athletics, soccer included.[66] In all, 89 per cent of all quoiters and 90 per cent of all soccer players of known social class were drawn from working-class backgrounds, proportions far in excess of those in any other sport except for athletics (86 per cent).[67]

In some respects quoiting's contribution to the emergence of an organised sporting culture among the working classes was clearly greater than even that of soccer. For one thing, quoiting developed formalised club structures and regularised rules of play very much earlier than soccer which did not proceed beyond folk forms of football until the 1860s and 1870s. For another, unlike soccer which owed much of its institutionalisation and codification to the initiatives of men of educated, public-school, middle-class origins, the development of clubs and adoption of common rules in quoiting were initiated chiefly by working-class men themselves. To the limited extent that middle-class males were involved, they were drawn principally from the lower echelons of middle-class society – from the ranks of tenant farmers, independent tradesmen and craftsmen of modest means whose education, income and life-styles were more akin to those of skilled workers than to those of other, more prosperous middle-class groups.

More so than soccer or any other sport quoiting was a thoroughly working-class game in composition, practice and outlook, with none of the hostility towards professionalism among its players and gambling among its spectators which characterised the early evolution of sports like athletics, rowing and soccer. Most striking of all is the fact that of all sports which attracted working-class participation quoiting alone seems entirely to have escaped the efforts of middle-class society to fashion a sporting culture based on strictly amateur ideals according to which winning mattered far less than the joy of simply taking part. For this, if for no other reason, we need to know more about it if we are ever fully to understand the process by which organised sport developed among the working classes of nineteenth-century Britain.

Notes

1 The area chosen for this study encompasses a fifteen- to twenty-mile radius of the town of Stirling, covering a population of over a quarter of a million by 1901. To the north and west of Stirling communities were generally small and largely agricultural or residential. To the south and east of Stirling the area was more heavily industrialised and urbanised and the average size of communities larger.

2 See N.L. Tranter, The social and occupational structure of organised sport in central Scotland during the nineteenth century, *The International Journal of the History of Sport*, 4, 3 (December 1987), p. 303.

3 In this respect the sport of athletics – highland games events, pedestrianism, harrying or cross-country running as well as amateur athletics – might also repay closer scrutiny. Between 1880 and 1883 86 per cent of a small group of athletes for whom occupations are known were working class men of one kind or another. *Ibid.*

4 G. Redmond, *The Sporting Scots of Nineteenth-century Canada* (East Brunswick, 1982), p. 38. J. Arlott ed., *The Oxford Companion to Sports and Games* (Oxford, 1975), pp. 805–6. See also W.J. Baker, *Sports in the Western World* (New Jersey, 1982), p. 49.

5 *Devon Valley Tribune* 4 October 1900. *Stirling Journal (S.J.)* 22 July 1830, 2 September 1830.

6 *Stirling Observer (S.O.)* 8 June 1837.

7 *S.O.* 22 July 1836.

8 *Alloa Advertiser (A.Adv.)* 24 August 1850.

9 *Falkirk Herald (F.Her.)* 9 August 1860. *S.J.* 24 August 1860.

10 *S.J.* 17 July 1863.

11 *S.J.* 31 August 1888.

12 *S.O.* 19 June 1879.

13 *F.Her.* 12 July 1890.

14 S.J. 16 July 1897.

15 S.J. 14 October 1898, 20 October 1899.

16 See, for instance, the eighteen-a-side match between quoiters from the Falkirk and Stirling districts in July 1830 (S.J. 22 July 1830), the eight-a-side game between Stirling district and quoiters from Doune and Dunblane in August 1833 (S.J. 16 August 1833), a six-a-side match between representatives of Falkirk and Larbert parishes in September 1834 (S.J. 19 September 1834) and two four-a-side games between the villages of Craigmill and Causewayhead in July 1836 (S.J. 15 July 1836, 22 July 1836). Subsequently, with the emergence of quoits clubs and inter-club contests, the institution of open-handicap quoiting tournaments and the proliferation of money matches between individual quoiters, the frequency of inter-community and inter-district games declined.

17 The league comprised six clubs: Bannockburn, Bridge of Allan, Carron, Fishcross, Sauchie and Stirling. S.J. 28 April 1899. The Association was made up of twelve clubs: Alva, Banknock, Bannockburn, Camelon, Carron, Denny, Fishcross, Haggs, Kinbuck, Longcroft, Redding and Stirling. S.O. 22 September 1899. In 1900 it began a Challenge Cup competition.

18 Inter-club matches for money stakes were relatively infrequent. But see Doune versus Alva in 1838, Doune versus Rumbling Well in 1839 (for a £2 stake), Haggs versus Bannockburn in 1859 (for £10), Braco Ardoch versus Buttergask in 1860, Buttergask versus Dunblane in 1861 (for £1) and Doune versus Deanston in 1882 (for 'a handsome sum of money').

19 See below p. 53.

20 S.J. 1 July 1836, 15 July 1836, 22 July 1836.

21 S.J. 7 August 1840, 4 September 1840, 9 September 1840.

22 S.J. 14 May 1841. The largest crowd ever recorded at a quoiting match in nineteenth-century Scotland was five thousand, at Melaugh's quoits ground, Glasgow, in January 1870 for a game between Walkinshaw of Alexandria and Graham of London for £100 a side and the championship of Great Britain. Matches between Walkinshaw and Whittacker of Manchester at Melaugh's in June 1867 for a £100 stake and the British championship and between Connel of Darvel and Watters of Lochgelly at the Glasgow Bridgeton quoits ground in June 1896 for the twenty-one-yard championship of Scotland attracted around two thousand spectators. A crowd of fifteen hundred watched Simpson of Glasgow play Graham of London at Melaugh's in July 1871. The attendance at the Walkinshaw-Whittacker contest was described as 'enormous, far exceeding anything ever seen at a quoiting competition before' and that at the Connell-Watters match as 'the largest . . . seen at a quoiting match for many years'. S.J. 7 June 1867, 26 June 1896. Typically, however, depending on the weather, the fame of the competitors and the size of the stakes, the most important Glasgow quoiting contests appear to have drawn crowds of between several hundred and a thousand, the latter considered 'very large'. S.J. 1 October 1897.

23 S.J. 8 August 1834.

24 S.O. 15 September 1853. *Clackmannanshire Advertiser* 15 September 1855.

25 The one thousand crowd at a match between Stewart of Perth and Rae of Carronshore at Bainsford in October 1862 was considered 'immense' by local standards. *S.J.* 17 October 1862.

26 The exception was a match between Hepburn and Shaw in November 1894 to raise funds for the Stirling Quoits Club at which 'afternoon showers' resulted in a 'not very large' attendance. *S.J.* 16 November 1894.

27 In October 1869, for example, 'a great many people' watched Jack Gowan and James Stevenson of Bannockburn compete for a stake of just £1 a side. *S.J.* 8 October 1869. At least at the most important games spectators were expected to pay for the privilege of watching. At a match between Rennie and Ewing of Pollokshaw on the Bruntsfield Links, Edinburgh, in 1851 600 spectators paid sixpence each for admission to the ground. For a match between Adam Hunter of Alva and Alex. Kirk of St Ninians at St Ninians in 1879 admission was two pence. Whether or not admission charges were normal is not known. Open-handicap tournaments for individual players were also popular with spectators. An Alva handicap tournament, played over three successive Saturdays in July 1871, attracted two hundred spectators on the first day, 'a large number' on the second and 'a very large turnout despite heavy rain' on the third. *S.J.* 7 July 1871, 14 July 1871, 21 July 1871.

28 The largest amount of stake money known to have been wagered on a quoiting match in Scotland was £200 a side, on games between John Rennie and William Hodgson of Lancashire at Edinburgh in 1854 and Robert Kirkwood – William Watters of Lochgelly at Glasgow in 1900. Usually, the most important games, pitting Scot against Scot for the Scottish championship or the Scottish champion against the English champion for the British championship, involved stakes of from £50 to £100 a side. As in central Scotland, however, the majority of matches played in Glasgow, Edinburgh and elsewhere were for much smaller stakes.

29 See below pp.57–8.

30 *S.J.* 6 September 1833.

31 *S.J.* 14 October 1898.

32 Dealers, chiefly hoteliers and publicans, comprised 44.4% of twenty-seven donors of land of known occupation and 31.6% of nineteen individuals of known occupation who supplied prizes to quoits clubs. Local merchants and tradesmen were particularly generous in their donations of prizes to the Deanston and Doune clubs. The Alva handicap tournament was managed by the proprietor of the Crown Hotel and the Denny tournament by the proprietor of the Anchor Inn at Dunipace. The same Anchor Inn hosted the £5-a-side contest between Hugh Williamson of Dunipace and James McCann of Carron in 1880 and the Alva Temperance Hotel one of the two matches for £10 a side between Thompson of Alva and Stalker of Galashiels in 1878. An innkeeper like William Wright, patron of the Doune Quoits Club, was no doubt one of the many who regarded the patronage of quoiting as a profitable undertaking.

33 *S.J.* 20 October 1899.

34 Much less frequently forty-one, fifty-one, seventy-one, eighty-one and

even 101 shots. Of seventy-one matches played in central Scotland between individual quoiters for which the number of shots needed for victory are recorded by the press sixty-two (87.3%) were sixty-one up, four (5.6%), forty-one up, three (4.2%) fifty-one up and two (2.5%) seventy one up. A match between Thompson of Alva and Kirkwood of Haggs at Bannockburn in July 1874 was described as 'the usual 61 up'. *S.J.* 31 July 1874. At open-handicap tournaments, where players completed on a knock-out basis, each game was won by the first player to twenty-one shots.

35 *S.J.* 24 August 1849.

36 *S.J.* 15 April 1870, 3 June 1870.

37 There were, of course, some teenage players. John Rennie, later to become Scottish and British champion, was already a noted player at the age of twenty. In 1842 the Alva and Doune Juvenile quoits clubs consisted entirely of youths aged between sixteen and twenty. At Bannockburn in 1860 Robert Goldie and John Thomson were defeated by Charles Eadie, a youth of sixteen. In 1866 Robert Bryant, aged eighteen, was killed by a blow on the head from a quoit thrown during a match in which he was playing. In 1886 the Braco Quoits Club awarded six prizes for competition among members aged under eighteen.

38 *S.J.* 1 August 1851.

39 *S.J.* 9 September 1864.

40 *S.J.* 6 January 1888.

41 John Rennie was reckoned especially adept at ensuring that both the quoits he threw each 'end' scored points. His opponents, when throwing first, seldom succeeded in scoring more than one point with their two shots. The level of skill displayed by leading quoiters was little short of awesome. During an exhibition match at Cambusnethan in 1873 John McGregor, a national champion at the eighteen yards distance, ringed sixty-two out of seventy-seven quoits thrown in twenty-five minutes.

42 Also, the heavier the quoit the less it was affected in flight by wind. In a game between married and unmarried members of the Doune Quoits Club in 1865, won by the former, the bachelors 'were not skilful enough to move the quoit through the air making allowance for a . . . troublesome wind'. *S.J.* 21 July 1865. Sometimes, of course, the use of heavy quoits proved a disadvantage. In 1861 Taylor of Alva, the 'immense favourite' at the start of the match, lost to Hardie of Bainsford because 'his quoits were too heavy for him and rarely reached the mark'. *S.J.* 16 August 1861.

43 A two-a-side contest between Goodall and Rigby, the English champions, and Turnbull and Dunlop, of Scotland, in October 1844, was fixed for quoits not exceeding 10lb as a result of complaints by the English pair that their defeat at the hands of Weir and Dunlop the previous July had been caused by the excessive weight of Weir's quoits.

44 In 1900 the Stirling Quoits Club, too, reported 'sound finances'. *S.O.* 2 March 1900.

45 In the case of the Craigton club in 1896, 2s 6d for full members and 1s for boys and honorary (non-playing) members.

46 As revealed by a decision of the Braco Quoits Club in 1886 to ban from the

quoiting pitch anyone who was not a member of the club or 'otherwise authorised'. *S.J.* 16 July 1886.
47 *S.J.* 8 May 1885. The Doune Bowling Club levied an annual subscription of 6s. New members were charged only 1s for each of their first three years but were required to pay an entry fee of £1.
48 *S.J.* 13 December 1844. His earnings from quoiting enabled him to move from Ayrshire, where he had worked as an agricultural labourer, to Glasgow, where he became proprietor of the Tradeston curling and quoiting green.
49 Though less dominant in subsequent years, Rennie continued to compete successfully until 1858.
50 *S.J.* 24 July 1868.
51 *S.J.* 11 July 1873.
52 *S.J.* 10 September 1875, 29 October 1875.
53 Andrew Hunter winning four of them. In the first four months of 1878 Hunter competed in four money contests, the fourth against Adam Hunter of Skinflats at Alva for £10 a side.
54 At the Killearn Strathendrick open-handicap tournament of 1870, which attracted eighteen competitors – many of them 'among the cracks of Scotland' prize money ranged from £3 10s for the winner to £2 5s for the runner up, £1 for third and 10s for fourth. First round losers played in a special competition for prizes of 15s, 10s and 5s. The Denny Bridgend tournament of 1877 which drew fourteen contestants, offered prizes of £1, 12s 6d, 7s 6d and 5s..
55 Occasionally encouraged by the adoption of handicap procedures to even up the chances of victory among players of differing abilities. Thus, Nielson of Kilmarnock received a twenty shot start in a sixty-one up, £25-a-side game against Murray of Carron at Falkirk in 1867. For references to betting among spectators see *S.J.* 5 September 1862, 2 November 1862, 6 September 1867, 21 July 1871, 6 June 1873, 3 October 1873, 2 July 1875. *Devon Valley Tribune* 5 June 1900. In July 1898 George Thomson, a Cowie miner, took legal action against John Martin, a Bannockburn quarryman, for the recovery of a £2 stake wagered on the result of a match between Peter Wilson and David Brown at the Stirling quoits ground. *S.J.* 8 July 1898.
56 *S.J.* 13 September 1861, 15 September 1871.
57 *S.J.* 11 August 1865. *Devon Valley Tribune* 3 July 1900.
58 *S.J.* 22 August 1851.
59 *S.J.* 11 April 1873.
60 At the height of soccer's popularity, in the 1890s, there was one soccer club for every 365 inhabitants of central Scotland, one for every 178 males of all ages, one for every eight males aged 15–44 and one for every fifty aged 15–29. During the final decade of the century roughly 25 per cent of all males aged 15–29 were members of soccer clubs. Quoiting at its most popular (in the 1890s) provided one club for every 4,593 inhabitants, one for every 1,007 males aged 15–44 and attracted between one in ten and one in twenty of all males aged 15–44 into club membership. Measured in this way, quoiting was less popular than cricket or curling, approximately

as popular as bowling and more popular than angling. None of these latter sports, however, had such a large representation of working-class players as quoiting or soccer. See Tranter, *The Social and Occupational Structure of Organised Sport*, pp. 303, 306–7.

61 *S.J.* 22 July 1836.

62 *S.J.* 27 July 1838.

63 *S.O.* 27 April 1898. Quoiting was never entirely a working-class game. According to Charles Roger, it was one of the games 'frequently played by visitors' to the spa village of Bridge of Allan, most of whom were of prosperous upper-middle and middle-class backgrounds. C. Roger, *A Week at Bridge of Allan*, Edinburgh 1851, p. 26. See also Table 3.7.

64 With minor exceptions, the occupational and social classifications adopted in these tables are those recommended by W.A. Armstrong. The use of information about occupation in E.W. Wrigley (ed.) *Nineteenth-century Society* (Cambridge University Press, 1972), pp. 191–310.

65 See Tranter, *The Social and Occupational Structure of Organised Sport*, pp. 301, 304–5.

66 Athletics 22.7%, soccer 5.7%, cricket 6.2%, curling 2.5%, bowling 1.8%, angling 4.5%, tennis nil and golf nil. *Ibid.*, p. 303.

67 See note 2.

4

Working-class sport in Manchester between the wars

Stephen G. Jones

The purpose of this chapter is not to enter directly into the continuing and complex debates over 'hegemony', 'social control' and 'class expression' in popular working-class culture, which I have examined elsewhere. The aim is rather to set such discussion in the context of a grass-roots survey of the actual extent and variety of sporting activity in a mature conurbation – in this case Greater Manchester – which had a population approaching two million between the wars. The city of Manchester itself officially had only 766,378 inhabitants in 1931, but, as J.B. Priestley observed, 'the real city sprawled all over South Lancashire' forming 'an Amazonian Jungle of blackened bricks'.[1] Economically, inter-war Greater Manchester presented a curious mixture of growth and diversification in new sectors such as electronics, finance and insurance combined with severe difficulties in older ones, especially recession in the textile industry. This ambiguity, though familiar to economic historians of the inter-war years, is still worth stressing as the idea of general decline is so deeply rooted in the popular mind. In fact, there was a surprising overall buoyancy in the local economy, even in the 1930s. Purchasing power in Manchester was impressive, only just behind Greater London and far in excess of the depressed areas in south Wales, the north-east and Scotland. The central shopping area was a hive of activity – there were over twenty thousand shops by the 1930s. Arguably, the origins of our contemporary leisure patterns and of modern consumer society are to be found in this period as the sale of cosmetics, fashions, furnishings, household gadgets and motor vehicles rose sharply, though until recently inter-war social history has tended to overlook such changes.

Into this category of leisure consumption came sportswear and equipment which was part of a wider growth in leisure consumption. According to trade directories, by the 1930s there were a number of retail outlets which catered for the fancies of sportsmen and women; not only the big high-street stores such as Lewis's, but also specialist outlets. For example, in 1929, there were seventeen athletic outfitters, some of which had quite large operations in the city centre: Finnigans was located in Deansgate and Market Street; Spalding in Oxford Street and Lower Morley Street, and Alec Watson – outfitters to Manchester City FC – in Piccadilly and Oxford Street. A range of sports goods from football and cricket gear to boxing gloves, golf clubs, hockey sticks and tennis nets were thus readily available. Additionally, by 1929, Manchester had spawned a sports manufacturing sector – six billiard and bagatelle table manufacturers (presumably supplying the city's thirty-seven billiard room proprietors), six fishing-tackle makers and dealers, three golf club producers and two sports goods manufacturers, including Alec Watson. Given the fact that the Census of Production for 1930 recorded only eight sports firms (with more than ten employees) in Lancashire and Cheshire, this is quite an impressive return.

The growing consumer market in sports goods presumably had a symbiotic relationship with spectator sport. As spectator sport rose in popularity, it stimulated the purchase of sports goods, and vice versa in a self-reinforcing process of growth. At any rate the evidence suggests that enthusiastic working-class participants were also keen spectators. For those sections of the working-class benefiting from higher real wages, together with a shorter working week (secured during the bitter industrial confrontations of 1919–20) and a Saturday afternoon break, there were more resources and time for sport.[2] Even if sportswear and equipment were beyond the lower range of working-class budgets, this could hardly be said for spectator sports, one aspect of which was the promise of an occasional escape from the monotony of deprivation. The *Manchester Evening News* felt that depressed trade and unemployment made no difference to the Grand National which 'seems to grow in favour year by year'.[3] By the same token, the *Manchester Evening Chronicle* mused that 'although things are bad, it is amazing the amount of interest in boxing'.[4] Theatres and music halls were still well patronised despite the recession whilst the number of cinemas in Manchester City rose from 88 in 1919 to 129 in 1939. Films were an important alternative to sports, especially for women, who found in the 'dream palaces' new opportunities outside traditionally male-dominated recreational spaces. Nonetheless, participant and spectator sport boomed in inter-war 'Cottonopolis'. Indeed Manchester's Chief Constable, John Maxwell, in his *Annual Report* of 1932 maintained that the growth of various forms of sport, including tennis, bowls and country rambling, was behind the general decrease in drunkenness.[5]

Not surprisingly, association football was the most popular spectator sport in the city, although the inter-war years were mixed ones for Manchester United and Manchester City. For United the 1920s and 1930s were lean decades; nine seasons were spent languishing in the Second Division and in 1933-4 there was the threat of relegation to the Third. Indeed, at the start of the 1930-31 season, after United had experienced twelve opening consecutive League defeats (still a First Division record), a meeting of some 1,500 supporters at Hulme Town Hall threatened to boycott the next fixture against Arsenal.[6] Organised discontent on this level was a rarity, and a loyal hard core of supporters remained. Nationally, attendance at Football League matches rose steadily and crowds at Old Trafford showed an upward drift, rising from an average of 23,372 in 1913-14 to 25,200 in 1927-8 and 28,667 in 1938-9.[7]

For Manchester City the period was more rewarding. They reached three Wembley finals, eventually winning the Cup against Portsmouth in 1934, and were First Division champions in 1936-7. After opening their new stadium at Maine Road in 1923 the club built up new support.[8] When 'City walked away with the Second Division Championship in 1928', over one million entered Maine Road during the season, averaging approximately 38,000 per match and £54,812 was taken at the turnstiles.[9] Furthermore in the season 1929-30 the club recorded a profit of £8,429 'due principally to increased gate receipts'.[10] By 1934, the season in which Maine Road registered its record attendance of 84,569, the club chairman, Albert Hughes, whilst acknowledging that the clubs faced 'counter-attractions', went on to praise the 'rekindled enthusiasm' and the need for further grand improvements and ventures into the transfer market. The championship victory of 1937 was a just reward. Manchester had become a great name in English football.

The sports columnist of the *Daily Express*, Henry Rose, and the sports cartoonist of the *Daily Mail*, Tom Webster, were particularly effective supporters of the Manchester boxing scene. Like horse-racing, boxing had links with both the working class and the aristocracy, at least at national level. In Manchester, however, it was largely in the hands of one or two powerful promoters, together with various 'penny capitalists' and trainers. By the early 1920s, the influence of the boxing establishment in London, especially the aristocratic National Sporting Club, was being eroded as local promotions and coverage in the sporting press increased.[11] Even the formation of the London-based Boxing Board of Control in 1929 failed to undermine the dominance of local figures. The leading Manchester promoter in the 1920s was Jack Smith, who from his well-appointed offices, ran contests at the old Free Trade Hall, the Alhambra and the Adelphi Sporting Coub. The Free Trade Hall alone accommodated over two thousand spectators with admission prices ranging from 1s 2d to 7s 6d. For such sums, the paying customer could expect to see three 15-round contests and possibly two 6- or 8-rounders. By the 1930s, Smith had been joined by Harry 'Kid' Furness who, on behalf of the Broadhead theatre circuit, staged bouts throughout the Manchester district, and by Jack Madden, the matchmaker at Belle Vue's new King's Hall. It was the King's Hall with its seven thousand seats which hosted a number of Lonsdale Belt, European Title and World Title deciders.

Thus Manchester had a number of boxing venues; not only the more salubrious Free Trade Hall and King's Hall, but also the 'small halls' like the Smithfield Market Boxing Club and Churnett Street Public Hall. It was these smaller clubs and venues which nurtured some of the most promising young boxers, who invariably came from tough working-class neighbourhoods and learnt their 'trade' in the back-street gyms of Collyhurst, Hulme or Salford. Some managers had a paternalistic attitude to their stable, though there was a great deal of corruption and injustice. The fact that 'bread-and-butter' boxers endured poor conditions of employment, serious illnesses and low rewards, led the local fighter, Billy Allen, to protest that boxers were exploited in the same way as the factory proletariat.[12] A number of boxing booths travelled the Manchester district, the most notable of which was run by the local black boxer, Len Johnson. Having entered the game in 1921 as a middleweight, Johnson rose to beat a number of champions and future champions, including the great Len Harvey. However, his poor eyesight and, more notoriously, the effective colour bar imposed by the National Sporting Club and the British Boxing Board of Control forced him to retire in 1933. Even so, his links with the game were maintained when he became proprietor of a travelling boxing booth with its accommodation for perhaps a thousand spectators to watch or even challenge one of Johnson's relatively well-paid booth fighters. With the Second World War the boxing booth was wound up. Personal injustice as well as close links with working-class poverty led Johnson to become an active member of the Communist Party.[13] In fact, as Fleming recognises, the Second World War seems to have signalled the end of the golden age of boxing in Manchester.

The 1920s also witnessed the rise of two new commercial sports – speedway and greyhound-racing. Speedway or dirt-track racing originated in Australia, and had become firmly established in Manchester by the end of the decade. The main sites were at Belle Vue with seats in covered stands for 28,000 at 1s, and the White City with covered accommodation for forty thousand and admission prices ranging from 6d to 3s. Additionally, there were speedway tracks at Salford, Audenshaw and Hardforth. As daredevil Glen Becker, a leading rider of the period, recalled: 'As a sport it was a huge success. I have in mind the first North of England track at Audenshaw, where the racing started at 2 pm, went on all afternoon, and often was not over at 9 pm.'[14] However, from the beginning of the next decade the large initial audience for the sport began to wane, though the speedway test match at Belle Vue still attracted a capacity crowd in 1932 and league matches continued until the end of the decade.

In the case of greyhound racing there was no diminution in popular support throughout the 1930s. Manchester had its own course for horse-racing at Castle Irwell, but for seasoned gamblers the intermittent meetings, such as the renowned November Handicap, did not offer sufficiently regular opportunities for on-course betting. This was partly solved in 1926 when Alfred Critchley, with the support of American backers, opened a greyhound racing track – 'the poor man's racecourse' – opposite Belle Vue Gardens. It was an immediate success, and by the end of the year 333,375 attendances had been recorded. With the development of similar interests in London, Critchley and the other promoters formed a public limited company, the Greyhound Racing Association Trust.[15] Under its umbrella various sites with totalisators were developed throughout the country, including the London White City track and the Albion Track in the Manchester region. In aggregate terms, the number of spectators attending greyhound races in Manchester rose only slowly from around one and a half million to one and three-quarters million during the 1930s, though the increases in London and Glasgow were far greater.[16]

Sport and the working class in modern Britain

Unfortunately, it is difficult to be precise about the social composition of inter-war sports crowds as no proper surveys were conducted. Certain grounds were built in proletarian districts – Maine
Road in Rusholme, the King's Hall in Gorton – and as John Maxwell
observed, 'there are three dog tracks in the Manchester district, and
they are all in the working-class residential areas'.[17] Yet, predictably
such spectator sports were controlled by a variety of middle-class
interests. Analysis of the capital and share register of the Manchester
Racecourse Company Limited for 1925, for example, reveals that the
preponderance of representatives from a diverse grouping of the
commercial, financial and professional classes, including solicitors and
surveyors alongside butchers and manufacturers.[18] In football,
formal control via the board of directors may also have been in the
hands of the commercial middle class but, as Charles Korr has noted
in his excellent study of West Ham United, 'the club had become
almost a captive of the community in which it existed and which the
directors purported to serve'.[19] At least the price of admittance to
sports grounds was low enough to attract large sections of the
working class: one shilling, between one-fortieth and one-sixtieth of
an ordinary weekly wage, would gain entry to Old Trafford, Belle
Vue, the White City, the Ice Palace and many other sporting venues.
Social segregation of crowds was achieved by pricing policies. Fight
fans could thus choose tickets ranging from 2s 4d to 31s 6d for the
British lightweight championship contest held between Al Foreman
and George Rose at the King's Hall in October 1930.[20]

Also suggestive is the fact that before the Second World War it was
usual for sportsmen to live within the same communities as their
fans. This was clearly the case with boxers and to a lesser extent also
with footballers. Harry Godwin, a former Manchester City scout,
recalled that in his council house he was 'surrounded not only by City
supporters but also their players'.[21] After all, most footballers grew
up in northern working-class communities. Research on the 1934
Manchester City side shows that no first-team regular had been born
in the so-called 'affluent' south. More substantively, footballers'
wages, which were regulated by the notorious retain and transfer
system, were comparable to those received by skilled labour aristo-
crats. Run-of-the-mill boxers considered themselves fortunate to pick
up the average industrial wage, whilst accusations were made that
even speedway aces were exploited by E.P. Spense, the dictatorial
head of the Belle Vue track.

How fans travelled to attend their favourite sport may also offer some indication of social identity. Belle Vue, Maine Road, the Manchester racecourse and the Birch Park Skating Palace made great play of the fact that they were easily reached by public transport. Indeed, though many sports venues had private car parks, the vast number of spectators used the tramway system – designed specifically for the popular classes – to reach their destination. Interestingly enough, both the police and the Manchester Corporation Transport Department made special arrangements for football traffic. For instance, the department's traffic superintendent laid on a hundred additional trams for Manchester United's home game against Birmingham City in February 1922.[22] There is also evidence that local employers were pressed by their labour force to concede earlier closing on those Saturday mornings when a big football match was being staged.[23] Finally, here, impressionistic evidence, especially photographs and the use of language in press reports and the like, all reinforce the conventional wisdom that spectator sports in Manchester were proletarian and male-centred.

This last point is worth developing. Rosemary Deem and other feminist scholars have argued that recreational opportunities for women are patently constricted by their subordination to men.[24] Certainly in the context of the inter-war years, as Margery Spring-Rice's classic study testified, working-class wives found it difficult to enjoy sport for even limited periods as the overall responsibility for domestic labour and child care remained theirs alone.[25] However, a few sports promoters were attempting to woo female spectators, offering, for example, reduced admission prices at the Salford speedway and the Albion greyhound racing track. Protests over greyhound racing point to the growth of female support. As William Bower of the Manchester and Salford Federation of Brotherhoods lamented:

> I have been to the Salford Albion dog races. On the last occasion when I was present there were about 3,000 people. It was an evening meeting, and there were 25 bookmakers to look after the people and take the bets. Amonst the people were young boys and girls of 14 or 15 years of age. In the case of one boy in particular, his own mother was giving him money to put on. For a time there was a part of the ground where the mothers could take the baby in and leave the carriage. At Salford Greyhound racecourse I have seen the mothers taking the babes in the carriage into the ground.[26]

The extent of such female behaviour is not known at present and would repay further study. Despite the possibility that the period saw a rise in certain forms of female sports spectatorship, the football ground, boxing hall and speedway track remained firmly and unquestionably male preserves.

Voluntary organisations did offer an alternative to spectator sports. With their emphasis on participation rather than spectatorship, they genuinely hoped that sport in Manchester would not fall under the total control of commercial forces. However, many groups protested that they were fighting an uphill battle. Certainly the evidence suggests that various established organisations were losing membership. For instance, the number of boy scouts in the district fell from 8,975 in 1931 to 7,168 in 1938 whilst the famous Ancoats Recreation Movement and Hugh Oldham Lads' Club were in decline due to 'the widening choice of leisure activities'.[27] Significantly, the competition posed by commercialised sport to voluntary and religious organisations led to a certain degree of moral condemnation. Moralists akin to the Victorian rational recreationalists found in the 'newer' sports a further cause for concern.

This was particularly true of those sports, like greyhound racing, associated with betting. After all, according to the Census of Population, the number of bookmakers in Manchester rose from 108 in 1921 to 367 in 1931. We have already referred to the critical comments of William Bower. He was not alone. Peter Green, the Canon of Manchester, regularly attacked the spread of the gambling habit. W.D. Cobley of St Paul's Literary and Educational Society would not have the term 'Christian' 'applied to followers of horse-racing, dog-running and the like, which exist simply and solely for betting purposes'.[28] By the same token, the local Watch Committee, in discussing 'the evils arising from the great amount of betting that takes place on greyhound racecourses', called for preventative legislation to be enacted.[29] The local Labour MP for Gorton, Joseph Compton, was also scathing about greyhound-racing, precisely because of its connection with gambling. Speaking during the Dog Racing and Racecourse Betting Bills of 1928, Compton at first welcomed the new sport, but as soon as he realised the true intentions of promoters, who were riding 'roughshod' over local interests, he insisted that it would 'propagate poverty' and lead to 'the ruination of the homes of thousands of people'.[30] Such moral crusades predictably failed to undermine the popularity of the dogs. The will of the people to gamble together with the ability of entrepreneurs to respond to new market opportunities ensured that greyhound racing would remain one of the most popular recreational habits in Manchester until the outbreak of the Second World War.

Moralists, social engineers and particularly sabbatarians were more successful in their campaign against Sunday sport, although boxing and dirt-track racing certainly took place on Sundays. A local councillor called Sunday speedway at the Audenshaw track a 'second Sodom and Gomorrah'.[31] Hence, church groups were particularly keen to prevent the introduction of Sunday games in public parks and open spaces. Agitation over this question dates back to the mid-nineteenth century and earlier. During the inter-war years the sabbatarian lobby were certainly much more efficiently organised than those advocates of Sunday opening.[32] As the *Manchester City News* reported on the eve of the 1922 local elections, 'organised opposition to such games is, at present, quietly active' whilst other contributions to the paper stressed that organised religion was the 'rock of defence against the desolating blasts of materialism'.[33] As late as December 1937 a motion calling for 'games to be played in the public parks and recreation ground on Sundays during the period of official summer time' was defeated at a meeting of the Manchester City Council by sixty-one votes to fifty.[34]

Clearly religious pressure groups and voluntary organisations were determined to struggle against the commercialisation and secularisation of the age. In addition, a wide range of working-class neighbourhoods continued to band together and provide sport for themselves on their own terms. By the twentieth century there were a myriad of neighbourhood football teams based on the workplace, the pub or simply the street. It was these, as an 'affirmation of collective identity', which offered a means for democratic control in leisure, so often denied in commercialised sports and by the atomising tendencies of a mature industrial city.[35] Despite the paucity of sources, working-class clubs were commonplace in inter-war Manchester. For instance, according to the annual reports of the Baths and Wash-house committee, some thirty-four swimming clubs subscribed to municipal pools in 1921–2, rising to forty-eight in 1936–7. Likewise, by this latter date the city parks accommodated some four hundred football and hockey teams and some one hundred and fifty cricket teams. Indeed, reports in the local press indicate that organised amateur sport was prolific. To take but one example, at the start of the 1937 season, there were numerous football leagues: the Rusholme and district league had seven divisions in all with an average of fifteen teams in each; the Chorlton League had three divisions with thirty-nine teams in all; and the Eccles league had two divisions with fifteen teams in each. Additionally there was a Manchester and district league, a Wythenshawe league, a Parks' league and leagues organised by the Co-operative and Wholesale Society (WS), Sunday School Union, Catholics and the rest. Though provision for women was not so wide-ranging, it appears that hockey was more popular than its middle-class private-school image might suggest. The Sunday School Union Women's Hockey League contained six divisions with eleven teams on average in each. Broadly speaking female access to sport was very much structured by the family life cycle with young women without domestic responsibilities forming the nucleus of active participants. Of the 3,250 members in the thirty-five local clubs affiliated to the National Council of Girls Clubs in 1933–4, 62 per cent were under eighteen years of age.[36]

Employer and labour organisations also catered for sport. In the Manchester district certain cotton mills, most notably those associated with the bigger combines like the Fine Cotton Spinners' and Doublers' Association and Tootal Broadhurst Lee, sponsored recreational facilities for their workforce. Obviously cotton makers were motivated by the need to improve labour productivity and industrial relations, though research indicates that operatives themselves were often able to gain control of such facilities.[37] Outside the cotton industry, a number of other companies had sports clubs: Armstrong Whitworths, Hans Renold and Metropolitan Vickers were involved in ventures such as the Workshops Bowls League and the Manchester Business Houses Cross Country Championship.

On the other side of the labour-capital divide, the Co-operative movement and certain trade unions branched out into sport. In fact, labour or socialist provision has to be viewed to some extent as a response and alternative to the rise of commercialised leisure and company sport. At any rate, to take but one example, in 1928 the Manchester Sports Association was formed, and by the 1930s, it had acquired its own sports ground, formed two football leagues and sponsored competitions in bowls, gold, swimming and ladies' cricket.[38] As the *Co-operative News* noted in reference to the football league: 'It was the aim of the executive to make the league as respected in Manchester football circles as the CWS was in its trading operations, and with the support of the teams in the league there was no reason why that aim should not be realised.'[39] Also, by 1930 the

Collyhurst district of Manchester had a branch of the Communist-inspired British Workers' Sports Federation (BWSF). With the use of a 'huge room' at the back of a bakers' shop and access to the local swimming baths, a predominantly male membership formed boxing, running, skipping and swimming groups and a football team.[40] Yet, it is very clear that the club had significant competition for potential membership. The local Guild for Social Service, which met at the Collyhurst Recreation Rooms, as well as the Parish Church, had sections for indoor recreation, football, cricket, swimming and ladies' hockey.[41] In fact, the BWSF's claim to fame was as the rambling group responsible for the Mass Trespass on Kinder Scout in 1932. By specialising in open-air activities the Manchester BWSF had in fact fortuitously concentrated on an activity which was increasingly controversial and in the public eye.[42]

Numerous labour sympathisers were enthusiastic about the open-air movement. In the mid 1920s, the Plebeian Ramblers emerged out of the Manchester and District Labour College, while a number of Independent Labour Party sections organised rambles, picnics and the like.[43] Aside from labour groups, there was an array of societies and associations catering for those interested in the open air. Manchester supported branches of such national organisations as the Cyclists' Touring Club, National Cyclists' Union, Camping Club of Great Britain and Youth Hostels Association.[44] The Manchester and District Federation of Ramblers was perhaps the most important local open air organisation formed in the aftermath of the Great War. By 1928 there were over a hundred clubs in the Federation. That year a demonstration four thousand-strong protested against restrictions on access to the countryside imposed by the landed élite – a struggle which continues to this day.

In the inter-war years local authorities had a good deal of autonomy, and as such had responsibilities for the regulation and licensing of leisure. This is an important point to make for developments in sport were often shaped by particular local government policies whether in the form of police coercion or municipal provision. Although the local authorities were constrained to some extent by the financial stringencies imposed by central government and worked with such official bodies as the National Fitness Council, Manchester Corporation independently sponsored numerous sports facilities.[46] By the end of the 1930s there were 35 swimming baths in the city, seven of which had been built since 1920. Special concessions were introduced for schools, the unemployed, and mixed bathers, whose numbers increased from 14,259 bathers in 1919–20 to 77,344 in 1936–7.[47] The new popularity of swimming is partly shown by the rise in the number of swimming galas and water polo matches from 62 in 1921–2 to 142 in 1929–30 and 199 in 1936–7. Similarly, many amenities were provided in open spaces and recreation grounds, as at the famous Heaton and Wythenshawe parks. By 1938 there were as many as 398 tennis courts, 201 football and hockey pitches, 76 cricket pitches and 79 bowling greens.[48] Judging from the range of organisations and leagues which used these facilities, they were of central importance in the city's sporting life. Additionally, in the mid-1920s the local council, working in conjunction with the Lord Mayor's Relief Committee, began to provide sports facilities and indoor recreation for the unemployed. This intervention brought 'a certain modest humaneness into the dull round of the unemployed', though the Conservative-controlled council mush have been perturbed by the growth of communist influence and may have regarded leisure provision as a palliative.[49] If the council's aim had been one of 'social control' of the unemployed through municipal leisure provision, this was far from being fulfilled. For Manchester was the scene of some of the most militant demonstrations and active organisation through the communist-dominated National Unemployed Workers' Movement and TUC Unemployed Associations in the early 1930s.

In fact, public bodies found it difficult to penetrate the dense network of informal recreations supported by the local community which ranged from the myriad hobbies and cheap literature taken in the home to the lively world of the street corner with its betting and banter. Joseph Farrington recalled how he used to sell football programmes around the streets near Maine Road and Belle Vue whilst entertainments and games were very much part of the carnival atmosphere of Saturday night food markets.[50] The street was of course the recreation venue *par excellence* for working-class youth. Always a place of social conflict and 'negotiation' between rival claims for control, the street supported a plethora of sports and games, nicely evoked in Anthony Burgess's recent autobiography, *Little Wilson and Big God*.

A survey of Hulme in the late 1930s – perhaps the most notorious slum area in the city with 44 per cent of families in overcrowded conditions and an above-average infant mortality rate – showed that family life was conducted chiefly in the kitchen. Recreation, at least for men, was taken outside the home. Although there were twelve public dance halls, eight cinemas, as well as various other public places of amusement and clubs, it was claimed that adolescents spent a lot of their spare time in the street.[51] This meant that youngsters invariably played football, 'ide' (hide and seek) and other games in the street, bringing them into conflict with the law.[52] The temperance advocate, Ernest Winterton, provided a vivid glimpse of local society on his visit to the area in 1932: 'Later in the evening we saw some of the social results of those prosperous little public houses in Hulme. Blossom Street, a very narrow street, was full of children and adults listening to a frightful row between drunken women, in which the most terrible language was used.'[53] Little wonder then, that in the same year the city's chief constable, John Maxwell, recommended that five streets in Hulme be closed to traffic and used as children's play areas. Despite such developments there were still 129 offences recorded in 1936 for playing games in Manchester Streets.[54]

The Chief Constable did notice a diminution in the incidence of street gambling in 1936 though this may simply have arisen from the growth of legalised gambling on greyhound races as well as the rise of lotteries and fruit machines. The fact that the number of street gambling prosecutions rose from 1,064 in 1920 to 1,170 in 1930, probably tells us more about detection than about the prevalence of street gambling. In fact, as Maxwell acknowledged, 'police action is to all intents and purposes ineffective owing to the great demand for betting facilities'. Arrests were only made when plain-clothes officers, often disguised, moved in. The reason for such a problem appears to have been the community nature of street betting, which involved women, children and adult men, and was organised in a fairly sophisticated way with illegal bookmakers – of which there was perhaps three hundred in the early 1930s – and a network of agents, scouts, and 'runners'.[55]

This chapter has only been able to cover a part of the sporting life of inter-war Manchester. Cricket, a Lancastrian passion, is an obvious omission in the land of Neville Cardus, and so too is rugby. How important, for example, was Lancashire County Cricket or Broughton Rangers rugby club in the recreational life of the city? What significance is to be attached to sports like roller skating, table-tennis or billiards? What is clear is that a relatively buoyant local economy underpinned a wide range of sporting forms, which were more predictably structured by class, gender, age and also ethnicity –

a regrettable absence from this paper are Manchester's considerable Irish and Jewish communities. Certainly income, work and housing conditions determined the ways in which people experienced sport. Poverty restricted access to equipment whilst patriarchial relations in the home still limited women's opportunities in sport, especially after marriage. Ordinary people were able to resist official intervention into their sports and pastimes in the local community with surprising effectiveness – as manifested by the success of streetbetting. By the same token spectator sports in Manchester were 'owned' by workers in spirit if not in fact. United and City supporters refused to regard their teams as the legal possessions of their directors alone. What remains to be investigated is the extend to which changes in the work process and the social relations of production – as forged by economic growth and diversification – altered the contours of non-work life. Older patterns of work and leisure were being re-defined as the expansion of unskilled and semi-skilled jobs in the newer trades increased labour-market flexibility. Together with developments in transport and housing policies, this fed gradually into the creation of new communities, whether based on suburbia or council estates. The kind of information presented in this brief survey of popular sports now requires both considerable expansion and a more systematic integration into the shifting and complex relationship between work and leisure as well as local and national structures of power.[56]

Notes

1 J.B. Priestley, *An English Journey* (Penguin edn., London, 1977), p. 239; on the local economy see H. Clay and K. Russell Brady (eds), *Manchester at Work: a Survey* (Manchester, 1929), pp. 3-4; Board of Trade, *An Industrial Survey of the Lancashire Area (Excluding Merseyside)* (HMSO, 1932).

2 See S.G. Jones, *Workers at Play: a Social and Economic History of Leisure* (London, 1985), ch. 1.

3 *Manchester Evening News*, 23 March 1923, p. 4.

4 *Manchester Evening Chronicle*, 30 August 1930.

5 The Chief Constable of Manchester, *Annual Report*, 1932, p. iii.

6 *Manchester Evening News*, 18 October 1930, p. 2.

7 Calculated from C. Zahra et al., *Manchester United: a Pictorial History and Club Record* (Nottingham, 1986), pp. 96, 124, 146.

8 *Manchester Evening News*, 24 August 1923, p. 6.

9 Eric Thornton, *Manchester City: Meredith to Mercer – and the Cup* (London, 1969), p. 2.

10 Manchester Central Reference Library 797.4 M1, Manchester City Football Club Limited, Report and Balance Sheet Year ended 10 May 1930.

11 This account is based largely on D. Fleming, *The Manchester Fighters* (Manchester, 1985).
12 *Daily Worker*, 20 March 1930, p. 11.
13 Michael Herbert, 'Len Johnson, black Mancunian, uncrowned king of boxing, committed internationalist', paper presented to the Northern Labour History Society, 1986.
14 *Worker Sportsman*, 1 May 1932, p. 4.
15 D.J. Jeremy, 'Critchley, Alfred Cecil (1890–1963). Greyhound racing: promotor and industrialist', in D.J. Jeremy (ed.), *Dictionary of Business Biography* (London, 1984), pp. 828–9.
16 Public Record Office, London, Home Office papers 45/15853.
17 *Minutes of Evidence Taken Before the Royal Commission on Lotteries and Betting* (HMSO, 1932), pp. 58–9.
18 Manchester Central Library Archive Deposit, L115/9, Manchester Racecourse Co., Register of Shares 1902–1928.
19 C. Korr, *West Ham United: the Making of a Football Club* (London, 1986), p. 27.
20 *Manchester Evening News*, 18 October 1930, p. 2.
21 *The Guardian*, 19 March 1980, p. 10.
22 Manchester Central Library Archive Deposit, M 29/22596c, Traffic Superintendent to General Manager, 22 February 1922.
23 See, for example, Manchester Central Library Archive Deposit, M 127/1/18, English Sewing Cotton Company Executive Minutes, 21 March 1923.
24 See, for example, R. Deem, *All Work and No Play? The Sociology of Women and Leisure* (Milton Keynes, 1986).
25 M. Spring-Rice, *Working-Class Wives: their Health and Conditions* (London, 1939).
26 Minutes of Evidence Taken Before the Royal Commission on Lotteries and Betting (HMSO, 1932), p. 316.
27 W.G. Jackson, 'An historical study of the provision of facilities for play and recreation in Manchester', M.Ed., University of Manchester, 1940, pp. 142–8. J.I Rushton, 'Charles Rowley and the Ancoats Recreation Movement', M.Ed., University of Manchester, 1959. Manchester Central Library Archive Deposit, M 7/29, W.A. Richardson, Manuscript History of Hugh Oldham Lads' Club 1888–1958, p. 6.
28 Manchester Central Library Archive Deposit, M 38/4/2/73; W.D. Cobley, 'The ethics of sport', *Odds and Ends*, LXXIII, p. 290.
29 Proceedings of the Manchester Watch Committee, 27 October 1927; Proceedings of the Manchester Education Committee, 16 July 1928.
30 *House of Commons Debates,* 5th Series, CXVII, cols 552–5, 11 May 1928; CIXX, cols 1805–7, 6 July 1928; CXX, cols 545–8, 675–6, 18 and 19 July 1928. See also *Labour* (May 1934), p. 210.
31 *Ashton-Under-Lyne Reporter*, 12 July 1930 p. 6.
32 See S.D. Simon *A Century of City Government, Manchester 1838–1938* (London, 1938), p. 310.
33 *Manchester Evening News*, 2 September 1922, p. 4.
34 Proceedings of the Manchester City Council, 15 December 1937.
35 See R. Holt, 'Working-class football and the city: the problem of continuity', *British Journal of Sports History*, III (1986), pp. 5–17.

36 Madeline Rooff, *Youth and Leisure: a Survey of Girls' Organisations in England and Wales* (Edinburgh, 1935), pp. 236–7.
37 See S.G. Jones, 'The survival of industrial paternalism in the cotton districts: a view from the 1920s', *Journal of Regional and Local Studies*, VII (1987).
38 *Peoples Year Book*, 1928, p. 61; 1930, p. 63; 1932, p. 61.
39 *Co-operative News*, 16 May 1931, p. 6.
40 Rebecca Casket (née Goldman) interview with the author, 17 August 1981.
41 See *Annual Reports* of Guild for Social Service, Collyhurst Recreation Rooms, 1930–35; also St James's, *Parish News*, 1931–1933.
42 See, for example, B. Rothman, *The 1932 Kinder Trespass: a Personal View of the Kinder Scout Mass Trespass* (Timperley, 1982).
43 *Labour's Northern Voice*, 1 May 1925, p. 7; 8 May 1925, p. 1; 21 May 1926, p. 7; 13 August 1926, p. 7.
44 W.H. Shercliff, *Nature's Joys are Free for All: a History of Countryside Recreation in North East Cheshire* (Poynton, 1987).
45 See A.W. Hewitt, *The Ramblers Federation: Nineteen Years of Progress in Manchester and District* (Manchester, 1938); *Northern Rambler*, May 1936, pp. 86–7.
46 *How Manchester Is Governed*, 1939, p. 161; Public Record Office, Board of Education Papers, 113/8, National Fitness Council, Lancashire and Cheshire Area Committee Report, 4 February and 17 October 1938.
47 See R. Hill (ed.), *The City of Manchester and How It is Managed* (Manchester Corporation, 1938), pp. 165–9.
48 *Manchester Corporation Parks and Cemetries Department Short Historical Survey*, 1938.
49 See F.J. Rosamond, 'The social and economic effects of unemployment in Manchester, 1919–1926', University of Manchester MA thesis, 1970, pp. 136–7, 328.
50 N. Gray, *The Worst of Times: an Oral History of the Great Depression in Britain* (London 1985), p. 15; A. Davies, ' "The air of carnival and the entertainment of shopping": Saturday night markets in Manchester and Salford, 1840–1939', *Manchester Region History Review*, I, no. 2 (1987).
51 H.E.O. James and F.T. Moore, 'Adolescent leisure in a working-class district' (reprinted from *Occupational Psychology*) (1940).
52 See Fred Davies, *My Father's Eyes: Episodes in the Life of a Hulme Man* (Swinton, 1985), p. 3. Harry Watkin, *From Hulme All Blessings Flow* (Swinton, 1985), pp. 29–34.
53 *Minutes of Evidence Taken Before the Royal Commission on Licensing (England and Wales)* (HMSO, 1930), p. 1915.
54 Proceedings of the Manchester Watch Committee, 14 November 1932; Manchester Chief Constable's *Annual Report*, 1936.
55 Manchester Chief Constable's *Annual Report*, 1936.
56 R. Whipp, 'Labour markets and communities: an historical view', *Sociological Review*, XXX (1985), pp. 767–90; S.G. Jones, 'Work, leisure and the political economy of the cotton districts between the wars', *Textile History*, XVIII,

(1987), pp. 33–8; P. Joyce, 'The historical meanings of work' in P. Joyce (ed.), *The Historical Meanings of Work* (Cambridge, 1978), pp. 1–30.

5

Parks and baths: sport, recreation and municipal government in Ashton-under-Lyne between the wars[1]

David Bowker

Despite the recent growth of sports history, surprisingly little is known about the municipal provision of baths, parks and playing-fields during the inter-war years. Wider studies of leisure, recreation or popular culture make but passing reference to municipal sports provision while at the local level works of a largely antiquarian nature often contain scant, uncoordinated and uncritical material. There are, of course, scholarly exceptions in the field of municipal analysis: the work of Helen Meller, John Walton and Richard Roberts spring to mind.[2] But for valid reasons these writers do not focus specifically on sport and recreation. Conceptually, despite vigorous criticism, broad notions of 'social control' remain implicitly and explicitly rooted within the vocabulary of leisure studies based on nineteenth-century material.[3] The lack of inter-war evidence leads to a rather distorted debate in which the moral reform of workers and the idea of respectable citizenship was largely confined to Victorian society. Yet moral reform through leisure lasted well into this century. Any question of municipal efforts at social control in the field of recreation imply some understanding of the extent of provision and 'take-up' rate as well as the underlying attitudes and values of the authorities. The modest aim of this paper is to use local newspaper sources and council minutes to provide a survey of municipal sport and recreation facilities in Ashton-under-Lyne between the wars, and then to briefly consider some of the attitudes and motives that were bound up with that provision and usage.

The Pennine foot-hill town of Ashton-under-Lyne, some seven miles north-east of Manchester, with a population which rose from 47,172 in 1911 to 60,331 in 1931, was a classic product of the industrial revolution. Although the number of cotton firms in the town fell from thirty-eight to twenty between 1911 and 1937, cotton remained the dominant industry. In 1931 the textile industry was by far the largest single employer of labour, especially for females, employing a workforce as large as that in metalworking, transport and communications, commerce and finance, personal service and miscellaneous occupations combined. For many Ashtonians the inter-war period was a gloomy one. In 1931 20.0% of men and 27.9% of women were unemployed. Over a number of years short-time working was common. From about 1935 unemployment levelled-off returning to the mid-1920s average of about 9.6% of the working population. By 1937 the District Juvenile Employment Committee and some trade unionists suggested that industrial diversification was robbing the cotton industry of juvenile labour. It may be that the local economy was less devastated than previous orthodoxy suggests; problems of the cotton industry have been skewed and overstated whilst industrial diversification and recovery from about 1936 onwards have been minimised. Whilst sustained deprivation was the fate of the unemployed, a shorter working week and paid holidays had been achieved in other sections of the community by the end of the inter-war period. Ashton's industrial and economic base was relatively buoyant, at least in comparison with areas such as South Wales, Tyneside or even parts of Lancashire itself.[4]

Despite the democratic and industrial struggles of the first half of the nineteenth century, during the later Victorian and Edwardian periods the politics of Ashton were far from radical. The electorate of Ashton returned a Conservative to Westminster for most of the period 1868 to 1935 with a predictable Liberal interlude from 1906 to 1910. Despite success in parliamentary elections in 1929 and 1935, Labour could not gain control of the Council Chamber; the Conservatives remained the majority local party throughout the inter-war years. Allowing for annexations and boundary changes the full Council comprised more or less forty seats, the Conservatives usually holding no less than twenty of them. Although there was political change in prospect as the Liberals weakened and Labour demanded more say in the shape of Committee Chairmanships – the Baths and Recreation was among Labour's targets – the balance of power meant that these aspirations did not become a political reality.[5]

During the nineteenth century the provision of baths, parks and libraries gradually ceased to be regarded as controversial and came to be seen much more as essential elements in the general process of public and personal improvement. Stamford Park, which straddles the borders of Ashton and Stalybridge, was opened on the first public park in 1873 and parks provision was further extended in 1893 when the West End Pleasure Ground (3.4 acres) was opened at the opposite end of the town. The Corporation Baths were opened in 1870 and the Public Libraries Act was adopted in 1880.[6] Some 'municipal' provision originated from finance provided by industrial benefactors and public subscriptions. For example, Hurst incorporated into Ashton in 1927, had its own recreation ground of almost 6.0 acres which had been built as a memorial to a local cotton master. It was opened in 1913 by Lady Beaverbrook, wife of Ashton's former MP, Max Aitkin, who 'wanted all children when they went there to play to promise they would leave all their troubles and sorrows behind them, and fill their hearts with the great joy that was awaiting them'.[7]

Thus parks and bathing facilities were prominent areas of municipal activity long before the inter-war period, which, however, saw a major expansion in the scale of their operations. At the end of the Great War Ashton Baths was a well established concern of some fifty years which bore towering witness to the Victorian passion for personal cleanliness as a condition of civilised life. The large brick building with its tall imposing chimney was said to look 'more like a Church than a public bath', and up to the mid 1930s was also partly used as a police station.[8] It housed a main pool of one hundred by forty feet as well as other subsidiary facilities. This was a substantial municipal operation, costly both in terms of running and maintenance. Between the wars total expenditure as shown in the revenue accounts amounted to approximately £80,000 with a rate contribution of about £45,000 and income from receipts of around £30,000.[9]

There was a dramatic increase in the provision of municipal bathing facilities in Ashton between the wars. In general terms this seems to have been in response to a considerable degree of working-class demand. In 1932 the Baths Committee Chairman indicated that the baths were 'mainly patronised by artisans . . . and we have patrons not only from Ashton, but from Droylsden, Littlemoss, Dunkinfield, Stalybridge and Denton'.[10] The 1920s was the decisive decade. The number of swimmers almost trebled between 1921 and 1930 remaining more or less static thereafter (see Table 5.1). One of the most striking features of baths usage was the decline in the relative importance of private bathing against the increase in those who used the Baths mainly for swimming. A comparison with 1921 to 1938 shows that in the former year 46.0% of all users took private baths whereas in 1938 the figure was 17.2%. Private bathing remained a significant social phenomenon but swimming, both recreational and competitive saw a remarkable growth which was not confined to boys and men as were most other sports.

Mixed bathing may have been a major reason for the increase in swimmers. Between the wars mixed sessions were increased on three occasions so that by 1929 there were sessions on Monday, Tuesday and Friday evenings and on Sunday mornings. By that year the pool was allocated for public use as follows:

Monday 9 am to 1 pm men only, 2 pm to 4.45 pm mixed bathing;
Tuesday 9 am to 1 pm men only, 2 pm to 7.45 pm mixed bathing;
Wednesday 9 am to 8 pm women only;
Thursday 9 am to 8 pm men only;
Friday 9 am to 4.30 pm men only,
Saturday 9 am to 1 pm men only, 2 pm to 4.30 pm mixed bathing;
Sunday 7.30 am to 8.45 am mixed bathing.[7]

A further inducement to use the baths was to be found in the long overdue provision of improved facilities. It was not until 1915 that a filtration plant had replaced the weekly water change when 'fresh water days' were Tuesday, Wednesday and Thursday and warranted a 6d admission, whilst Friday, Saturday and Monday were 'dirty water days' and brought a reduced admission of 2d. In 1927 the filtration plant was updated and in 1937 a chlorinator was installed to further sterilise the water, and incidentally to produce the distinctive 'baths atmosphere' that many will remember. The maximum charge remained at 6d during the inter-war period, but there were 4d and 2d admissions dependent upon age, choice of changing and other facilities. Concessions, usually 1d, were granted variously over the period to school groups, military personnel, the unemployed, some holders of life-saving awards and swimming club members. Also during the period some fifty or so private changing cubicles were built, bringing greater privacy and leaving the communal, though sexually segregated, changing rooms (known locally as the 'ice-box') to be used mainly by school children. During this first phase of building improvements the *Reporter* noted that showers were being installed to allow 'school children and others to wash themselves under running showers of over 100 degrees'. Simultaneously 'the

Table 5.1 Number of users of the Ashton-under-Lyne Corporation Baths, 1920–39[a]

Year	No.	%	Private baths No.	%	Turkish baths No.	%	Total users No.	%	Education Committee Scheme Boys	Girls
1921	32,809	49.9	30,224	46.0	2,653	4.0	65,686	99.9		
1922	38,775	57.0	26,766	39.3	2,511	3.7	68,052	100.0		
1923	42,243	56.8	29,040	39.1	3,024	4.1	74,307	100.0	14,189	7,616
1924	59,214	62.3	32,780	34.5	3,064	3.2	95,058	100.0	14,028	6,560
1925	77,466	67.2	35,048	30.4	2,751	2.4	115,265	100.0		
1926	78,720	67.7	34,842	30.0	2,767	2.4	116,329	100.1		
1927	83,386	68.1	36,099	29.5	2,906	2.4	122,391	100.0		
1928	72,950	64.6	37,032	32.8	2,930	2.6	112,912	100.0		
1929	78,670	67.8	34,512	29.8	2,796	2.4	115,978	100.0		
1930	94,800	73.6	30,956	24.0	3,030	2.4	128,786	100.0	10,619	5,911
1931	91,791	79.6	21,983	19.1	1,519	1.3	115,293	100.0	10,619	5,911
1932	96,210	79.9	23,129	19.2	1,096	0.9	120,435	100.0	11,696	8,494
1933	108,887	82.4	22,249	16.8	1,084	0.8	132,220	100.0	10,360	6,705
1934	96,117	81.0	20,972	17.7	1,573	1.3	118,262	100.0	8,624	6,539
1935	90,345	79.8	19,535	17.2	3,388	3.0	113,268	100.0	7,487	5,434
1936	91,017	79.6	21,489	18.8	1,804	1.6	114,310	100.0	7,487	5,434
1937	94,000	80.1	21,232	18.1	2,084	1.8	117,316	100.0	6,379	3,983
1938	96,239	81.0	20,515	17.2	2,197	1.8	118,951	100.0		

(a) *Source*: Ashton-under-Lyne Corporation Baths Committee Reports, 1920–1938.

wooden partition between the ladies and gentlemens shower bath is being replaced with white glazed brickwork'.[12] Readers were left to ponder whether the reinforcing of the barrier was a matter of hygiene or morals.

If mixed bathing was one reason for the increased usage, the success of the Swimming Club was another. Between the wars, but especially from about 1934 onwards, Ashton could boast an active and increasingly successful club, all said to be 'working boys and girls'. They staged annual galas and competed in several national and regional competitions and leagues both for 'squadron swimming' and water polo at senior and junior level. Life-saving awards were also organised by them. Towards the end of the 1930s several players represented country and county with David Grogan becoming the England water polo captain in 1937–8. As their success grew it was not unusual to find crowds of 1,000 spectating from the balcony.[13]

Quantitative information about parks and playing-fields is patchy and difficult to synthesise, not least since actual usage is virtually impossible to measure in a meaningful way. Nevertheless it is possible to show expanded provision. Nationally the years 1919–39 saw local authorities embark upon schemes funded from rates or more commonly from a combination of rates and grants from such bodies as the National Playing Fields Association who, during the years 1927–33 were involved in some 1,090 schemes, or towards the end of the period by the National Fitness Council, which up to 1939 disbursed some £337,211 for playing field grants.[14] In Ashton total spending as shown in revenue accounts can be listed under two headings: Stamford Park and 'other recreation grounds'. Administered jointly by Ashton and Stalybridge Corporations, Stamford Park, with its bandstand (which incidentally, made a loss of about £1,200 in the decade from 1925), conservatory, duck pond, clipped lawns, pathways and magnificent floral displays remained the civic showpiece. Between the wars expenditure totalled some £131,390 and Ashton's rate contribution was approximately £63,495. The low point in spending came in 1928–30 when it fell below £6,000 and two peak years were 1923 and 1938 when expenditure topped £8,000.[15] Stamford Park had a large boating and fishing lake of approximately 6.0 and 3.5 acres respectively. Tennis courts, bowling greens, a playing field and putting-green were developed during 1919–39. According to the Ordnance Survey of 1933 the park, including the water area, covered some 147 acres. But, of this only some 5.0 or 6.0

acres of land was given over to potential play and sporting usage, the remainder being a mixture of flower beds, lawns and wooded sectors.

The revenue accounts for other recreation grounds between the wars show a total expenditure of £7,538 with a rate input of some £75,296. In 1920 expenditure was a mere £446 but by 1922 this had risen to £2,195; in 1928 the £3,000 mark was reached and expenditure then climbed steadily until 1937 when £9,571 was spent to be followed in 1938-9 by spending of £12,000 plus.[16] This increased expenditure was manifest in the acquisition of three additional sites: Oxford Street Park (2.7 acres) and Richmond Street Playing Field (almost 30 acres) were purchased in 1926; King George V Playing Field (19 acres) was bought in 1936. The latter was officially opened in 1938 and Oxford Street Park was opened in 1932. Richmond Street Playing Field, seems to have come into use gradually from about 1930 onwards and was still unfinished in 1939. This delay was because the land had initially been bought in conjunction with the cleansing department to be used as a recreation ground only after infill was complete. Two or three smaller 'recreation areas' and the War Memorial Gardens were also developed between the wars and whilst they cannot genuinely be counted as parks they were so classified by contemporaries for accounting purposes. Added together the total expenditure on Stamford Park and other recreation grounds increased from £5,494 in 1920 to £20,409 in 1939 producing a total spending between the wars of £209,878. On the rate input side the 1920 figure of £1,951 had reached £16,395 by 1939 to give an overall input of approximately £138,192.[17]

The increased provision was, of course, used in various ways. In terms of formal games crown green bowling and tennis were popular with park users whilst putting was not particularly well patronised except at special holiday pastimes such as Whitsuntide (the town is in the centre of the 'Whit-walk' area) and Wakes Week. But by the end of the inter-war period, at Stamford Park during August (which included Wakes Week) all three of these pursuits yielded less in total revenue than the boating lake skiffs. Pleasure boating was a great attraction at Stamford Park and a true municipal success. Several of the parks had bowling clubs which by the 1930s competed in local leagues and arranged internal competitions. Two or three parks had 'veterans pavilions' and by 1937 there was at least one ladies' bowling handicap tournament. During the mid 1930s the major sites at Oxford Street and Stamford Park installed 'Peter Pan' children's play equipment.[18] It is difficult to be precise about the provision of specifically designated cricket and football pitches through lack of proper evidence. Working by a process of elimination and on the assumption that then as now many municipal grounds would simply change sports according to season, it seems that there was not much in the way of municipally provided football and/or cricket facilities in the town. The Ordnance Survey of 1932–4 shows that by the latter date only Richmond Street had any changing accommodation. Using maps alongside scattered local press information and Council Minutes it appears there were probably about four or five pitches on this site from the mid 1930s onwards. When the King George V Playing Fields were designed in 1936 three pitches were included. There was virtually no public provision of pitches until the 1930s, and then only an estimated eight or nine with about a half of those coming into use on the last quarter of the decade.

There are other references to a serious shortage of playing fields. At the Ashton Sunday School Football League Dinner in 1937, where Sammy Cowan of Manchester City presented the trophies, the League President made a 'strong appeal for the provision of more playing fields' and 'his sympathy went out to the secretaries of clubs, because he knew something of the difficulty of securing suitable grounds, one of the greatest problems of junior football'.[19] At a similar function for the Sunday School Cricket League some seven months previously the newly elected Chairman of the Corporation Finance Committee and Honorary Secretary of the local Chamber of Trade hoped that

> in a short time they [the council] would be able to provide some decent playing fields in the town. He had been flogging a . . . dead horse for many years. Some 10 or 12 years ago the Corporation bought land for the Richmond Street Field, but [there had been problems – especially drainage] and it would have taken a lot of money to put it right. They had to be very careful about spending money out of the rates.[20]

In fact, the estimated drainage costs were £1,000, a sum which the council were plainly reluctant to spend on what was perceived as a low priority. Yet in terms of the inter-war spending on parks and recreation this was a fairly small sum. Recreation was clearly being given priority over sport. Parks were for a family stroll not a muddy scuffle. Pressure on pitches was so great that at the beginning of the 1937 season Sunday School Cricket officials appealed to the neighbouring towns of Dukinfield and Stalybridge to provide facilities. The difficulty in securing decent grounds had become so acute that a policy of grouping 'A' and 'B' sections within each division was devised so that each had a sprinkling of 'better' playing conditions. Preceding the 1937 season the Secretary of the Sunday School League noted that 'the playing conditions of the Sunday School league for the past quarter of a century have been a standing joke. To play under such conditions needs a deep seated interest and love of the game'.[21] Another informed observer 'did not know which was worse, the bumpiness of the cricket pitches or the wetness of the football pitches. It said a great deal for some clubs that they completed their fixtures under the existing conditions'.[22]

It seems that a great deal of Sunday School cricket and football was played on green-field sites belonging to local farmers or other privately owned land. At least five or six grounds in the town appear to fall into this category whilst another two or three venues were military property, such as the field at Ladysmith Barracks which covered some 9.8 acres. Respectable religious connections were presumably an asset in the search for a playing field, even a poor one. Most teams had to travel to the outskirts of town, and at least one cricket team was forced to play in Stalybridge whilst the ladies' hockey team occupied a ground mid-way between Ashton and Oldham. When the King George V Playing Fields were constructed in 1936-7 the project was unfinished with large areas of potential playing surface left uncultivated or merely levelled with spoil from a local colliery. Despite a £4,000 Ministry of Health loan, £1,000 in contributions from the Carnegie Trust, Jubilee Trust and National Playing Fields Association together with £2,500 from the King George V Foundation, the municipality failed to make a major commitment to team sport.[23] Sunday School League officials were aware that the shortage of grounds could be reduced by the sharing of school playing fields. The two main sites in this category were the Grammar School and Stamford Boys Secondary School, each about 8.0 acres. However, these were under the control of the Lancashire County Council. Ashton Council made tentative, and apparently half-hearted, inquiries about the possible use of this land but the County Council refused to make it more widely available for the sporting needs of the community.[24]

The municipal provision of sporting and recreational facilities in Ashton between the wars was not the simple product of public philanthropy. Attempts were made to influence working-class behaviour and thinking, partly by giving the park priority over the pitch. Sport, it seems, was not really accepted as a 'national recreation'. Territorial control, civic pride and promotion, the interest of local employers and the pursuit of economic benefit, social harmony and citizenship were inextricably linked in the minds of Councillors and those who expressed their views about sporting and recreational provision. This view was reinforced by a sympathetic local press. This was nowhere more evident than at the park or playing field where clear directives were attempted, though not necessarily achieved to regulate when, where and how play would occur. Bye-laws with intricate restrictions and prohibition notices, internal and external boundary fences, the conspicuous placing of monuments to local dignatories and industrialists, the locking of gates overnight and the monitoring of behaviour by park-keepers were all designed to influence park users. When an application by the Infirmary Workpeoples Committee to hold its Annual Gala Day was made in 1933, it prompted a resolution that 'Lawns not to be used for dancing or any other purpose and nothing of a heavy nature to be allowed in the park such as roundabouts etc.'[25] Plainly this was to be a 'respectable' affair and the preservation of the horticulture was uppermost in the minds of the Stamford Park Joint Committee – Infirmary Charity or not. The very fact that 'permission' was necessary emphasises the sometimes overlooked fact that parks were not 'public' in the widest sense but supervised places for the public to go to enjoy themselves in a respectable, healthy, sober family atmosphere.

Whether or not this kind of public morality had any real influence is a quite different question. Take, for example the anguished statement made by Alderman Broadbent in July of 1937: 'the other night I saw between 50 and 100 youngsters playing (on municipal gardens) trampling over flower beds and yet in the vicinity, not 50 yards away, is a proper recognised playing ground'.[26] There was at Stamford Park an annual 'Tulip Sunday', the day in the year when an event was made out of the conspicuous display of the gardens. Only a matter of days before this event in 1933 vandalism and theft of plants made it necessary for an appeal to be made to users to be vigilant and to report the culprits.[27]

Parks were a community resource to promote gentle relaxation and a salutary breath of fresh air amid attractive floral surroundings. The heatwave of 1933 found the *Reporter* plugging away at the idea of the park as a source of pastoral sociability for the town dweller: 'In the evening parks have been crowded, and cool spots under the trees have been eagerly sought. The bowling greens and recreation grounds have been filled with old and young alike anxious to benefit from the sun's health giving rays.'[28]

Parks were directly linked to morality and citizenship in the minds of certain dignitaries. When the land for the Oxford Street and Richmond Street Playing Fields was purchased, the Mayor R.S. Oldham, commented that: 'the Corporation was spending consider-able sums . . . in providing recreation grounds to take men and boys off the streets, and to enable them to grow into healthy citizens instead of idling their time away'.[29] Linked to keeping males off the streets and away from crime there was the question of traffic flow as well as road safety. In 1932, for example, Ashton streets were the scene of 473 accidents, four of them fatal. Some magistrates, despite their apparent vigour in the prosecution of youths for obstruction or street games (including football), were not blind to the problems of youth. A Labour Alderman and avid sports supporter sounded a note of self-reproach at the opening of Oxford Park: 'I have a guilty conscience on many occasions when boys are brought before the Bench for playing in the streets. We know it is wrong . . . but I do feel a responsibility for these boys.'[30] Conscience and responsibility are key words here and keeping people off the streets was part of wider municipal ideology of orderliness, public decency and improvement. As the Chairman of the Recreation Grounds Committee indicated at the same ceremony:

> Probably there will be people in the town who will consider this to be extravagant expenditure. But I don't think so. It is the duty of a corporate body to consider all sections of the community and the greatest responsibility of a Corporation is the health of its inhabitants. Without open spaces and parks, and opportunities for recreation the district would soon become a slum. . . . In opening this park we have been considering the physical well being of its inhabitants. We are out to give them pleasure and enjoyment and at the same time we are trying to beautify this town of Ashton.[31]

The implied reluctance to spend ratepayers' money on free recreatio-nal facilities unless for reasons of 'usefulness' and 'health' was also evident at the baths. As the statistical and social importance of bathing declined in the 1930s the question of whether pleasure in the form of swimming could be legitimately subsidised by the rate-payer was raised:

Do Ashton unemployed want to use the Corporation Baths from a hygiene point of view or from a recreation point of view?. . . The Baths Committee say that if the unemployed desire to use the plunge [swimming] bath there will have to be a small charge, but if they use them for private baths they can use them free.[32]

In the event the unemployed were able to use the second-class private swimming bath at prescribed times during the day for the cost of 1d. The low take-up rate, however, suggests that the majority were not bothered about the baths which accords with frequent observations about the passivity and demoralisation of the unemployed in the 1930s, though some may have simply wished to escape the indignity of publicly surrendering unemployment cards at the pay office. Belief in bathing for health and hygiene persisted. The turkish bath was finally replaced by the more economical 'Zotofoam' bath in 1937 which was perceived as 'remedial' and 'health giving'. Spending on improvements in water quality and shower installations were all essentially executed from a health perspective rather than for the encouragement of swimming as a competitive activity. Swimming itself would in any case presumably be regarded as a 'healthy sport'. Life-saving had definite connotations of citizenship and harked back in the nineteenth-century concern about death from drowning voiced by the Humane Societies.

Civil rivalry and prestige was a further motive in provision. When the new filtration plant was installed the chairman insisted that 'Ashton Corporation Baths have a filtration system which is second to none and there are no cleaner baths in the whole of England'.[33] Similarly when the turkish baths were under threat of closure one Alderman argued for their retention on the grounds of local pride: 'Otherwise we shall have to go to Stalybridge and we do not want to go to Stalybridge for owt'.[34] Indeed civic rivalry between Ashton and Stalybridge in water polo led to an early 'friendly' match being abandoned because of violent play. Local prestige was also evident in debates about the proper use of Stamford Park. Occasional requests to use the boating lake for training purposes were made by long-distance swimmers, usually entrants to the Morecambe Bay race. Permission was generally granted only to local people who were acknowledged competitive swimmers and stood a chance of gaining honours for the town. This provoked a hostile response from one correspondent to the *Reporter* who wanted to know 'Why should it be necessary for [outdoor swimmers] to have to go to one of the

Manchester Parks when Stamford Park Boating Lake can supply the ideal spot?'[35]

Civic pride, the promotion of citizenship, respectability and the importance of public health were connected ideas as in the wider promotion of the town as successful and efficient in municipal matters as well as in industry and commerce. When the proposed merger of Hurst and Ashton National football clubs was discussed, the mayor noted that 'there would be tremendous advantages if we had a Third Division team in the town. I am speaking in regard to trade in the town'.[36] Another speaker thought 'there was no doubt that a good football club would advertise the town. . . . Towns with football teams were put on the map'.[37] In the event lack of capital and a reluctance on the part of Hurst to relinquish its independence – itself perhaps indicative of the importance of sport and local identity at a time of local government amalgamation – meant that the proposals came to nothing. Football with its national following and press coverage was one thing but, it seems, the more modest image of swimming was another. When the Ashton water polo team experienced a lean time in the mid-1920s the following plea appeared in the *Reporter*:

> whilst in Hyde and Stalybridge – to go no further – Mayors, Councillors, Chief Constables and prominent townsmen of all classes patronise the weekly gala – especially 'at home' in Ashton generally speaking, very few of these people are seen as patrons except at the annual gala. May I make a special appeal to our own Baths Committee? The swimmers have made the baths popular . . . Their 'gate' is their only asset. They have to pay their way in away matches, and they have aspirations in new fields of conquer. They have potential talent of both sexes, probably unequalled by any town of our size . . . I appeal to all to help our swimmers and the day may come when the neglected talent of Ashton baths may make Ashton more famous than even cricket or football has done.[38]

In fact the swimming club put Ashton on the map by securing a visit from the Austrian international team in 1937. Also around that time the Ashton players Grogan and Laycock were England water polo internationals. This success, also signalled when the English Water Polo Championship was staged at the baths and covered by BBC radio, meant that the talented squad could draw crowds of a thousand to spectate from the pool-side and balcony. The publicity surrounding these events seems to have encouraged some functionaries to improve their attendance. Success in water-polo may not have been like winning the Lancashire League but it did give a useful fillip to local shops and at the baths' turnstile.

Those expecting to find strident party political conflict over municipal sporting and recreational provision will be disappointed. The political culture of Ashton was based upon a tradition of working-class Conservatism. But even with the rise of Labour in parliamentary and municipal terms in the 1930s, there was little evidence of ideological arguments over recreational and sporting provision playing any major part in this process. Indeed it is difficult to clearly distinguish party lines over sport and recreation issues at local level given the various statements of Alderman Broadbent (Conservative) and Alderman Massey (Labour). As one local journalist remarked: 'If there is one side of life where Ashton is a model for the towns, it is its local politics. In too many other places, the work of the Town council . . . is hampered by obstructive party tactics. That is not the spirit in this town.'[39] Labour failed to gain overall control of the Council in the 1930s but there is scant evidence that greater electoral success would have meant better municipal provision. Employment and housing were higher on the socialist agenda than the providing of more facilities for working-class sport.

In conclusion the rather inadequate evidence available suggests a somewhat parsimonious corporation which responded patchily to a three-fold increase in the number of swimmers and constant demand for playing space. An average annual spending of just over £11,000 on all parks and recreation grounds over the period tends to confirm the view that municipalities between the wars were still cautious about extending the scope of their activities. Closer examination also reveals that much municipal provision focused upon 'rational recreation' rather than popular sport. Use of public land was overwhelmingly 'non-sporting' even towards the end of the period when attempts were made to establish more pitches for cricket and football. The Victorian legacy of sport as a private activity enjoyed by individuals at their own expense was strongly entrenched. A large percentage of pitches were not controlled by the corporation. Moreover, the baths, which was probably the most popular single-site municipal sporting venue, received only a modest amount of rate support at an annual average of £6,667 over the years 1919–39. Here, despite undeniable public enthusiasm, cleanliness and health seem to have taken precedence over swimming as a sport in its own right. Councillors may have publicly indulged in self-congratulatory rhetoric together with expressions of duty and civic pride, but the funding and extent of provision fell short of the proclaimed ideal.

The major developments in sports provision took place outside the municipal sphere. There were initiatives from the voluntary sector such as the recreational centre for the unemployed set up by the National Council of Social Service in 1935 with a membership of 600; the Co-op provided facilities for sport meetings as well as whist-drives, dances and concerts; the older traditions of Church and Chapel recreation survived and prospered. The Sunday School Football League signed up 500 players in 1936 with twenty-seven cricket teams adhering to the Sunday School Cricket League in the same year. There was also a 'workshop' league with cricket teams from engineering, chemicals as well as the cotton mills and the 'Golden Shred' team of Robertson's marmalade. There was a Tuesday cricket league for retail and entertainment trades too. Alongside this dense network of participation there were also important commercial spectator initiatives. A boxing hall was opened in 1930, which drew up to 1,200 spectators for mid-week fights, and even more striking were the crowds, of five to six thousand, who gathered to watch speedway and from 1932 to follow in even greater numbers the new sport of greyhound-racing. There were two Cheshire League football teams, one of which briefly signed the famous Scottish winger Alex Jackson, and a Central Lancashire League cricket side who were well supported despite the ease with which Ashtonians could go to Manchester to watch City or United or to see county cricket at Old Trafford. Municipal provision, therefore, despite its undoubted value, was never more than a small part of a rich and diversified sporting culture and had a relatively small impact on the habits and values of this particular northern industrial town.

Notes

1 I am indebted to Dr R.J. Holt for his assistance in preparing the final draft of this paper and to the late Steve Jones who was mentor and friend during earlier stages of research.

2 See works such as H. Meller, *Leisure and the Changing City* (London, 1976); R. Roberts, 'The corporation as impresario: the municipal provision of entertainment in Victorian and Edwardian Britain', and J.K. Walton, 'Municipal government and the holiday industry in Blackpool 1876–1914' in J.K. Walton and J. Walvin (eds), *Leisure in Britain 1780–1939* (Manchester, 1983).

3 For example: H. Cunningham, *Leisure in the Industrial Revolution* (London, 1980); J.M. Golby and A.W. Purdue, *The Civilization of the Crowd* (London, 1984); J. Hargreaves, *Sport, Power and Culture* (Cambridge, 1986); S.G. Jones, *Workers at Play* (London, 1986); S.G. Jones, *Sport, politics and the working class* (Manchester, 1988).

4 *Census* 1911, 1921, 1931. *Ministry of Labour Gazette,* 1920-39 passim. M. McNama, 'A study of local responses to the Means Test and unemployment in Ashton-under-Lyne, 1931-34', unpublished dissertation, University of Salford, 1983. *Worral's Directory* for selected years. A welcome and long-overdue short survey of the cotton industry in the town is I. Haynes, *Cotton in Ashton* (Tameside, 1987).

5 *Ashton Corporation Manuals,* 1919-39 passim. *Ashton-under-Lyne Reporter,* 9 November 1929.

6 W.M. Bowman, *England in Ashton-under-Lyne* (Altrincham, 1960), and D. Grogan, *Centenary Brochure: Ashton-under-Lyne Public Baths Department 1870-1970* (Ashton-under-Lyne, 1970), give useful background to nineteenth-century municipal growth in the town.

7 A. Parry, *A History of Hurst and Neighbourhood* (Hurst, 1908). *Hurst Urban District Council Minutes,* 1909-27 passim. *Ashton-under-Lyne Reporter,* 7 June 1913.

8 D. Grogan, *Centenary Brochure,* p. 12.

9 *Ashton-under-Lyne Corporation Baths Committee Reports,* 1920-39.

10 *Ashton-under-Lyne Reporter,* 25 January 1936.

11 *Ashton-under-Lyne Reporter,* 19 April 1932.

12 G. Foster, *Ashton-under-Lyne: Its Story through the Ages* (Ashton-under-Lyne, 1947). *Ashton-under-Lyne Reporter,* 5 November 1932.

13 D. Grogan, *Centenary Brochure.* G. Foster, *Ashton-under-Lyne. Ashton-under-Lyne Reporter,* 17 March 1934.

14 S.G. Jones, *Workers at Play,* pp. 88-100.

15 *Ashton-under-Lyne Parks and Recreation Committee Minutes,* 1919-39 passim.

16 *Ibid.*

17 *Ibid.* G. Foster, *Ashton-under-Lyne,* pp. 79-83, gives dates of purchase.

18 *Stamford Park Joint Committee Minutes,* 1930-35.

19 *Ashton-under-Lyne Reporter,* 7 May 1937.

20 *Ashton-under-Lyne Reporter,* 6 November 1936.

21 *Ashton-under-Lyne Reporter,* 4 June 1937.

22 *Ashton-under-Lyne Reporter,* 6 November 1936.

23 *Ashton under-Lyne Reporter,* 25 January 1936. *Ashton Corporation Parks and Recreation Committee Minutes,* 1936-7.

24 D. Bowker, 'Aspects of municipal leisure provision in Ashton-under-Lyne, 1919-39', unpublished MA dissertation (CNAA), Manchester Polytechnic, 1986.

25 *Stamford Park Joint Committee Minutes,* 13 May 1938.

26 *Ashton-under-Lyne Reporter,* 16 July 1937.

27 *Ashton-under-Lyne Reporter,* 6 May 1933.

28 *Ashton-under-Lyne Reporter,* 10 June 1933.

29 *Ashton-under-Lyne Reporter,* 19 June 1926.

30 *Ashton-under-Lyne Reporter,* 7 May 1932.

31 *Ibid.*
32 *Ashton-under-Lyne Reporter,* 6 May 1933.
33 *Ashton-under-Lyne Reporter,* 3 May 1932.
34 *Ashton-under-Lyne Reporter,* 12 March 1932.
35 *Ashton-under-Lyne Reporter,* 8 July 1934.
36 *Ashton-under-Lyne Reporter,* 3 March 1928.
37 *Ibid.*
38 *Ashton-under-Lyne Reporter,* 23 May 1926.
39 *Ashton-under-Lyne Reporter,* 7 January 1934.

6

Recreational cricket in the Bolton area between the wars

Jack Williams

Social distinctions found in county and test match cricket reveal much about the complexities of class and gender divisions over the past century. Yet cricket played for recreation can make an equally strong claim to be a relevant area of enquiry for historians of sport and of British society in general. No survey of leisure in twentieth-century Britain can be complete without an assessment of sport's social role, which, in turn, will not be fully understood until the recreational variants of different sports are examined. Local studies with their depth of detailed analysis provide the most effective method of explaining how different sports were played for recreation rather than for results or for profit. An added justification for undertaking localised studies of recreational sport is that they seem likely to be a way of evaluating in microcosm the impact of sport upon class and gender divisions, sociability and the creation of community. Sport provides a means of penetrating the seemingly closed world of male working-class culture between the wars with its fierce local patriotisms and friendships.

The great concentration of cricket played by men and youths around Bolton between the wars makes this an appropriate locality for considering the game's social ramifications.[1] Almost all cricket played on a regular basis in this area was organised into leagues which can be divided into those for high-quality clubs playing virtually semi-professional cricket and those whose cricketers participated for the sheer joy of playing (though, of course, most of those playing more seriously also enjoyed their cricket). In the 1920s the First Division of the Bolton and District Cricket Association (BDCA) constituted the highest form of league cricket in the area, but after the 1929 season twelve of its strongest clubs left to form the Bolton League which has remained the locality's premier cricket league. The leading clubs between the wars usually hired one professional player and also paid some or possibly most of their amateurs. In 1921 an aggregate around a hundred thousand paid to watch semi-professional league cricket in Bolton. In the 1930s attendances were probably below fifty thousand yet above those of less well supported county clubs.[2] By the late 1930s most clubs in the First Division of the BDCA had stopped employing professionals but they still represented a very high level of cricket. For the purposes of this paper recreational cricketers will be regarded as those who played cricket solely as a leisure interest and for clubs not competing at these higher levels. What, then, was the basic structure of 'leisure' cricket?

By 1922 over seventy teams were playing recreational cricket in the Bolton area. In the early 1930s they reached a peak of around 120 but by 1939 had fallen to just over 110. Most clubs playing recreational cricket within the County Borough of Bolton in the 1920s belonged to the A, B or C sections of the BDCA's Second Division and the three sections of the Junior Second Teams association which became the BDCA's Third Division in 1930. Their combined number of teams was sixty-two in 1922, forty-four in 1930 and thirty in 1939. Approximately half of these teams had grounds within the county borough. The Walkden Amateur League catered for clubs beyond the southern and western boundaries of the county borough. This collapsed in 1918 when the grounds of its member clubs were used for food production but was resurrected in 1925. It always had two divisions with each member club having to field teams in both divisions. It had eight clubs in 1925 and sixteen in 1931, but in 1932, the seven furthest from Bolton county borough left to form the Tyldesley League, which disbanded after the 1938 season. By 1939 the Walkden League had sixteen clubs.

The Sunday School Cricket League of Radcliffe, situated between the county boroughs of Bolton and Bury, had also collapsed during the First World War but resumed its competition in 1922. This had two divisions, the second being for reserve sides. Almost all its clubs fielded two teams. In 1922 fifteen teams competed in its two divisions. Only once in the 1930s did these numbers drop below twenty and in 1939 reached a peak of twenty-five. In Horwich, an urban district adjoining the north-western boundary of Bolton County Borough, a Sunday School Cricket League held its first competition in 1923 with ten clubs. In 1927 and 1928, a second division was organised for reserve teams but in the 1930s there was only one division with between eight and ten clubs.[3]

Great variations existed between the playing standards and facilities of recreational clubs. Playing records of clubs which moved between different leagues indicate that the highest quality of recreational cricket was played in the A section of the BDCA's Second Division. For the 1921 season, five clubs were admitted from the A section and one from the B section to extend the Association's First Division but three of these six clubs had belonged to the Walkden League in 1914. Only one of these six promoted clubs was elected into the elite Bolton League after its formation in the winter of 1929–30. Playing standards of the resurrected Walkden League in the 1920s appear to have been a little below those of the A section in the BDCA's Second Division. Two of the three clubs which left the Association for the Walkden League came from its B Section. Oral evidence reveals a belief that the two Sunday School Leagues had the lowest playing standards but these were probably not worse than those of weaker clubs in the Junior Second Teams Association or the BDCA's Third Division. In the 1930s the Horwich Parish Church Club fielded its first eleven in the B section of the BDCA's Second Division and its reserve team in the Horwich Sunday School League. Most clubs from the B section of the BDCA played their reserve teams in the B section of the Association's Third Division.

Clubs playing in the BDCA's Second Division and the Walkden League appear to have enjoyed good facilities. In 1923, St Peter and Paul's CC spent £70, a far from trifling sum, upon improving its ground after promotion to the A section and in 1936, All Souls CC, one of the stronger A-section clubs, paid a groundsman to look after its pitch.[4] Scattered press comments suggest that the £15 spent by Farnworth St John's CC in 1936,[5] was just a little above the expenditure on ground maintenance by most A section clubs. Press photographs of teams in the Walkden League invariably show them seated outside wooden pavilions of a size roughly equivalent to two modern semi-detached bungalows whilst the regular reports of the League's grounds inspection sub-committee reveal an intention to improve facilities still further. The worst facilities were in the Sunday School Leagues. In the 1920s pitches in the Horwich League were considered dangerous.[6] Bushes and long grass in the outfields of grounds at Radcliffe led to a special rule forbidding more than four runs being run when a ball became lost without having crossed the boundary.[7] Frequent low scores, despite the presence of a few players with great natural ability, are also evidence of poor-quality pitches in the Sunday School Leagues. In 1925 the highest individual score in the Radcliffe League was only forty-three whilst in its First Division six bowlers had taken over thirty wickets at less than four runs apiece.[8] Yet even at this humblest level of recreational cricket facilities were better than in other parts of Lancashire. Almost all teams played on grass wickets whereas Sunday School Leagues in Burnley and Oldham had separate sections for clubs with cinder or shale wickets. By the late 1930s clubs in the Horwich and Radcliffe Sunday School Leagues had erected by the voluntary labour of team members small wooden pavilions with separate changing rooms for each side and a central area for serving teas, though some of these were little better than sheds.

Oral evidence indicates that almost all who played recreational cricket in the Bolton area belonged to what can be described loosely as the lower-middle and working classes. Most blue-collar workers who played tended to have some degree of skill and, not surprisingly, many were employed in cotton textiles or engineering though mining workers were found among teams to the south and west of Bolton county borough. Building workers such as plumbers and electricians were often a significant minority but what proportion were self-employed, or employed others, is not clear. The largest lower-middle class groupings were office workers and usually it is their place of employment rather than the nature of their work which is recorded or remembered. Sons of small businessmen formed a group whose social status is hard to define. As so very few with reliable memories of the early 1920s can be found, it is difficult to detect whether major changes in the social backgrounds of recreational cricketers occurred between the wars. By the late 1930s several Sunday School teams included two or three who are remembered as the first generation of their working-class families to have received secondary education. Sons of local industrialists did not usually play for recreational clubs but instead gravitated to more socially exclusive clubs such as Bolton CC or Worsley CC. Occupations of officials for clubs in the BDCA were broadly similar to those of players.

Although cricket can be played until relatively late in life, the average ages of recreational cricketers tended to be lower than for those in the highest level of league clubs. Average ages were usually youngest at the humblest levels of cricket. In 1921 the Dixon Green Congregational second team had an average age of twenty-three and eight players under twenty (although the captain was forty-five) and was thought to have been the youngest side ever to have won the B section of the Junior Second Teams Association.[9] In the late 1930s teams in the Sunday School Leagues often contained a nucleus of players in their late teens. In 1939 the captain of the Radcliffe Parish Church club was in his forties but to the rest of the players appeared very much 'the old man' of the team.[10] At the All Souls Club in 1938, players were older; ten of its first team, which was among the stronger sides in the A section of the BDCA's Second Division, were aged between twenty-six and thirty-five with one in his mid-forties, whilst nearly all the second eleven were between twenty-four and thirty-six except for one aged about fifty.[11] The absence of family commitments was a major reason for the relative youthfulness of recreational cricketers whilst those with the greatest ability usually gravitated to clubs of a higher level as their skills matured. The local press reported that rough pitches in the Horwich Sunday School League might have been tolerated by younger but not by older men.[12]

A combination of factors made recreational cricket into a sport for the lower- middle and working classes. Cricket playing was not expensive. Players' subscriptions were often no more than half a crown, which was probably not prohibitively expensive for those in work. Clubs provided all equipment except footwear and clothing. Almost all who played regularly between the wars are remembered as wearing whites but it has been pointed out that these could be acquired second hand or made from the bottom halves of white overalls.[13] Those interviewed often expressed amazement that they, like most others who played in the Sunday School leagues, did not wear boxes when batting despite the poor quality of pitches.

This comparative cheapness of cricket playing helps to explain why economic depression had little pronounced effect upon the sport. The numbers of teams playing regularly reached their peak in the early 1930s, which the Ministry of Labour Local Unemployment Index indicates were the years of heaviest unemployment in the Bolton area. Unfortunately, there is no method of establishing what proportion of recreational cricketers may have been unemployed. Oral testimony confirms that those who played for the Stand Unitarian Club of the Radcliffe Sunday School League in 1927 and 1939 were in work or full-time education.[14] On the other hand the majority of Lee Congregational CC of the Horwich Sunday School League were unemployed but passed their time working on the club's wicket[15] – a tendency also noted among clubs belonging to the BDCA's First

Division in the 1930s.

The numbers of works clubs playing recreational cricket in the Bolton area rose from four in 1927 to seventeen in 1939. This modest expansion of works clubs increased opportunities for some to play regularly but only concerns with large numbers of employees could support works clubs. No firm in the Bolton area was sufficiently large to have an inter-departmental cricket league between the wars. Most works teams playing recreational cricket were from cotton mills or engineering firms, but by the late 1930s a tannery and factories making aeroplane propellors and mass-produced clothing had teams. The high proportion of teams based on workplaces in medal or knock-out competitions for scratch teams, where facilities were provided by a sponsoring club from the highest level of local cricket, suggests that playing alongside workmates was popular. More works teams might have played in leagues had works managers provided funds and equipment. On the other hand, certain employees were sensitive to overt employer involvement in leisure. The playing field provided by Sir John Holden, a cotton manufacturer, was little used by his employees and its cricket club played in the BDCA only from 1928 to 1932.[16]

The ethos of recreational cricket also encouraged working-class involvement. Almost all recreational cricket played on a regular basis took place in leagues or knock-out competitions organised by leagues. All matches were fiercely contested. Those whose playing careers stretched across the full spectrum of league cricket in the Bolton area recall that matches in Sunday School Leagues were contested just as fiercely as those in the Bolton League. Indeed, the competitive spirit was heightened by those on opposing sides being so well known to each other and accords well with other observations of the ethos of working-class sport. Men played to win not just to take part, in sharp contrast to the declared objectives of public schoolboys for whom cricket was raised to the status of a moral code. Competitiveness meant that all clubs wished to do well which in turn sometimes led to the recruitment of players primarily for playing ability rather than on the grounds of personal worthiness or local loyalty. The Brunswick United Methodist Club of the Horwich Sunday School League could not find a regular place for one of its most enthusiastic members who was always eager to help with pitch preparation or bag carrying but had little cricketing ability.[17] All the same, in the Radcliffe Sunday School League, where almost all clubs had two teams, it was usually possible for all who wished to play to be found a place.[18]

The determinants of lower-middle and working-class involvement are inseparable from those which influenced the creation of the league system as the preferred form of competition. As in other sports, loyalty to locality lay at the heart of recreational cricket. The BDCA had launched the first cricket league in Lancashire in 1890 and by 1900 almost all clubs in Lancashire except those of the social and economic elite were playing in league competitions.[19] In the Bolton area competitions were so well entrenched that among the lower-middle and working classes leagues were regarded as the 'natural' forms of inter-club competition. The league system itself was a stimulant to club formation just as much as the founding of new clubs helped the leagues. The process was cumulative and self-reinforcing. When leagues were created it was essential to have a viable number of clubs, and organisations playing other sports were invited to form cricket sections. The decision to relaunch the Radcliffe Sunday School League for the 1922 season led to the re-establishment of four clubs, each with two sides, which had not played since 1914. In August 1922 all churches in Horwich were invited to enter teams in the proposed Sunday School League and this resulted in the formation of at least three new church clubs. The desire to retain a viable number of clubs may also have underlain the decision of the BDCA to allow the St Peter and Paul's Club to play all its matches away from home because of difficulties in finding a ground for the 1927 season.[20]

The geographical distribution of clubs helps to explain the social and economic determinants of recreational cricket. At all levels much more cricket was played outside than within the county borough of Bolton. In 1929 the BDCA's First Division of twenty clubs contained only four from within the county borough. In the 1930s only three clubs from the county borough played in the Bolton League. None of the three clubs from inside the borough playing in the First Division of the BDCA in 1930 was still doing so in 1938. At the recreational levels of cricket, no clubs in the Walkden League or the Horwich and Radcliffe Sunday School Leagues came from the county borough. In 1930 only half of the forty-two teams playing in the BDCA's Second and Third Divisions were from the county borough, though in 1938 a slightly higher proportion of a smaller total number – eighteen out of thirty-two teams – originated from within the formal boundaries of Bolton.

The expansion of house-building and the consequent increase in competition for land restricted recreational cricket in the county borough. Most recreational cricket clubs rented their grounds but landlords often found it more profitable to sell land to housebuilders. Losing tenancy of its ground usually meant that a club collapsed because so little alternative land was available at rents which clubs could afford. In 1927 *The Buff* commented that at least one junior club collapsed each year through losing its ground.[21] In 1934 Bolton Playing Fields Association listed fourteen recreational clubs which had disbanded since 1924 because of difficulties over grounds.[22]

Within the county borough this shortage of land was exacerbated by the reluctance of the council's Parks Department to lease municipal land to cricket clubs. By 1934 39½ acres of municipally owned recreational land had been laid out at Hall-i'th'Wood with grants from the National Playing Fields Association and the Carnegie Trust. Although original proposals for this scheme included five senior and four junior cricket pitches for fourteen- to eighteen-year olds, these were not used by BDCA clubs before the Second World War.[23] The only municipal land used by recreational clubs was at Leverhulme Park. From 1921 until 1930, one club per season occupied a pitch there, with Trinity Wesleyan CC's tenancy from 1926 until 1930 being the longest. No club played there again until 1933. From 1935 to 1939 two clubs played their home matches at Leverhulme Park but as these had only one team each, they may have used the same pitch on alternative Saturdays.[24]

Officials of the BDCA made repeated attempts to have more municipal land set aside for cricket clubs but the failure of the council's Parks Committee to respond reflected differing views about proper uses for municipal land. In 1934 the Bromilow and Edwards club found that a pitch on municipal land could not be booked for a whole season but had to be claimed each matchday by club representatives arriving early and practising upon it. On one occasion its players had prepared and rolled a wicket and were practising on the edge of it when another side arrived and claimed it.[25] Clubs wishing to rent municipal land usually wanted pitches reserved for their exclusive use each Saturday and on two mid-week evenings for practice but the view of the Parks Committee, as expressed by Councillor Grealey in 1935, was that it could not consent to municipal land being used exclusively by a single club. Municipal facilities, in his view, existed for all the borough's population and exceptional provision could not be made for particular clubs.[26] The responsibility of the Parks Committee was to assist everyone as far as possible but with a due regard for the spending of rate-payers' money.[27]

The attitude of Bolton Council contrasted sharply with that of councils in neighbouring urban districts. The Farnworth and Radcliffe clubs, two of the area's leading clubs, rented their grounds at comparatively low rents from their councils whilst church teams were allowed to lease council grounds in Horwich and Radcliffe. In 1939 councillors of all political parties in Worsley united in unsuccessful attempts to persuade Manchester Collieries not to sell the ground of Whittlebrook Methodist CC which played in the BDCA's First Division.[28] Such instances of local political goodwill towards senior clubs and to the greater number of recreational clubs appear to have arisen from a sense of local patriotism which transcended class and party political divisions in areas outside the county borough. Success for teams from outside the county borough in the BDCA's First Division during the 1920s or in the Bolton League during the 1930s were occasions of communal celebration. Oral evidence shows that self-employed tradesmen and shopkeepers were prepared to boost club finances, and consequently prospects of playing success, by becoming members or vice-presidents out of a desire to be associated with popular local activities.[29] Even the more cynical interpretation that such actions were prompted by a determination not to risk losing the goodwill of customers can be seen as evidence of extensive local support for clubs playing at the highest level of league cricket. Wealthy industrialists and landowners were prepared to become patrons of such clubs. Colonel Hardcastle, the major employer in Bradshaw, gave the Bradshaw club its ground in 1920 in memory of wartime sacrifices.[30] In 1937 wealthy patrons of Little Lever CC, including a colliery proprietor, owner of a bus company and a colonel, bought the club's ground on the understanding that it could be purchased from them whenever the club wished.[31] Executive committee minute books often record that leading clubs approached local industrialists to provide jobs for unemployed players or to tempt players from other clubs.

Radcliffe CC perhaps demonstrates most clearly how leading clubs reflected and strengthened local loyalties. In 1925 the club launched an appeal for a new tearoom. Each week names of subscribers and the amount of their donations were advertised in the local press. Within a month 147 donations totalling £250 had been received. After four months the £450 needed had been collected. All local firms and businesses appear to have subscribed. Of course, publishing names in the local press can be described almost as a form of blackmail. The fact that some businesses were afraid of being seen not to subscribe, testifies to the depth of local support for the club. In 1938, at the opening of the club's new pavilion, the mayor praised 'the good relationship' which existed between the newly created municipal borough and the club. He thanked the cricket club 'for their efforts during the past decade in providing the town with sport of such a high character . . . they have done their best to put Radcliffe on the map and that is what we want. . . . We hope further successes will attend the efforts of the club and enhance the importance of Radcliffe in the county'.[32] Even allowing for a degree of exaggeration in such a speech, this combination of local sentiment and community support created a climate of moral approbation which led councils to encourage more humble levels of cricket playing.

Bolton County Borough, on the other hand, had no single club which could stimulate a sense of municipal loyalty. The three clubs which joined the Bolton League – Astley Bridge, Heaton, and Tonge – all attracted large numbers of spectators but never appeared likely to become the major focus of loyalty for cricket enthusiasts within the borough. Bolton CC did not generate the same degree of town loyalty as did Oldham CC or Burnley CC in other parts of Lancashire. This was partly because it played in the Manchester Association, an organisation which, by allowing clubs to arrange their own fixtures, refused to adopt a full-blooded league apparatus and consequently did not have the same popular appeal as more competitive cricket leagues. Despite its splendid ground, few spectators watched the matches of Bolton CC.[33] Most players and officials belonged to the wealthier sections of local society, which gave the club an aura of social exclusiveness. There is little evidence of a desire to convert the club into a Bolton equivalent of either Burnley CC or Oldham CC.

Schools cricket does not seem to have been a major stimulus to recreational cricket. At Bolton School, the leading private grammar school in the locality, cricket squares had been laid out in 1903 and 1905. In the 1920s a pavilion was built and Albert Ward, a former Lancashire county professional, was engaged as a part-time coach. The standard of its cricket was remembered as 'often very good indeed' but few of the ordinary inhabitants had links with it. In 1924 it had only 384 pupils.[34] Cricket was also played regularly at Farnworth Grammar School. Opportunities to play at elementary schools, which the great majority of boys attended, were far more restricted. The Bolton and District Schools Athletic Association had been formed in 1898. Within weeks it organised seven inter-school soccer leagues.[35] Though the association was also running athletics, rounders and swimming contests in the 1920s, an elementary school cricket knock-out competition was not started until 1933 following initiatives from officials and players of Bolton CC.[36] By 1935 inter-school cricket leagues were established but in 1936 cricket was described as the Association's 'Cinderella activity'.[37] The Lancashire County Schools Cricket Association was set up in 1922 and organised matches between teams representing elementary schools of local education authorities but Bolton had not affiliated to the LSCA by 1939.[38] The extent of elementary school cricket outside the county borough varied considerably. By 1926 the Worsley District Schools Association had an annual competition for schools from Walkden, Boothstown and Little Hulton;[39] whilst Radcliffe council agreed in the same year to requests from the local elementary schools association that recently acquired public land be used for schools cricket.[40]

A shortage of playing fields slowed the development of inter-school cricket in the Bolton area. As late as 1944 only four schools in the county borough had playing fields and until the development of playing fields at Hall-i'th'Wood little publicly owned land was available for cricket playing. An additional factor could have been reluctance among teachers to organise inter-school matches on a regular basis, especially as cricket matches could last so much longer than football games. In 1935 J.M. Massey, who was connected with the BDCA and Eagley CC, offered to act as secretary if elementary schools in Turton UD formed a league but complained that the headmaster in Bromley Cross was not interested.[41] Except for Bolton CC, whose initiatives were presumably of a paternalistic kind, most clubs took little interest in sponsoring schools cricket, though the lease of Radcliffe CC's ground required it to provide coaching for schoolboys. Yet the weak state of schools cricket did not prevent cricket from having a strong place in youth culture. Oral evidence shows that great numbers of boys and youths played knockabout games of cricket each summer evening on any available space. The young working-class cricketer, however, was not well served by local politicians and some of those involved in a senior capacity in education.

The great majority of teams playing recreational cricket were affiliated to churches or Sunday Schools and this did much to determine the social character of the sport. For most of the 1920s, three-quarters of teams had such affiliations with a figure of around two-thirds for the 1930s. All clubs in the Sunday School Leagues belonged by definition to churches as did four-fifths of those in the Walkden League. In 1924, forty-two of the fifty-five teams playing in the BCCA's Second Division and in the Junior Second Teams Association were church sides. By 1939, however, only eleven of the thirty teams playing in the Second and Third Divisions belonged to churches, a decline brought about largely by church clubs losing their grounds. Throughout the inter-war period church clubs were much rarer at the highest levels of league cricket. In 1921 the twenty-four clubs of the BDCA's expanded First Division included only four church clubs plus that of the YMCA and by 1929 only two of the twenty First Division clubs were affiliated to churches. In 1920 the re-constituted First Division contained three church clubs plus the YMCA but by 1939 only one remained. No church clubs played in the Bolton League.

Church involvement with almost all sports in the Bolton area was so marked before 1914 that it was taken for granted churches were organisations onto which sports clubs could be grafted. This legacy of Victorian moral reform through leisure activity does much to explain the strong church presence in recreational cricket. The Bolton Sunday School Social League had been established in 1893 and by 1936 was the country's largest Sunday School sports organisation with over 3,000 in winter and 2,500 in summer playing sports under its auspices. It organised rounders, tennis, hockey, billiards, table tennis, association football, swimming and badminton competitions but its cricket section had collapsed before 1914, probably because so many church sides played in other leagues.[42] Districts such as Farnworth, Radcliffe and Walkden had their separate Sunday School football leagues.

The role of Sunday School leagues in stimulating the formation of clubs has already been noted but how far clergymen took the lead in setting up teams is unclear. Clerics were often presidents of clubs and attended their annual meetings but otherwise they appear to have taken little active part in club affairs and only a few played for church teams. In 1922 the Reverend W. Popplewell, an Anglican, testified 'in no uncertain manner to the value of cricket in connection with parochial work', but a year earlier the Secretary of Junior Second

Teams Association had observed that more Sunday School teams could have been formed if those 'largely connected' with them had 'set the ball rolling'.[43] Although it is likely that the letter from St Mary's Catholic Church declining an invitation to join the local Sunday School League was composed after consultation with the priest, no firmer evidence has been found of a cleric opposing the establishment of a church cricket club. Comments by clerics about how cricket promoted character and helped to combat attitudes hostile to organised religion also tend to suggest that clergymen welcomed cricket clubs being formed at their churches. Regulations of church clubs and Sunday School leagues requiring all players to attend religious services regularly were obviously a further attraction for clergymen.

Almost all denominations encouraged the formation of church-affiliated clubs. Eighty-eight Church clubs played for at least part of the inter-war period. Many fielded two and a few three teams. Thirty-two were connected to Anglican churches and thirty-nine to the various strands of Methodism. Nearly half of the Methodist Clubs were Wesleyan and nine Primitive Methodist. There were eleven Congregationalist and three Unitarian clubs but none from the Presbyterians or Baptists though comparatively small religious groupings such as the Swedenborgians and Spiritualists had one club each. The Anglican presence was disproportionately small at the highest levels of cricket. Not one of the six churches which played in the First Division of the B.D.C.A. at various points between the Wars was Anglican. *Tillotsons' Bolton Directory*, which included most of the surrounding districts but not Radcliffe or Atherton, shows that Anglicans and Wesleyans had the highest numbers of places of worship but a greater proportion of Wesleyan churches had cricket teams. Only seventeen of the fifty-one Anglican churches from the area covered by the directory had cricket clubs whereas fourteen of thirty-one Wesleyan churches or missions did so. The proportion of Congregationalist places of worship with cricket teams, seven out of seventeen, was roughly similar to that of the Wesleyans. Within the area of the directory the Primitive Methodists with eight out of fourteen and the Independent Methodists with three out of five had the highest proportion of teams. The Anglicans had the greatest number of churches without teams.

Only one Catholic church, St Peter and Paul's, from Bolton county borough, had a cricket club between the wars and this played only from 1922 until 1937. Numbers of Catholic clubs were also very low in the Oldhan and Burnley areas. In part the small number of Catholic clubs can be attributed to a reluctance among Catholic clergy for closer links with other denominations. In the Bolton area, Anglicans and Non-conformists held joint processions of witness but those for Catholics were held separately and on different days. Within the county borough, only one Catholic church played in the Sunday School Social League's football competition and in the 1920s a Catholic Football League was set up.

The comparative lack of interest in cricket among the Irish may also have contributed to the tiny number of Catholic clubs. It seems likely that St Peter and Paul's CC owed much to the enthusiasm of Father Leighton, a noted cricket enthusiast and the only cleric among the BDCA's vice-presidents in the 1920s. The Secretary of the Radcliffe Sunday School League in the 1930s recalled that hostility to Catholics was not so strong that an application from the local Catholic church would have been refused.[44] No doubt the virtual absence of Catholic church teams in the Bolton area meant that Catholics had fewer opportunities to play than other denominations but Catholics are remembered as playing for non-church teams.

The strong church presence helped to determine the social profile of recreational cricket. The great numbers of church clubs would seem to account for the absence of pub teams, though a few pub sides entered medal or knock-out competitions organised by the leading clubs for scratch elevens. However, they hardly ever bore the name of a pub. The great majority who played for church teams belonged to 'respectable' families. Very few 'boozers' or 'roughs' played for church teams and the church presence in cricket may have discouraged those who felt uneasy in institutions with strong connotations of respectability. Moreover, the strength of Sabbatarianism in the Bolton area, which was so closely interwined with organised religion, meant that the playing of cricket on Sundays was unthinkable and this must have restricted opportunities to play. Not surprisingly those who worked on Saturday afternoon, such as shop assistants and transport workers, did not usually play cricket. Attempts to form a Bolton Wednesday League in the 1920s came to nothing though employees of co-operative stores in Bolton, Farnworth and Radcliffe played in the Manchester Wednesday League.

The church presence did not have a great impact upon the spirit in which recreational cricket was played. Religious connections did not necessarily guarantee fair play. Those who played cricket at all levels recalled Sunday School matches being just as competitive as the Bolton League, partly because a desire not to be bettered by those from the same neighbourhood engendered fierce rivalry.[45] Even the humblest leagues found it necessary to have matches umpired by those not connected with either side. In the 1930s umpires for the Horwich Sunday School League complained about players questioning their decisions, unpleasant remarks, muttering throughout matches, behaving childishly and failing to signal when balls had crossed the boundaries. A form of sharp practice in the Radcliffe Sunday School League was for fielders to run out batsmen by pretending to have lost the ball in the long grass of some outfields.[46]

Precise measurements of recreational cricket's impact upon social relationships within the Bolton area cannot be made because of the insurmountable difficulty of isolating its influence from that of other factors, and probably more powerful factors, such as wage levels, unemployment, trade-union militancy and alternative leisure interests. Still, it is possible to identify social tendencies which it strengthened. Though recreational cricket was played by working-class men and youths from a variety of occupations, it did not promote working-class solidarity but instead deepened existing divisions within a fragmented working class. The massive church presence in recreational cricket meant it was a sport played predominantly by 'respectable' sections of the working class and this helped to deepen gulfs between those who were not considered 'respectable'. The large number of church clubs can be interpreted as strengthening institutionalised Christianity in the Bolton area by encouraging church attendance. Oral evidence shows that not all church teams were able to enforce rules about regular church attendance for players, especially when this made it difficult to raise sides. Strict enforcement would have denied regular attenders who wished to play the opportunities to do so. Yet it is clear that many players did attend church or Sunday school men's classes, partly perhaps because the previous day's match could be discussed before or after the service. As many players were in their late teens, church attendance was promoted at an age when it often fell away.

The presence of young men, who were cricketers, often led young women to continue attending church, whose presence in turn attracted other young men who were not interested in cricket. Conversely, oral evidence provides instances of young men joining churches attended by their girlfriends and then being pressed to play when it became known that they had an aptitude for the game. Many recreational cricketers first met their wives at church. Wives were usually present at interviews with former players and often displayed an equally detailed knowledge of the occupational and family backgrounds of other players. Regular attendance at church service, of course, is not proof of religious conviction, though religious leaders have often stressed conviction requires attendance. But it can be argued that recreational cricket by stimulating church attendance helped to promote class co-operation. Although church leaders at the local level represented a wide variety of attitudes to working-class political activism, almost all churches advocated inter-class collaboration. There is no method of establishing how many of those attending church accepted such teachings but church clubs helped to increase the numbers of those exposed to intellectual and social forces attempting to reduce class antagonism. Though the almost total absence of Catholic teams stressed the distinctiveness of Catholics as a separate religious group and church teams in general emphasised denominational loyalties, regular matches between sides of different churches helped to promote inter-denominational goodwill and social cohesion.

Semi-professional clubs, especially those outside the county borough, stimulated and sustained local bonds which cut across class barriers and tended to work against unity between working-class groups in different parts of the Bolton area. Though most players and spectators of semi-professional clubs were working-class, such clubs fostered collaboration with other social classes. Several clubs were patronised by the local elite of wealthy industrialists who were often also landowners.[47] At least four leading clubs acquired their grounds between the wars through the generosity of this elite and club committees often asked local industrialists to find jobs for players. Owners of smaller businesses such as shopkeepers were usually prepared to contribute to club finances by becoming members or vice-presidents. Such sponsorship of semi-professional clubs would not have occurred had the elite or the 'shopocracy' seen cricket as threatening their economic and social influence. Clubs playing at the recreational level did not require or receive similar financial assistance from the elite and smaller businessman. Yet there were important links between the higher and lower levels of Bolton cricket. Although semi-professional clubs ran third teams to develop young players, the maintenance of their playing standards was equally dependent on talent recuited from below. Without this flow of players from recreational clubs, the semi-professional game would have been less healthy and less likely to become the focus of localised inter-class goodwill. Middle- and upper-class support for a largely working-class leisure interest reflected and confirmed a measure of cohesiveness within local society, which is easily overlooked in more conventional accounts of the 1930s.

Cricket played for recreation in the Bolton area was almost exclusively a leisure interest for males and demonstrated the social dominance of men. In the 1930s a few women began to play regularly. Bolton Ladies' CC was formed in 1931 and played for the rest of the decade whilst in 1935 there were press reports of at least four other women's teams playing occasionally. Yet women formed a significant minority of spectators at men's matches. In the late 1930s a witness from Mass Observation found that fifty out of 700 spectators at a Bolton League match and a third of the 350 at the Cup Final for the First Division Clubs were women.[48] In 1926 even a local sports journalist had to concede that most women spectators 'know a bit about the game'.[49] Moreover, women were vital to the financial well-being of semi-professional clubs. All leading clubs had 'ladies' committees', consisting usually of wives and mothers of players and executive committee members, who prepared teas, sold refreshments and helped with fund raising activities such as dances, whist-drives, bazaars and gala days. Sums raised by ladies' committees were often the third largest source of club income after gate receipts and members' subscriptions. In 1932 Farnworth Ladies' Committee raised £107. Tonge ladies contributed over £1,000 between 1926 and 1938.[50]

Despite their importance to semi-professional clubs, ladies' committees had little formal power. A few women were members of clubs and some attended annual meetings but they do not appear to have been elected onto executive committees. Yet no club could afford to antagonise its ladies' committee. Women were exploited in a manner which reflected their treatment in other spheres. The types of tasks allotted to ladies' committees helped to reinforce perceptions that only work related to domesticity was appropriate for women. At recreational clubs women made teas but the scale of their involvement was far less than at the highest levels of league cricket. Yet it may be that women were most effective as opponents of the game. Oral evidence reveals that many men stopped playing cricket because of family commitments or opposition from wives or girlfriends.

There appears to be no way of determining whether increasing numbers of men stopped playing as a result of such pressures and it is difficult to be sure if this part of a trend towards less inequality between the sexes.

An examination of recreational cricket in the Bolton area suggests that it did more to preserve than to change local social relationships. It helped to perpetuate divisions within the working class between rough and respectable; it also augmented the influence of organised Christianity. Hence the work of 'rational recreation' went on surreptitiously long after it had ceased to be a prominent ideological issue at the national level. Semi-professional cricket cultivated local loyalties and bonds which transcended class divisions fostering closer links with the local middle classes. It does not follow, of course, that recreational cricket had sufficient influence to neutralise economic and cultural forces with contrary social tendencies towards class conflict. Investigating recreational cricket and its social impact, if nothing else, amply demonstrates the enormous complexity and variegated nature of social relationships at the local level and the wide range of factors which need to be included in explanations of social cohesion and social change in the industrial centres of inter-war Britain.

Notes

1 The terms 'the Bolton area', 'Bolton and its surroundings' refer to the pre-Radcliffe-Maude county borough of Bolton, the municipal borough of Radcliffe plus the urban districts of Adlington, Atherton, Blackrod, Farnworth, Horwich, Kearsley, Little Hulton, Little Lever, Turton, Tyldesley, Westhoughton and Worsley. In 1921 and 1931 total population was nearly 255,000 with just about half residing inside Bolton county borough. Industry was the basis of the economy in all parts of the locality. Though the metropolitan borough of Bolton absorbed most of this area in the early 1970s, Little Hulton and Worsley were merged with Salford, Atherton and Tyldesley with Wigan and Radcliffe with Bury. The distribution of clubs across this area affiliated to the BDCA and the Bolton League made it an entity from a cricketing viewpoint.
2 Precise statistics of paying spectators at league cricket in the Bolton area are not available. Estimates can be based on gate receipts but men paid higher admission fees than women and children and totals of gate receipts do not distinguish between amounts paid by men and women or children. Gate receipts suggest that paying spectators at home county championship matches for Essex CCC were below 25,000 in 1925, 1936, 1937 and

1938. For league and county cricket there is no indication of how often club members, who were admitted free, attended matches.

3 Numbers of clubs in cricket leagues are derived from press reports, Annual Handbooks of the BDCA and minute books of the Bolton League, the Horwich Sunday School League and the Walkden Amateur League.

4 *Buff (Bolton Evening News* Saturday sports edition), 10 November 1923, 10 October 1936.

5 *Buff*, 17 October 1936.

6 *Buff*, 26 May 1923.

7 Interview with Sir Robert Southern, 3 August 1987.

8 *Radcliffe Times*, 3 October 1925.

9 *Farnworth Weekly Journal*, 14 October 1921.

10 Interview with A. Burnham and J. Pickstone, 2 April 1987.

11 Information supplied by A. Hargreaves.

12 *Buff*, 26 May 1923.

13 Interview with T. Needham, 30 January 1987.

14 Interview with Sir Robert Southern.

15 J.A. Hester, E. Ward and L.E. Perry, *Horwich Churches Welfare League 1922-72* (1972), p. 11.

16 A. Hargreaves, *Cricket in My Life. A Story of Cricket in the Bolton District 1917-83* (Swinton, 1984).

17 Interview with S. Webb, 14 July 1987.

18 Interview with A. Burnham and J. Pickstone.

19 R. Cavanagh, *Cotton Town Cricket* (BDCA, 1988), p. 3.

20 *Buff*, 5 March 1927.

21 *Buff*, 5 March 1927.

22 Bolton Playing Fields Association, *Report and Statement of Accounts for the Period ending 31st December 1934* (Bolton, 1935), p. 4.

23 Bolton County Borough Town Clerk's Office. Correspondence with the National Playing Fields Association concerning the Application of a Grant from the Carnegie Trust for Purchase of a Plot of Land at Hall-i 'th'Wood for Playing Fields.

24 Annual Handbooks of the BDCA give locations of grounds.

25 Bolton Playing Fields Association minutes, 18 May 1934.

26 Bolton Playing Fields Association minutes, 27 February 1935.

27 *Bolton Evening News*, 16 March 1935.

28 *Farnworth Weekly Journal*, 31 July 1925, 24 March 1939; *Buff*, 5 November 1938.

29 Interview with A. Smale, 15 March 1987.

30 J.B. Taylor, *Bradshaw Cricket Club* (Bradshaw CC, 1984), p. 36; *Buff*, 24 January 1920.

31 *Farnworth Weekly Journal*, 12 February 1937.

32 *Radcliffe Times*, 7 May 1938.

33 Interview with H. Scholes, 16 February 1987.

34 J.L. Glover, 'Physical Education at Bolton School 1516-1980', University of Liverpool M.Ed. thesis, 1986, pp. 23, 45, 86-7. Letter from 'A Headmaster' in *The Journal of Education* (February 1947).

35 C.A. Bentley, 'Provision of physical education in Bolton between 1870 and

1940', University of Manchester M.Ed. thesis, 1978, pp. 102–3.
36 *Buff*, 10 August 1935. Interview with H. Scholes.
37 *Buff*, 24 June 1936.
38 *Lancasshire Schools' Cricket Handbooks, 1933–1952.* H.F.B. Thomas, *Schoolboy Cricket in Manchester. A Short History of the Manchester Schools Cricket Association* (Salford, 1947).
39 *Farnworth Weekly Journal*, 23 July 1926.
40 *Radcliffe Times*, 15 May 1926.
41 *Buff*, 10 August 1935.
42 *Farnworth Weekly Journal*, 10 August 1928. *Bolton Journal and Guardian*, 5 June 1936.
43 *Buff*, 19 November 1921, 18 November 1922.
44 Interview with Sir Robert Southern.
45 Interviews with A. Burnham and J. Pickstone and with former players of Horwick RMICC, 10 July 1987.
46 *Buff*, 2 June 1930, 2 June 1934. Interview with Sir Robert Southern.
47 The political and social views of Bolton's elite are considered in P.A. Harris, 'Social leadership and social attitudes in Bolton 1919 to 1939', University of Lancaster Ph.D. thesis, 1973. This thesis does not discuss the elite's patronage of cricket.
48 Mass Observation Worktown Survey, Box W2, File D, Worktown: Cricket, Mass Observation Archive, University of Sussex.
49 *Farnworth Weekly Journal*, 2 July 1926.
50 *Buff*, 28 January 1933, 3 December 1938.

7

League cricket in the North and Midlands, 1900–1940

Jeffrey Hill

The profound changes in the provision and organisation of sport, which occurred between the late nineteenth century and the Second World War, produced two spectator sports that may fairly be described as 'working-class': these were, of course, Association Football and, in the north of England, Rugby League. Both were firmly fixed in the public's mind with the proverbial 'cloth cap' image. Cricket, on the other hand, though often regarded at this time as 'the national game', articulated quite different meanings. In all its forms – from the rituals of its play on the field to the representation of the game in literature and the mass media – it was heavily coded to connote upper classness. Cricket symbolically depicted the nation's social structure: gentlemen amateurs leading working-class professionals. Paradoxically, though cricket had played a pioneering part in the development of sporting professionalism in the mid-nineteenth century, and had anticipated football by well over a decade in the inauguration of a league competition, the game proved resistant to the pressures which in many other sports led to commercialisation.[1] Its governing elite made few attempts to exploit cricket as a spectator sport until the 1960s, and its basic form of play – the three-day match – remained for the most part attuned to a middle-class clientele rather than a working-class one. There seems, in cricket, to have been a conscious wish to prevent the game's becoming a *mass* sport, with all that was implied – politically, socially and aesthetically – in that notion.

But did all cricket conform to this philosophy? By shifting our gaze away from 'first-class' cricket we may perceive other developments in the game. In the late nineteenth century there emerged a diverse series of 'league' cricket competitions in the industrial districts of the north and midlands. In many ways the clubs involved in this branch of the game represented a quite distinctive cricket culture, communicating meanings different from those conventionally associated with the game.[2] It is the aim of this essay to explore some aspects of this cricket, in particular its personnel and styles of play, in an effort to discover whether we should begin to reassess our conceptions about the role played by cricket in English society in the first half of the twentieth century.

The project is not without certain difficulties. In contrast to first-class cricket – the growth of which is documented in an ample (albeit mainly descriptive) literature – virtually nothing has been written on league cricket.[3] This is perhaps not surprising considering the immense variety of this branch of the game and the attendant problems of making worthwhile generalisations about it. For example, in one northern town, Burnley, in the 1920s there were no fewer than six cricket leagues of varying quality in operation, ranging from an extensive Sunday School League (the basis of so much of the cricket in the north of England), through a Tuesday League, played on early closing day by members of the retail trades, to the Lancashire League, one of the country's premier leagues, famous for its star professional players, in which the club bearing the town's name competed.[4] There is no reason to suppose that Burnley is at all exceptional in this respect. The problem of cohering this complex hierarchy of clubs into a meaningful whole is added to by the predictable difficulty with sources. It is one thing for the social historian to ask questions about the nature of league cricket but quite another to provide the answers. Recording the sporting achievements of the clubs would be a relatively straightforward task, given the often excellent coverage of matches in the local press; but when it comes to yielding information about the social composition and role of the clubs the sources – whether newspapers, club records, commemorative histories or oral recollections – are often infuriatingly opaque. In the face of such problems the present essay settles for modest objectives; instead of attempting to sketch in the broad picture it has been decided to focus discussion upon two clubs for which a reasonable range of sources was available. They are the Nelson Cricket Club (Lancashire League) and the Durham City Cricket Club (Durham Senior League).[5] From this case-study basis some generalisations about the nature of league cricket are offered, though a couple of initial qualifications should be lodged. First, both clubs occupied leading positions in their respective areas, at the apex of the local cricket hierarchy; they therefore represented something quite different from the brown boots and braces sport played by chapel, school, works and neighbourhood, which probably constituted a more demotic form of the game. Secondly, given the gaps in the sources, a good deal of what follows is inevitably speculative.

I

'Working-class' sport, so called, was often in practice influenced by middle-class leaders and organisers. This was certainly true of professional football,[6] and a similar feature is discernible in league cricket. In their recent study of popular culture in nineteenth-century England, Golby and Purdue make some interesting observations on this point, contrasting a convivial, populist form of cricket which developed in the south with a more serious, competitive form of the game established in the north by a university-educated business elite.[7] Without specifying the exact form of cricket under discussion (county or league) these two authors may nevertheless have identified a key feature of league cricket in the twentieth century: namely, the importance of middle-class leadership. This was certainly given support by former players and administrators of the Dudley Cricket Club, interviewed by the present writer in 1987.[8] All expressed the view that league cricket in the Black Country had close associations with the professional classes, especially in the sphere of club management. And, interestingly enough, in the records of that particular club there is a clear indication that, at least until the 1920s, the principal source of recruitment to the club had been the local grammar school.[9] The Nelson and Durham clubs, for which more detailed information was available, similarly reveal a strong middle-class presence among those who held leading positions in club affairs, either as officials or members of the executive committees.

In the case of Durham City CC this feature is perhaps most clearly illustrated in the figure of H. Cecil Ferens. For most of the inter-war period Ferens was the club chairman and captain of the first eleven. He also played for the Durham county side as well as other leading amateur teams. Not only did he figure prominently in the administration of the club but on occasions assumed an almost seigneurial role, as when, during the 1930s, he and his family dug deeply in their pockets to carry the club through difficult financial times. Cecil Ferens was a notable figure in Durham civic life, a solicitor of standing as a partner in the family firm of H.E. Ferens and Son, Secretary to the Bishop of Durham, solicitor to the Cathedral Chapter and, from 1934 onwards, a member of the City Council. His father, Alderman H.E. Ferens, had established the family's prominence by virtue of his public service, having sat on the City Council since the 1890s and held several honorary positions in prestigious local institutions, including the Durham Rugby Club, the Girls' High School and the University Council. Of similar status was Henry Shaw Harrison, head of a leading firm of organ builders in Durham, who took over the position of President of the Cricket Club in the late 1920s from John McCartan, a well known local solicitor.[10] People of an equal social and economic standing held the presidency of Nelson CC during the same period. James Ridehalgh and, from the early 1930s, David Tattersall, held the office between the wars; both were members of influential mill-owning families, and as may be imagined, served as Justices of the Peace. So too did T.E. Morgan, editor of the *Nelson Leader*, who was the club chairman during the whole of this time.[11]

In a rather less patrician form a similar social tone prevailed in the committee membership of the two clubs. Nelson CC elected a committee of fifteen from 1923 onwards and (as many members were re-elected from year to year) an analysis of membership in a sample twelve years of the inter-war period produces a total of just 30 names.[12] Of these, 22 can be identified sufficiently clearly from local directory sources for them to be roughly categorised socially. The results reveal a preponderance of middle-class occupation (Table 7.1). The committee of seven which administered the Durham City CC at this time is, unfortunately, more difficult to place in these terms; aside from the presidents and chairman only 7 members from 5 sample years of the 1920s and 1930s could be identified adequately, and their occupations were: cashier, clerk (two), draper, schoolmaster, rate collector and cabinet maker.[13] Though there is clearly a strong petty bourgeois element here the evidence is too flimsy for any hard and fast conclusions to be drawn. But at least, in considering committee membership, there are indications that the control of the two clubs was in the hands of a middle-class group, and this helps to substantiate some of the points made by Gerald Howat, in his study of Learie Constantine, on the respectable middle-class life and connections of the league cricket professional in the 1930s.[14]

It is no doubt to be expected that persons from this social group would be associated with organisations which themselves occupied a prominent place in local life. Mason has noted this relationship in connection with professional football clubs[15] and doubtless a similar mixture of economic, social and political motives was responsible for

Table 7.1 Nelson CC: Occupations of committee members, 1920s and 1930s

Manufacturing and business	
Manufacturer	6
Businessman	1
Retail business	1
Professional and managerial	
Mill manager	1
Theatre manager	1
Schoolmaster	2
Self-employed/clerical	
Agent (cotton yarn)	1
Clerk	1
Factory employees	
Warper	1
Loomer	1
Overlooker	1
Miscellaneous	
Secretary, Women's Institute	1
Secretary, Liberal Party	1
'Engineer'	1
Son of middle-class parents (occupation unspecified)	1
Former club captain; served in Guards regiment in First World War (occupation unspecified)	1

Source: NCBC, *Secretary's and Treasurer's Reports*, 1919–27, 1932–4; P. Barrett and Co., op. cit. 1919–34

attracting business and professional people to league cricket clubs. It seems very likely, for example, that the politically ambitious Nelson solicitor J.H.S. Aitken consciously cultivated close connections with the cricket club as a way of fostering his political objectives. The club afforded him a valuable point of contact with the electorate in his parliamentary campaigns for the Liberals in Nelson and Colne in the 1920s.[16] In fact, in both towns under consideration, the cricket club seems to have been linked in with other institutions as part of a local middle-class network. Durham, with its historic ecclesiastical, administrative and educational functions was a city of strong Tory

Anglican traditions, markedly more middle-class in character than the industrial towns and villages surrounding it. The cricket club, significantly sited on the racecourse on the more affluent eastern side of the city, alongside the tennis club and the University's athletic ground, was naturally a part of the local 'establishment', as the activities of the Ferens family show. Nelson, on the other hand, was a very different town. It had developed rapidly as a cotton-weaving centre from the 1870s onwards and was predominantly working-class in social terms, possessing a strong trade-union movement. The area had long traditions of nonconformity and radicalism but from the early years of the twentieth century had become a stronghold of independent Labour. By 1905 both the municipal council and the parliamentary seat were Labour-controlled,[17] with the result that the Liberal manufacturing elite had been largely ousted from its position of political power. In the post-war years, in response to Labour's dominance, an anti-socialist coalition of Liberal and Conservative forces emerged. The cricket club committee was aligned with these developments, in political as well as social terms, representing an enclave of middle-class influence in contrast to the new political power radiating from Weavers' Institute, the hub of Nelson's labour movement.

It would, however, be misleading to portray cricket clubs as closed middle-class institutions. Membership was open to all who could afford the subscriptions and, whilst these might on occasions be beyond the reach of the working man and woman, there was usually a degree of popular participation. In fact, the depth of public involvement was a frequently commented on feature of league cricket, especially by those who came to it from the outside. Fred Root, the old Worcestershire and England bowler who joined the Lancashire League club Todmorden as professional in 1933, was particularly impressed by the enthusiasm shown for the cricket club among the people of the town:

> Everybody seems to be a member of their respective Lancashire League club. They would rather miss joining the Co-op than the cricket club, and when bad times make money scarce their sacrifices to enable them to pay their annual subscription are almost pitiful. In addition to paying their subscriptions, they do anything in their power to assist the club. They will be very annoyed if not included in the 'roller XI' – as they call the squad which is never tired of 'ironing out' the pitches – and I have seen men do as much voluntary work on Lancashire League grounds in a week as a paid groundsman in county cricket does in a fortnight.[18]

Constantine, writing a few years earlier, had made similar observations about the strength of support at Nelson, where he became professional in 1929.[19] From what we have seen of the social composition of the Durham and Nelson committees, however, the participation of 'ordinary' people in club affairs seems to have been limited, as far as the management was concerned, with working men like Edward Ashton and Ben Chadwick of Nelson noteworthy exceptions. Ashton, Secretary of Nelson CC from 1913 until his death in 1932, was still working as a warper in a local mill when he died, aged sixty-seven. An active Wesleyan and a noted raconteur, who entertained many a gathering at the annual cricket club dinner with his stories, Teddy Ashton was in many ways the typical self-taught Victorian working man.[20] His friend Ben Chadwick, the club Treasurer during the inter-war years, was also employed in the cotton trade, as a loomer, and like Ashton was prominent in the Liberal Party, standing as a candidate for the anti-socialist cause in municipal elections.[21] But if there was a working class element in league clubs it was more likely to be found in the broader mass of the membership than in the leadership roles. It is to the ordinary members that we should now turn our attention.

II

Unfortunately, the absence of any precise data on the social composition of ordinary members means that fairly crude indicators have to be used to gauge its characteristics. The most helpful clue is provided by considering levels of membership subscriptions. In doing so, however, some of the factors that impinged upon league cricket finances need to be borne in mind. In the forty or so years before the Second World War the expenses involved in providing cricket entertainment in the leagues were increasing considerably. In presenting his financial statement for the 1921 season, for example, the Nelson Treasurer compared the year's total receipts of £3,391 with those of £706 in 1914, commenting 'the Club is now a huge concern'.[22] Like many football clubs those of league cricket were caught in an upward spiral of costs. The competitive nature of the game created pressures to produce the results that would attract the spectators. With this in mind the engagement of a high-class professional player was seen by many clubs as a prerequisite for success. By the 1930s Nelson were paying their West Indian professional Learie

Constantine upwards of £1,000 a season, though this was exceptional.[23] Durham City nevertheless paid the former Kent player Joe Galley a basic £7 7s 0d a week for the 1921 season, and to secure the services of Bill Sadler for the 1926 season the club had to offer £5 a week over the whole year.[24] Once ensnared in this quest for players and spectators club treasurers faced perennial problems in maximising their funds. Gate receipts, which could prove a most rewarding source of income, were nevertheless extremely unreliable since they depended so much on good weather. A wet summer, like that experienced in Lancashire in 1938, could play havoc with even the best laid financial strategy. Ben Chadwick recorded the loss of several hours of cricket at Nelson in that season, including 'two of the most attractive matches of the season, which probably would have yielded over £200 at a modest estimate (and which) brought us in £1. 0s 6½d'.[25] As a guaranteed pool of income for the season, therefore, membership subscriptions came to assume a vital part in clubs' plans. The policy adopted in seeking to enlarge this source could have important repercussions on the nature of a club's membership.

Dudley CC provides an example of high subscriptions having an adverse effect upon membership. The club had incurred serious debts during the First World War as a consequence of an ambitious scheme, launched in 1910, to extend its ground facilities with a view to becoming a major venue for Worcestershire county fixtures. The scheme had failed and in 1920 the club felt that it had no alternative but to increase its subscription rates – to two guineas for players, and one guinea for non-players – in an attempt to clear its debts. The issue of subscriptions proved a frequent and contentious one in club meetings thereafter, as members sought an alleviation of the club's financial problems. Despite a raising and lowering of the rates the chairman was still reporting in 1928 the club's 'very poor membership', and it seems likely that by this time Dudley's policy of having relatively high membership charges had marginalised its working class supporters to the role of spectators paying at the gates.[26]

Nelson and Durham City, on the other hand, strove to bring the cost of club membership within the reach of working people. Early in the century Durham City had established a membership subscription of 10s a season for town members, and 5s for those from the county districts. These rates were not increased until the 1930s, when the club fell on hard times financially.[27] Well before this, though, there had been indications of declining membership, often attributed by club officials to short-time working and unemployment in the local economy.[28] Be that as it may, subscriptions could hardly have been more reasonable, at least for employed working men, even when increased in 1933 to a comprehensive 10s for all adults. Other factors may have been responsible for poor membership. Working men might have preferred to join clubs based on the industrial towns and villages in the county districts rather than stand the costs of travelling into Durham itself. They may also have been deterred by the club's social character. Whatever the reason, the club's membership appears to have been largely middle-class in nature. A fair guide to this is provided by the names of 140 people recorded in the club minute books of the inter-war period as new members. The occupations of eighty of these members can be found from local sources. Only seven could be regarded unequivocally as 'working people' (gasman, chauffeur, postman, labourer, and three junior members who were sons of a linesman, stoker and gardener). The remainder all fall into what would conventionally be regarded as lower-middle or middle-class status, ranging from self-employed artisans to clergymen, doctors, business managers and schoolmasters, with a rough equivalence between 'lower-middle' and 'middle'.[29] Presumably, with this clientele, the club could have afforded to set its subscriptions rather higher than it did, and by choosing not to do so was forced to make economies to offset loss of income. The most significant of these was the abandoning of the policy of engaging former county players as professionals, resulting in a decline of spectators and, therefore, gate receipts. Some members clearly saw this policy as short-sighted and advocated instead a programme of buying success by hiring a star player. But, as officials gloomily pointed out, the wages demanded by such players at this time were 'far beyond the present capacity of the Club'.[30]

Durham City's failure to broaden the basis of its membership contrasts with the success of Nelson CC. As Table 7.2 shows, the club had provided a variety of categories of membership since the late nineteenth century, each type suited to a different pocket and bestowing different privileges. With average wages in the local cotton trade around 25s a week at the turn of the century[31] these rates were reasonably affordable for working people, especially when it is considered that cotton offered employment opportunities for families, which were often not exclusively dependent on the earnings of the adult male. Membership rates, moreover, increased roughly in keeping with the rise in money wages, which approximately doubled in the cotton trade over the first thirty years of the century.[32] It might therefore reasonably be assumed that a good proportion of that vast majority of members enrolled at the popular prices were working-class, though some, of course, especially in the important women's category, would be better-off people taking advantage of cheap rates. On this basis the club financed an ambitious policy of engaging star international professionals in the inter-war years, beginning with the Australian E.A. MacDonald (1922-4), and reaching a zenith with Constantine (1929-37). Though such a policy had initially provoked doubts from the local press (despite being warmly praised by 'Tityrus' of the nationally circulating *Athletic News*)[33] it was vindicated by Nelson's financial and sporting success over the next fifteen years. The club demonstrated that it was possible to provide 'big cricket' without excluding working people, whose continuing involvement was ensured in the 1930s by the introduction of an instalments scheme to ease the payment of subscriptions.[34]

III

It was, nevertheless, as a spectator sport that league cricket made its strongest contribution to working-class life. John Kay, one of the few cricket writers alert to the characteristics of league cricket, has noted that game's particular appeal to the working people of Lancashire in the early part of the century:

> The workers settled for league cricket. It was played on Saturday afternoons when they were free, and, what is more, little was demanded from the travelling point of view. As one old-time cotton worker put it: 'Tha's got to be a man o'means to watch first class cricket . . . and, besides, tha's expected to wear a collar and tie when tha goes to Old Trafford.[35]

The leagues certainly displayed a capacity for evoking a passionate and extensive popular support. The Birmingham League players interviewed recalled 'gates' of five to six thousand in the 1930s, and the 1929 Lancashire League season, with the arrival of the brilliant Constantine, produced several gates of around ten thousand.[36] Enthusiasm of football-like proportions was not uncommon, given the highly charged local rivalry that was endemic in league cricket. A press report of the 1919 local 'derby' between Colne and Nelson is worth citing for the sense it conveys of the intense communal interest in the match:

Table 7.2 Nelson CC: Membership subscriptions and gate receipts 1896, 1908, 1924 and 1926

Category of member	Total numbers	% of total	Amount received (£sd)
		1896	
£2 2 0	2	0.4	4 4 0
£1 1 0	97	17.2	106 1 0
10s 6d	124	22.1	65 2 0
5s	318	56.6	79 10 0
2s 6d	21	3.7	2 12 6
	total 562		total 253 5 6
			gate 259 12 4½
		1908	
£5 15 6	2	3.4	11 11 0
£2 2 0	4	0.5	8 8 0
£1 1 0	123	17.9	129 3 0
10s 6d	114	16.6	59 17 0
5s	398	58.1	99 10 0
2s 6d	24	3.5	3 0 0
	total 685		total 311 9 0
			gate 619 4 0
		1924	
63s	6	0.7	18 8 0
42s	36	4.6	75 12 0
30s	1	0.1	1 10 0
21s	2	0.2	2 2 0
20s	1	0.1	1 0 0
15s	220	28.0	165 0 0
12s 6d	2	0.2	1 5 0
10s 6d	206	26.2	108 3 0
7s 6d (ladies)	235	29.9	88 2 6
6s	26	3.3	7 16 0
6s (youths)	50	6.3	15 0 0
	total 785		total 812 18 6
			gate 759 0 2

	1926		
63s	6	0.9	18 8 0
42s	40	6.0	84 0 0
30s	1	0.1	1 10 0
21s	1	0.1	1 10 0
20s	—	—	—
15s	191	28.7	143 5 0
12s 6d	—	—	
10s 6s	175	26.3	91 17 6
7s 6d	196	29.5	73 10 0
(ladies)			
6s	54	8.1	16 4 0
	total 664		total 748 5 6
			gate n.a.

Source: NCBC, Treasurer's Reports and Balance Sheets for Seasons 1896, 1908, 1924, 1926.

The match at Colne on Saturday was an 'old-timer' in every sense of the phrase. The day could not have been more propitious. There was a bright and genial sun which radiated pleasure all round, and it was an ideal day from the spectators' point of view. The influx of Nelsonians was the greatest for many years. The cars were crowded, and if there had been another dozen cars available the Nelson and Colne Tramways Committees would have reaped a rich harvest. As it was many of the Leeds Road section had to make the journey on foot, and there was so much struggling on the return that many walked home. The gate was £137 – £20 more than the previous record, and judging by the cheers there appeared to be as many Nelsonians present as Colunians. Nelson achieved a decisive victory, but as it was only accomplished about 11 minutes from time, excitement was kept up until the last.[37]

Especially in fine weather like this league cricket offered good entertainment for a small charge. Admission to cricket grounds could be obtained for around 6d in the inter-war period (including the much-hated Entertainment Tax); Dudley CC, for example, charged 5d in 1919, and 6d after 1925. Constantine and the Nelson team could be watched for 6d (enclosure extra), whilst Durham City charged 8d, as did the Blackburn Club, East Lancs.[38] Moreover, spectators were accommodated in some comfort compared to the provisions of football grounds. Seating on banked benches was usually available, unless the ground was packed when some would have to stand. Members sometimes had the privilege of watching from behind the bowler's arm, though pavilions were not always so advantageously sited. Many of the leading clubs' grounds were spacious and the clubs themselves sensitive to the concerns of their followers, especially for big matches:

> The Committee of the Nelson Cricket Club are making ample provision for the crowd that is expected for the visit of East Lancs, (September 1919). They are banking up the ground near the new refreshment tent and are also making another temporary enclosure to the left of the pavilion. The full holding capacity of the ground has never been tested but it certainly will be tomorrow if the weather is in keeping with the importance of the encounter. To relieve the pressure at the gates, it has been decided to sell tickets before the day of the match, and those who purchase them have the privilege of entering the ground at 12 o'clock. The doors for those who have not taken this precaution will be open at one o'clock, so that supporters of the Nelson club cannot complain if outsiders secure the best positions . . . large numbers are expected from other towns, and an application has already been received from Bolton for 24 seats. No seats, however, are being reserved.[39]

One of the attractions for those who turned up was, apart from the play, drinking. On large grounds as many as three bars might be open during the match, even in areas with a strong chapel community.[40] Refreshment points were an important source of revenue to the clubs, whether run by local traders or by the club themselves. Nelson CC, for example, contracted its refreshment services to a local caterer in the years before the First World War for around £40 a season, but after the war took on this service itself and, with the help of volunteers, frequently made a handsome profit on the sales.[41] In addition to drinking, small-stake betting was another institution of working-class life which made its appearance on league cricket grounds. Details of its operations are hard to come by, however, since it appears to have been conducted in an informal manner by the participants themselves rather than being organised by the bookmakers. Fred Root commented upon the role of the public houses and the working men's clubs in organising 'cricket pools',[42] and the practice of leading professionals taking bets on their own performances was probably quite common.[43]

Notwithstanding these activities the behaviour of spectators seems to have been exemplary. League crowds were, it is true, noted for their frank and critical appreciation of the events taking place on the field. Barracking was commonplace, most clubs possessing a mascot figure, like the famous Joe Brick of Dudley, who acted as a 'cheerleader', directing the club's supporters in partisan badinage with those of the opposition.[44] Physical confrontations, however, seem to have been few and far between. There are occasional press reports of disorderly incidents, as when, for example, the captain of South Shields in the Durham Senior League withdrew his team from a match against Philadelphia in 1912 'in consequence of the bad behaviour (i.e. verbal insults) of the spectators'.[45] The Bradford League match between Saltaire and Undercliffe ten years later ended with spectators coming onto the playing area as heated exchanges and, it was alleged, fisticuffs took place between players and officials following a tense climax to the game. But the League management committee took stern action over this incident, banning the players involved for a season and fining the home club for failing to restrain its supporters.[46] Birmingham League players interviewed on this aspect of league cricket were, however, able to recall only one instance of crowd misbehaviour over some thirty years of playing experience, and that resulted from a disputed run-out decision involving a professional.[47] Altogether, league cricket was watched, and played, in a good natured if frequently noisy atmosphere: 'keen but friendly', as one former player described it.[48] Above all it was characterised by a fierce local patriotism, never more clearly expressed than when a club won its particular league championship, as the little Lancashire town of Haslingden did in 1920:

> Headed by the Borough Prize Band, the team drove through the town with the cup in a char-a-banc. About twelve private motors with searchlights, and a large number of people on foot, accompanied the procession.[49]

Such an event was cause for genuine rejoicing, in the pubs, clubs and, no doubt, even the sarsaparilla bars.

On the field league cricket differed as a spectacle from the game played in county or test matches. The most obvious difference was, of course, in the limited duration of league matches; in keeping with the working and domestic arrangements of the population, play started at around 2 pm and lasted for five hours, with strict attention paid to punctuality.[50] Interestingly, though, the leagues conformed to the laws of cricket as laid down by the MCC; there were no adaptations of these rules to encourage 'brighter' play, as was to occur in later years with, for example, the restrictions placed on fielders' positions in some first-class one-day competitions.[51] The differences were essentially in the approach to the game. A marked feature was the emphasis on attacking cricket. More often than not conditions favoured the bowlers; batting could be a difficult art but its exponents were nevertheless expected to 'get on with it', to score quickly, improvising if necessary. The general mentality was neatly summed up by the experienced league player Cecil Parkin, writing in the 1920s:

> From the bowler's point of view, it is ten times easier in the league than in the county. I don't only mean that in the league a bowler has to play only one day a week. I mean that it is ten times easier to get wickets in the league than against county cricketers. For one thing, the pitches are not perfect in the leagues. Then it must be remembered that the pace league cricket is played at gives a batsman little or no chance of playing himself in. . . . A league batsman has to get busy with the runs from the moment he arrives at the crease. Consequently, he is always giving the bowler a chance. He will go after your off balls, and even if you keep a perfect length, he must still, in the interests of his side, continue to take risks. A league club has no use for the batsman who, like the county cricketer, can only score from loose bowling.[52]

In this rather frenzied mode of play, which often elicited a disdainful attitude towards league cricket from the purists ('likened in their own minds to a circus or music-hall version of the game')[53] much depended on the contribution of the professional player. In contrast to the inferior social status he experienced in first-class cricket,[54] the 'pro' was elevated to a position of great esteem, at times even adulation. Whilst many leagues included among their aims the fostering of amateur cricket,[55] all came to rely upon the services of professionals. Usually there was an agreement to limit the number to one for each club (the Bradford League exceptionally permitting four) and it was rare to find a club achieving success without professional help.[56] Indeed, reliance upon the professional could, on occasions, prove excessive, as matches became gladiatorial contests between the rival champions. The 1922 fixture between Church and Nelson is a case in point: Church bowled out for 59 (E.A. Macdonald, the Australian test player, 7 for 29); Nelson all out 44 (S.F. Barnes, the former England international, 6 for 19).[57] It was difficult to see how this encouraged amateur cricket, but on the other hand, the outstanding achievements of professionals attracted spectators. The more so when it was batting skill on display, such as Constantine's 124 out of 175 in seventy minutes for Nelson against Enfield in 1929, or Dennis Hendren's thrilling innings of 149 in two hours for Burnmoor just before the First World War.[58] This was entertainment, compared to the many dull fixtures, played on over-prepared wickets, that characterised the county game. Root, the former county and test player, was all too aware of the difference: 'Never have I played in any sort of cricket that provides greater thrills than the Lancashire League.'[59]

But despite these contrasts league clubs at no time evinced any sense of rebellion against the prevailing order in cricket. Whereas both football and rugby had experienced sharp internal divisions of class and regional loyalties during the course of their development – resulting, in the case of rugby, in the formation of distinct and rival organisations within the sport – this never occurred in cricket. League clubs accepted their subordinate position, often seeing as one of their chief purposes the provision of players for the first-class game; clubs took great pride in any subsequent rise to fame at test or county level of their former members.[60] The cordial relationships that generally prevailed between league and county clubs are well exemplified in the arrangement concluded in 1910, and reaffirmed after the war, between the Lancashire League and the Lancashire County Club for the mutual exchange of players. The League clubs made available their professionals for ad hoc county service, the county offered its reserve contracted players as substitute professionals when needed by league clubs. In very few instances did this arrangement create any ill-feeling.[61] Cordiality of this kind was further fostered by similar attitudes towards the 'spirit' of the game of cricket. The unwritten codes of fair play and gentlemanly conduct, for which the first-class game was a byword, prevailed equally in the leagues. There appears to have been little, if any, concern that the emphasis upon the professional, and the quest for spectator appeal, would produce the kind of 'win at all costs' mentality which many observers claimed to see in the development of football, epitomised in the concept of the 'professional foul'. Sometimes, of course, the codes were transgressed, as in the deciding match for the Lancashire League title in 1922, when the captain of Rawtenstall removed his team from the field in poor evening light in order to avoid the danger of losing. The opposition, Bacup, compounded the crime by refusing to resume the match on another day.[62] What is interesting about this incident, though, is the scandalised reaction it aroused from other clubs, notably Nelson CC where several of the speakers at the annual players' dinner of that year referred disparagingly to the episode. The Mayor of Nelson, Councillor Gibson, was particularly censorious: 'Whether they won or lost, he hoped they would all remember to be gentlemen in their games. He had been extremely sorry to hear about the fiasco in the League final. He thought such a thing was detrimental to cricket. Whatever was said about Nelson cricket, he believed from the captain downwards they were gentlemen. . . .' And following him Captain Albert Smith JP, former Labour MP for Nelson and Colne, concluded the evening with a sentiment taken from one of the game's most celebrated figures: 'To all players he would say in the words of Pelham Warner "Keep a straight bat and a modest mind" (Applause).'[63]

IV

Was cricket ever a working-class sport? From what we know about the first-class game (and we still, despite the extensive literature available, need more studies of it written from the perspective of the historian rather than that of the cricket lover) it seems unlikely that it occupied as all-consuming a place in working-class life as did football.[64] League cricket, on the other hand, probably proved more accessible to working men and women than its first-class counterpart, by virtue largely of its appeal as a spectator sport in the industrial districts. In this respect it was also, no doubt, an important cultural influence helping to shape people's sense of place and identity. But it should not be forgotten that league cricket clubs owed a good deal to the leadership and even patronage of middle-class people. Clubs might have provided opportunities for workers to rub shoulders with their bosses, but equally they might become rather exclusive institutions socially, and we should be wary of some of the more romantic images associated with league cricket.[65] It may have been the influence of a manufacturing and professional bourgeoisie, alongside the local 'shopocracy', that was responsible for the more pointedly commercial emphasis of league cricket by comparison with the 'semi-commercial' nature of county cricket. League clubs certainly endeavoured to cultivate their market more vigorously than county clubs by devising a form of play that was closely attuned to the recreational patterns of an industrial population. Indeed it was in the role of consumer rather than as active participants that working people were able to exert their strongest influence over the development of this form of cricket. Nevertheless, even in this role, the working class was able to imprint some characteristics on the game, making it distinctly different from – if not in conflict with – the first-class game. The local league cricket club might justifiably be seen as one of the many institutions of industrial society where class interests and influences converged; as Hoggart noted in his classic study of working-class culture: 'many of these activities are sponsored by "Them", but they would not survive were they not supported by a strong and genuine enthusiasm from working people'.[66]

Notes

1 See K. Sandiford and W. Vamplew, 'The peculiar economics of English Cricket Before 1914', *British Journal of Sports History*, vol. 3 no. 3 (December 1986), pp. 311–26.

2 See K.A.P. Sandiford, 'Cricket and the Victorian society', *Journal of Social History* (Winter 1982), pp. 303–16; Benny Green (ed.), *Wisden Anthology*, 1864–1900 (London, 1979), pp. 1–9.

3 The exceptions are: R. Genders, *League Cricket in England* (London, 1952). See also Jeffrey Hill, ' "First class" cricket and the leagues: some notes on the development of English cricket, 1900–40', *International Journal of the History of Sport*, vol. 4, no. 1 (May 1987), pp. 68–81. Don Mosey includes an interesting section on league cricket in Yorkshire in his recent *We Don't Play It For Fun: a Story of Yorkshire Cricket* (London, 1988), ch. 15.

4 *Burnley Express*, 12 August 1925.

5 Nelson Cricket and Bowling Club (Hereafter NCBC), Secretary's and Treasurer's Reports, 1899–1901, 1904–9, 1911–26, 1932–9; by kind permission of L. Wilkinson and D. Metcalfe. Durham City Cricket Club (hereafter DCCC) *Minute Books*, 1908–23, 1923–47; *Account Books*, 1914–29, 1929–42, miscellaneous papers, reports, correspondence 1922–40, at Durham County Record Office, (D/DCC 1–80).

6 See A. Mason, *Association Football and English Society, 1863–1915* (Brighton, 1980), ch. 2.

7 J.M. Golby and A.W. Purdue, *The Civilisation of the Crowd: Popular Culture in England, 1750–1900* (London, 1984), pp. 79–80.

8 My thanks to A. Fry, A.J. Grace, A. Hartill and R. Smith, all former members of the Dudley Cricket Club, with experience covering the period from the 1930s to the present, who very kindly consented to my questioning them on aspects of cricket in the West Midlands; Sedgley, 27 September 1987. (Hereafter BL interviews).

9 Dudley CC, *MS Minute Book*, 1910–80, 29 September 1926 (by arrangement with A.J. Grace, for whose help I am deeply indebted).

10 DCCC, *Minute Books and Accounts*, passim 1920s–30s; The Durham County Advertiser and General Printing Co Ltd, *Durham City Yearbook, Business*

Directory and Diary (Durham) 1922–27, 1930–31, 1938–39; A.L. Parsons, *Durham City Cricket Club History* (Durham, 1972).

11 NCBC, Secretary's Reports, 1922, 24, 32–4, 36, 38; P. Barrett and Co, *General and Commercial Directory of Burnley and District* (Preston), 1927–8, 33.

12 Using NCBC reports for years 1919–27, 1932–4 with Barrett and Co, *op. cit*, for appropriate years; also W. Bennett, *The History of Marsden and Nelson* (Nelson, 1957).

13 Sample years: 1923, 28, 33, 38, 39 (DCC, *Minute Book* 1923–47, 12 March 1923, 12 March 1928, 13 March 1933, 14 March 1938, 8 March 1939); *Durham County Advertiser* etc, *op. cit.*, appropriate years.

14 Gerald Howat, *Learie Constantine* (London, 1975) pp. 75–76, 79–81.

15 Mason, *op. cit.*, pp. 48–9.

16 See e.g., *Nelson Leader*, 22 February 1924.

17 See J. Hill, 'Working class politics in Lancashire, 1885–1906: a study in the regional origins of the Labour Party, unpublished Ph.D thesis, University of Keele, 1971, pp. 334–9.

18 F. Root, *A Cricket Pro's Lot* (London, 1937), p. 187.

19 L.N. Constantine, *Cricket and I* (London, 1933), ch. 7.

20 *Nelson Leader*, 5 August 1932.

21 *Ibid.*, 14 October 1932; Barrett and Co, *op. cit.*, 1933.

22 *Nelson Leader*, 20 January 1922.

23 NCBC, *Treasurer's Reports*, 1932, 33, 36; Howat, *op. cit.*, p. 87. See also Learie Constantine, *Cricket in the Sun* (London, n.d.), pp. 65, 92.

24 DCCC, *Minute Book*, 1923–47, (entry undated, *c.* 1921); 14 September 1925.

25 NCBC *Treasurer's Report*, 1938.

26 Dudley CC, *MS Minute Book* 1910–80, 22 September 1910, 18 May 1915, 3 May 1920, 11 April 1923, 20 April 1928, 10 April 1929, 24 March 1930, 31 March 1933.

27 DCCC *Rules*, 1908, 1933. This figure compared with an annual subscription of £1 0s 5d to join the adjacent lawn tennis club, whose membership was limited to 90 players. (Durham County Advertiser etc., *op. cit.*, 1938, pp. 99, 108.)

28 DCCC, *Secretary's Report*, 1925; *Durham County Advertiser*, 15 March 1935.

29 Information for years 1923, 25, 27, 28, 30, 33, 34 (DCCC, *Minute Book*, 1923–47); with *Durham County Advertiser* etc. *op. cit.*, appropriate years. The survey does not include thirty-one students of Bede College, Durham University, enrolled *en bloc* in 1925.

30 DCCC, *Statement of Accounts*, 1934; Executive Committee Report, 1935.

31 G.H. Wood, *The History of Wages in the Cotton Trade During the Past 100 Years* (London, 1910); Hill, 'Working class politics', p. xiv.

32 H.A. Clegg, *A History of British Trade Unions Since 1889:* vol. II, 1911–33 (Oxford, 1985), p. 560.

33 *Nelson Leader*, 17 March 1922; *Athletic News*, 10 April, 19 June 1922.

34 NCBC, *Treasurer's Report*, 1936.

35 J. Kay, *A History of County Cricket: Lancashire* (London, 1972) p. 43.

36 *Nelson Leader*, 13 September 1929: *The Cricketer Annual* (London, 1929–30), p. 66.

37 *Nelson Leader*, 6 June 1919.

38 Dudley CC, *MS Minute Book*, 1910–80, 15 April 1919. 29 April 1925; *Nelson Leader*, 3 July 1936; DCCC, Minute Book 1908–23, 22 March 1920; *Northern Daily Telegraph*, 17 May 1920.
39 *Nelson Leader*, 6 September 1919.
40 See, e.g., the reservations expressed about the sale of drink on cricket grounds by the Nelson CC caretaker, George Illingworth, interviewed in the *Nelson Leader*, 14 October 1932.
41 NCBC, *Balance Sheet for Season*, 1908; *Secretary's Report*, 1922; *Nelson Leader*, 20 January 1922.
42 Root, *op. cit.*, p. 188.
43 See, e.g., Sidney Barnes, *It Isn't Cricket* (London, 1953), pp. 107–9. Was this a practice introduced by Australian professionals? Bill Alley, who played for Colne in the late 1940s, was renowned for it. It is interesting that the Dudley players interviewed expressed mild surprise when asked about betting, and had few comments to make on it.
44 BL interviews. Nelson had a similar figure, Nightie, who specialised in taunting opposition supporters, especially those from Colne.
45 *Cricket*, 12 October 1912.
46 *Athletic News*, 29 May 1922.
47 The date could not be recalled; probably early 1950s.
48 BL interviews.
49 *Northern Daily Telegraph*, 13 September 1920.
50 Constantine, *Cricket and I*, p. 133; Genders, *op. cit.*, p. 16. Knock-out competitions were often played over the course of two weekday evenings.
51 League clubs seem to have co-operated willingly in rule changes proposed by the MCC. See, e.g., the response to the idea of introducing a lighter ball in 1927 (*Athletic News*, 25 April, 2 May 1927). Lancashire League clubs delayed using the new weight only until the stock of old balls had been used up.
52 Cecil Parkin, *Cricket Reminiscences: Humorous and Otherwise* (London, n.d.) p. 19.
53 Root, *op. cit.*, p. 185.
54 See John Hargreaves, *Sport, Power and Culture: a Social and Historical Analysis of Popular Sports in Britain* (Oxford, 1987 edn) pp. 46–7, 71.
55 See William Barlow, Secretary of the Lancashire League, on the aims of that League (*Athletic News*, 10 April 1922).
56 E.g. Philadelphia CC won the Durham Senior League in 1934 without the services of a professional (*Durham County Advertiser*, 3 May 1935).
57 *The Cricketer Annual*, 1922–23, p. 96.
58 *The Cricketer*, 8 June 1929; *Cricket*, 28 June 1913. For criticisms of professionalism by a writer sympathetic to the leagues see John Kay, *Cuts and Glances* (Altrincham, 1948), p. 132.
59 Root, *op. cit.*, p. 186.
60 See, e.g., Genders, op. cit., p. 157; *Burnley Express*, 22 August 1925; Les Hatton, *Cricket Grounds of Worcestershire* (Haughton Mill, Notts, n.d.), p. 13. William Barlow of the Lancashire League, in presenting the league championship cup in 1919, commented that he 'would like to see more (league) players rise to County fame'. (*Nelson Leader*, 19 September 1919).

Talented amateurs were never discouraged from pursuing their skills at county level.

61 Lancashire County and Manchester Cricket Club, *Minute Book*, 1914–21, general committee meeting 9 April 1920. The agreement was extended to the Central Lancs. League after the 1914–18 war. Some difficulties were encountered with the Rochdale club over the availability of Parkin in the early 1920s. (Permission to consult these records generously given by C. Hassell, Secretary of Lancashire CCC).
62 *The Cricketer Annual*, 1922–23, pp. 94–6.
63 *Nelson Leader*, 6 October 1922.
64 Working-class interest in the press coverage of cricket seems to have been quite intense. See C.E.B. Russell, *Manchester Boys: Sketches of Manchester Lads at Work and Play* (Manchester, 1913) pp. 59–61.
65 E.g., Root, *op. cit.*, p. 188: 'No social distinction – one common effort for one common weal.'
66 R. Hoggart, *The Uses of Literacy: Aspects of Working Class Life, with Special Reference to Publications and Entertainments* (London, 1957), p. 268.

8

A different kind of success: West Ham United and the creation of tradition and community

Charles P. Korr

The story of West Ham United is about the club that has had a mediocre, if sometimes flamboyant, playing record. Its greatest measure of success has been to establish a reputation amongst its supporters and the press to the effect that the club has a unique heritage that allows it to act according to its own lights. It supposedly represents the emotional hopes and sensibilities of a much broader community than those men and women who attended foothall matches. West Ham United has shown that a football club can redefine what is meant by success and that non-quantifiable, intangible qualities are both important and all too often taken for granted. The basis for much of its hold on its community and its strong role in local folk mythology was rooted in the events of the last six weeks of one remarkable season.

Any effort to discuss the impact of West Ham United in terms of a single local community distorts the history of the club and presupposes a homogeneity that has never existed in, what is loosely called, east London.[1] In its almost ninety-year existence, West Ham United (and its predecessor, the Thames Ironworks Football Club), has interacted with a variety of communities, each of which existed alongside the other and each of which played a role in shaping the way in which the club was developed. In turn, West Ham became a symbol of different things to different aspects of the population.

However, West Ham United has been an entity unto itself. The club has attempted to establish a set of its own standards and goals and to present itself as it wants to be seen by the public. For the most part of West Ham's history, what its leadership wanted to portray as 'the West Ham way' coincided with how the chairmen and directors actually believed the club operated. They took it upon themselves to define what 'the West Ham way' meant and that, in turn, was taken up by others who had little idea of how West Ham's ideals had been established.[2]

For the first twenty years of its existence, West Ham did virtually nothing to which its supporters could point to in order to show that it was either different or successful. The club survived in the mid ranges of the first division of the Southern League and had infrequent successes in the Cup. Its football was tough and bland, its management was conservative with an image to fit the harsh realities of life in the area from which it drew its earliest supporters. It did not give many of its supporters the chance to believe that it was important enough to challenge other Londoners who did not want to recognise there was anything, or anyone, of substance east of the City. That idea was deeply ingrained in East Londoners by the time United was founded. The club's decision in 1919 to abandon its contractual obligations to the Southern League and join the Football League was a critical move.[3] It was a dramatic act for the board; since it violated its sense of propriety and committed a very conservative organisation to an uncertain future where it would have to compete for better players, and against top-level competitives. It brought West Ham *closer* to the elite of English football, although there was no assurance that West Ham would ever get to play against the prestigious clubs of the First Division. The 1922–3 season was the turning point in West Ham's fortunes on the field, a time that enabled it to create a mystique for itself in the community. The club played beyond any reasonable expectations and won promotion to the First Division. It had reached the top and would be competing against clubs like Newcastle, Sunderland, Villa, and The Arsenal. But most people, including fervent supporters, do not even mention promotion as a high point of the year.

Nineteen twenty-three was the year of the West Ham Cup Final, the first Wembley Cup Final, the White Horse Cup Final and the electric tram. The excitement leading up to the Final propelled the club into the light of publicity it had not seen before. Newspapers throughout east London gave extensive coverage to the semi-final match and the run-up to Wembley even if they had not reported on the team at all before them. Stories appeared in the news section of local papers about the club, its management and its players. Syd King, the manager, had always been good for a quote or a witty remark, but in the spring of 1923, scores of reporters listened to him like a sage and turned him into a celebrity.

The excitement about the Cup Final (West Ham's first chance at national renown) helped to create an instant history of the club. The press accepted King's assertion's that success was merely the vindication of a long-term West Ham commitment to certain values. The local reporters who might have known better had no reason to challenge the over-simplifications of King's selective look at the past that made their local club look good; the rest of the press had no reason to challenge what appeared to be a good story.[4] West Ham's inability, or unwillingness, to attract good players via the transfer route was transformed into 'the West Ham way' of building from within and depending on local players.[5] The sale of the club's most prominent player, Syd Puddefoot, a year earlier, had caused tremendous ill will amongst the supporters and had led even some of the docile local press to question the commitment of the board to success.[6] In the glow of the coming Cup Final, the financial reasons for the sale was forgotten. The deal was interpreted to show West Ham's foresight in securing a place for Vic Watson, Puddefoot's successor. It was supposed to show King's ability to judge talent and outsmart the bigger clubs.[7]

West Ham was transformed from a mediocre club into a kind of ugly duckling that had moulted just in time for the opening of the Empire Stadium. The club's lack of previous success made it more romantic and accentuated the thrill of Bolton being challenged by a Second Division club was no past glories. Newspapers vied with one another for new ways to acclaim how West Ham was different and how it was tied to the values of the community which it supposedly represented and which the newspapers served. On the eve of the Final, the *Echo* bragged about the success of a club that had almost been insolvent less than twenty years earlier. West Ham was a team that was 'marked by togetherness, that has been committed to finding local players'. The newspapers asserted that the board and the managers represented all of east London when the club they created went onto the field.[8] The latter point was emphasised when the paper reminded its readers that *'win or lose,'* [my italics] there would be a civic reception 'at the West Ham town hall on Saturday and the next day at the East Ham town hall'.[9] Two weeks earlier, the same newspaper had commented that although some spectators might have complained over the years that the directors and King 'were not doing enough' they should have recognised that the directors were setting a harmonious tone for the club.[10] The *Stratford Express* was even more enthusiastic in its estimate of the season, proclaiming that 'West Ham is the wonder team of the year'. The club had come to its present success from 'virtual obscurity'. Even in 1922, almost everyone had given up on them, but the club perserved. The correspondent emphasised that the directors and the officials never seemed disturbed by setbacks. They just went about their normal routine and assumed that things would turn out for the best. That might strike many people as management according to Dr Pangloss, but the *Express* noted that 'few boards are as enthusiastic as 'West Ham's'.[11]

The other important feature noted by the *Express* was that King and Charlie Paynter, the trainer, were vital to the club because of the 'ties with the old days'.[12] There was no mention in the article about how good or bad the old days might have been. The struggles and virtual anonymity of the club were brought up only to show how it had overcome its past and now was on the brink of showing the world just how good it was. That was supposed to vindicate the standards of West Ham United and, by extension, the standards that prevailed amongst the population that read the *Express*. There was no reason to suggest that the modest history of the club was a sign of year by year failures. Unless the reader was supposed to assume that failure (or at best, mediocrity) was the necessary precursor to success, the adulation heaped on the Cup-bound West Ham was based on a convenient rewriting of the past.

West Ham's first major success helped to create a public perception of the club based on its instant new history. Wembley turned West Ham into a focus for civic pride and exposed it to thousands of people who previously paid little attention to either football or the local club. Newspaper coverage caused people to notice the club. The civic reception brought West Ham into the mainstream of local conversation. The tours of Town Halls meant that reporters had to say something about the club besides the obvious comments that it played football and was located on the border between West and East Ham.

The high point of West Ham's trip to Wembley was just being there or the pre-match drama of the White Horse clearing the pitch so that the match could be played at all. The 2–0 loss was painful, and the reaction to the match by players and club officials were a mixture of bitterness and amazement.[13] The headline in the *Stratford Express* summed it up: 'A Fiasco'. Interviews with West Ham officials showed how they were trying to shift the blame or downplay what had happened. Immediately after the match, Syd King, who loved to regale writers with quips and opinions restricted himself to saying, 'I am too disappointed to talk about it. I haven't got over it. I just want to forget about it.'[14] King changed his mind in a few days and spent the rest of his life talking about the 1923 Final and West Ham's role in the most dramatic match (and pre-match situation) that football had seen for years.[15]

Charlie Paynter had a more novel explanation for West Ham's defeat. Bolton might have adapted better to the conditions of the pitch, but it also had the advantage of *not* being a London club. The London crowd, had overflowed onto the pitch and the West Ham players had been slapped and pulled in unbridled joy before the match. That had unnerved the players and they never had been able to get into the routine of the match. Paynter was upset about the crowds at Wembley, but he was effusive in his praise for the one that assembled in east London that night and the next day: 'The players were greatly touched by the immense reception accorded to them on their return.'[16] After a while who won the Final did not matter anywhere as much as that West Ham had been part of it. The boroughs had a reason for massive celebration that night – an East-End "knees up" that extended for miles. The high point was an illuminated tram to commemorate the coming of age of this middling club from the poorest part of London.

It is impossible to overestimate the impact of the 1923 on the future of West Ham's operation as a football club and as the focal point of widespread local attention and involvement. Masses of non-supporters were caught up in the expectation of the Final and the celebration that followed it. The mayor and aldermen led the welcome at celebrations which were supposed to show that the club was a part of the boroughs and its people. Other politicians got involved later. Jack Jones, MP, questioned the Home Secretary on the floor of the House about inadequate policing at Wembley, observing that: They can turn out [police] 900 strong for a royal wedding, but when it comes to the *people's* amusement, there is, of course, a difference.[17] Mr Jones may have been correct about 'the people's amusement', but neither he, nor other local politicians had shown much interest in West Ham United until it had done something important.

The aftermath of the 1923 was much more than the memory of a glorious parade or even the mixture of local politics, civic pride and football. West Ham's promotion gave the club a chance to represent some of the aspirations of its community and to reassert the idea that east Londoners did not have to take a backseat to anyone. West Ham provided the most visible symbol of the 'us versus them' that had been present in that part of London for centuries. The next season West Ham supporters could gloat over the new status of the club. When Billy Brown, a 'young good player' was transferred to Chelsea, the press reported that supporters were surprised by the transfers. Rather than complain about another sale that might weaken the club, the *Echo* accepted Syd King's explanation that since West Ham was safe from relegation 'so the directors wanted to help Chelsea [which] shows a find sporting spirit on part of the Hammers'. The reporter hoped that supporters would be 'patriotic enough about London football', and enjoy the fact that 'Chelsea must have had to pay a pretty figure'. That combination of patronising Chelsea and charging them for the privilege must have appealed to east London sensibilities.[18]

The new visibility of West Ham meant that its players were thrust into the limelight. Many of them attended a Congregational Church service on the Sunday after the Cup Final. It had been planned long before the Wembley appearance, but extra preparations had been necessary for the church because attendance far exceeded that of a normal Sunday. The sermon was reported widely in the local press and represented the views that were acceptable to both the congregation and the West Ham officials who were present and had asked the players to accompany them. The minister began his sermon with his appreciation to the players and officials for their efforts and commend that they must have been super men to live under all of the pressure. Then he launched into a lecture on football, its history, and what lessons could be learned from it. The message in the sermon will not surprise anyone who has been exposed to the tenets of Muscular Christianity, but it is worth repeating because of the audience and the timing. 'The essential things in the game of football were the essential things of life.' Three specific ideals were chosen for elaboration: team spirit, discipline and unselfishness. Team spirit has 'saved the country in the dark days of war and would bring them through the peace which seemed even more difficult than the war'. Discipline had enabled West Ham players to get to the big matches. 'The faulty degeneration of the soul was the modern disease and there was no remedy for it except stern discipline.' Unselfishness was important because selfishness paid dividends in neither football or life. 'It might appear to be a good thing, but when they reached the touch line of life and the final whistle blew, it would be found that selfishness did not pay.'[19] The post-Wembley service took advantage of West Ham's success to use the club as a model for conduct. The minister was certainly not alone in drawing moral implications from the recent success of the club, or in stating that West Ham represented all that was best in the community of east London – hard work, loyalty and a sense of pride tempered with modesty. It was a message that would serve the club well over the succeeding years as it established itself as an integral part of the moral and social fabric of its broader community.

The year 1923 had immediate impacts on both the club and the public. Directors and management saw new obligations and opportunities. The directors achieved a new level of civic recognition. It was heady treatment to be fêted as local benefactors and have the press comment on the good judgement and restraint that they had shown in bringing the club to the top. Editorial comments forgot previous criticisms about the meanness of the directors, their fear of change, and their inability to win any honours. In the afterglow of promotion and Wembley, an undistinguished past was set aside as prologue. Seasons of defeat were explained as the tempering that was necessary to forge the solid organization that was now ready to represent its communities against the rest of the football world. The past mediocrity was not forgotten by the hard-core supporters, but they were engulfed in the almost universal approval of what the club had achieved in that one season. The magic year of 1923 enabled the club to obtain an audience that was interested enough to want a mythology of West Ham United around which to build its sense of commitment and identify. For the first time, it was necessary to talk about 'the West Ham way' of doing things because for the first time that could impress someone. The club wanted to bask in its success and the supporters and broader community wanted to know more about the organisation that had accomplished something. The club coped with success by convincing itself and others Wembley and promotion were the overdue accolade for having done things the right way all along. The themes that the directors stressed were those that mattered in their personal and business lives as well as their football existence. They had not changed when they had come into football and they had finally been rewarded for keeping to their values.

The year 1923 also produced a financial windfall for the club: profits that outstripped anything in the past.[20] But spending money on transfers was not what a frugal club like West Ham should be doing. Before 1923, it had not been able to afford to buy players, but after 1923 the refusal to buy players was transformed into the virtue of doing things their own way. The new profits did allow the directors to go ahead with plans they had tried to start just prior to the outbreak of the war.[21] Between 1923 and 1925, the club undertook a massive construction project at the Boleyn Ground. The idea had been resurrected in 1920, given a new impetus in 1922 when the club signed a thirty-four-year lease for the ground and set in motion when the money was available. The ceremony that accompanied the opening of the new stand in August, 1925, was much more than a football or a company event. It was civic 'boosterism', the cause for a public rally. But there was also a civic luncheon: a sedate, by-invitation-only affair where one segment of the local elite toasted another.[22] In the setting of local businessmen, political leaders, dignitaries and the elite of football, the directors of West Ham United were at home amongst their colleagues. The construction of the new stand was something to which the directors could point with great pride. It was a visible sign that the businessmen who ran the club could exercise sound judgement and build something that would outlive them. It would bring comfort to the spectators and, at the same time, be a civic monument. It was an accomplishment that satisfied all of the directors' presuppositions about themselves that they held the club in trust for a broader public. The newly constructed stand was supposed to forge a bond between the club and its supporters. The new comforts might keep some of the people who had been exposed to football by the successes of 1923. Many long-term supporters could not care less about the vast amounts of iron and concrete that had gone into its construction nor would they take advantage of the improved facilities in the stands. However, they did know that it was a huge project, unrivalled anywhere else in London. It was something to gain attention and to be treated with pride. If the new stand was a symbol to the directors that they had accomplished something, it was an even more visible sign to anyone who walked by it, or read about it, that the local club had no reason to feel that it was inferior to any organisation in London or anywhere else.

In recent years, many West Ham supporters, including officials of the club, have described this attitude as 'Cockney pride'. It is a catchy phrase, but it ignores the realities of London's geography and tries to place the club within the emotional confines of the traditional East End of London. The community in which West Ham United was founded had the horrors of poverty and deprivation with none of the sometimes romantically portrayed features of the East End. In 1929, the massively researched *New Survey of London* described the 'jerry built houses' of the workers who lived in the southern part of West Ham and concluded that: 'Poverty and overcrowding are distinctive of the greater part of the Canning Town and Silvertown areas, which make up what is perhaps the *largest area of unbroken depression in East London*' [my italics].[23] On the face of it, little seemed to have changed in the thirty years since Arnold F. Hills, the founder of the Thames Ironworks Football Club had written that 'the perpetual difficulty of West Ham is its poverty'.[24]

But there had been important developments between 1897 and 1929 – the situation in West Ham had grown worse in relation to the surrounding communities. By 1929, there was also the memory of the ephemeral prosperity that had existed as a result of the Great War. The industries on which West Ham depended were hit particularly hard by the economic slump and the restructuring of London's commerce. Ship-building disappeared from the Thames and the number of men involved in ship repairing dropped by 28 per cent between 1920 and 1928.[25] Almost one-third of the jobs in naval related engineering positions ceased to exist during the same period of time. The number of men trying for jobs on the docks had dropped by almost 15 per cent and the overall rate of unemployment in the borough had risen to more than 14 per cent. Between 1920 and 1924, the employed suffered a dramatic drop in their wages – dock labourers were down by 25 per cent, carpenters down by 26, and fitters down by 25 per cent.

The setting in which West Ham United operated had been changed dramatically in 1904 when it moved its ground from Canning Town in West Ham to Green Street in East Ham.[26] Twenty-five years later, the *New Survey* described East Ham as 'in the main, an upper working class area' including some middle-class elements. It was 'largely a dormitory' for clerks, shop assistants, mechanics and others who were employed elsewhere in London.[27] This situation had been apparent to the directors when they had moved the club to the Boleyn Ground. But East Ham was not as different from its neighbour as it might seem at first glance. The largest categories of employment in East Ham in 1928 were transport workers: dock labourers and men engaged in road and rail transport. There were obvious areas of poverty in the borough, but the kinds of the problems faced by West Ham were ameliorated by the number of residents in East Ham who were employed as clerks, shop assistants and in the building trades. During the 1920s, wage levels fell in East Ham, but not to the extent of the situation in West Ham. Unemployment in East Ham rose significantly, but it was still approximately one-third of what it was in West Ham.[28]

The economic picture was bleak in the areas of traditional support for West Ham United, but there was another community, or set of communities, that had an impact on the club. That area was further to the east and was the home of the directors of the club and their business and social acquaintances. Decisions on how the club would portray itself were made by men whose personal experiences avoided many of the worst excesses of the economic slumps in the traditional home of West Ham United.

On the eve of the 1923 Final, the economic situation looked bad in comparison with the boom days of the war. But it was only to get worse. Whilst the joy surrounding Wembley and promotion helped to combat the psychological impact of the post-war depression, the real impact of 1923 was felt over the next fifteen years. As the level of misery increased throughout east London it became all the more important to have something to look at that appeared to give a sense of hope. Past successes were magnified into past glories and were transformed into something to divert attention from the present and give some hope for the future.

Trained observers of the social and economic situation in London had a clear view of what was happening. The strengths of the *New Survey* were that its authors based their conclusions on verifiable data and with a firmly grounded historical basis. It was a conscious attempt to update the pioneering work of Booth and to comment on the importance of new developments. One area where the authors realised that significant changes had taken place was the role of leisure and leisure time in the lives of working men and women. One effect of the shortening of work hours for many workers was to give 'increasing prominence to the group of problems concerned with the use of leisure'. One of the issues that Booth had not considered was the rise of 'inactive forms of recreation, including the watching of football'.[29] The *New Survey* concluded that workers had more purchasing power for shorter hours and less physically exacting and unpleasant work. But they were subject to much greater risks of unemployment. The authors were sure that 'all the forces at work are combining to shift the main centre of interest of a worker's like more from his daily work to his daily leisure, whether that leisure be the margin of time available for rest and recreation after the day's work is done, or the compulsory leisure imposed by the total or partial failure of his means of livelihood'.[30] This detached, antiseptic description of the unemployment that would become the social and economic scourge of the next decade should not distract us from the validity of the observation about the growing importance of leisure to the working men and women, whether they were in work or not. That was especially true in east London, the area that had fallen under the sway of West Ham United. The club became critical to shaping the personality of east London during the harsh years between the wars.

After 1923, the future relationship between West Ham United and its external community would be shaped by, and judged against, three standards: success on the field, the continuation of the West Ham traditions, and whether the club also lived up to the standards of its broader community. The first appears to be the easiest to ascertain. The club either won or lost and could have to be judged by the points it achieved or its progress in the Cup. But, over the years, success meant more than just the score line. West Ham never won enough to create any realistically high expectations in its supporters. A respectable place in the table combined with wins in local derbies was enough to keep the supporters and the press behind the club so long as the other two criteria were maintained. West Ham officials pointed with pride that they were not going to get involved in a 'win at all cost' mentality. This philosophy had an appeal to supporters who resented the way with which some of the neighbouring London clubs, especially Arsenal, treated money with almost casual disdain. As the economic situation became graver in east London, this feeling about the extravagance of other clubs became stronger. But there was a thin line for the club to walk between being admired for good judgement and financial responsibility and being condemned for not spending money even when it was obviously necessary. Discontent with the club's refusal to spend money could also be assuaged by a periodic investment in the transfer market, a move that would show that the directors were not asleep at the controls. The most essential time to spend money was when the club gave the appearance of falling behind its obligation to *strive* for success. The club's relegation to the Second Division in 1932 was a cruel blow only to be followed in the next year by an equally disastrous season when West Ham finished twentieth in the Second Division. 1934 saw a shake-up on the playing staff and a rise to seventh position in the table. In 1935, the club showed its commitment to the future by entering the transfer market with two substantial purchases. One of them, Dr James Marshall, cost a record West Ham fee of £2,000.[31]

We must also recognise that the club was a community unto itself. The structure of the Board and the role of the Chairman were indicative of that feature. Their control enabled them to create stability, the maintenance of a conservative fiscal and management approach and resistance to change, sudden or otherwise. Since 1904 there have been five chairmen, including Len Cearns, the incumbent. The size of the Board has been close to its mandated minimum of five and vacancies have been filled with men with whom the board felt comfortable, men who shared their ideas and background. Two families, Cearns and Pratts, dominated the club from 1935 to 1980. The chairmen and vice chairmen came from one of them. This arrangement is part of what has led to the description of West Ham a 'family club'. Supporters point with pride to this feature of the club, usually describing it as representing traditional east London values and extending it to praise as unique and admirable the way West Ham treats its employees, and how it promotes from within its ranks.

One aspect about West Ham United that the press 'discovered' was its reliance on home-grown players: men who not only got their professional start with the club, but came from the supposedly football-rich areas throughout east London. This was something that club officials had been saying for years, but they usually mentioned it in response to the charges that they were not willing to buy good players. In its first flush of fame, the club wanted to remind people that its policy of nourishing local talent had nothing to do with being parsimonious. It was just their way to the top. The press was willing to go along with this approach; it gave reporters a way to join in the celebration of the club and the community that was apparent in 1923. An inquiring reporter could have asked about the local talent that had made West Ham what it was in 1923. Why had it taken so long and was it true? The former required a subjective judgement, the latter was a matter of checking numbers. A week before the semi-final, the

Stratford Express ran a feature story detailing the background of the eleven men who would represent West Ham. Hufton came to the club from Sheffield United, Henderson from Aberdare, Kay (the captain) from Bolton Wanderers and Belfast Celtic, Richards from Wolverhampton, Watson from a works club in Peterborough and Moore from Sunderland. Only Young, Bishop, Treasadern, Brown, and Ruffell had started with West Ham and were from areas of east London.[32] The *Express* thus stretched the facts a bit to describe the club as being based on a solid foundation of local talent.

By the end of the decade, part of the West Ham tradition was an assumption that went further than the idea of not being dependent on transferred players: it was that West Ham should build a winning side based entirely on local players. This idea was constructed on the twin beliefs that the east End was the breeding grounds of the best players in London and that most of them wanted to play for West Ham. Somehow, the tie between the community and the club was supposed to encourage the best players to flock to Upton Park. It was a comfortable belief for both the club and the supporter. There does not appear to be any statistical basis for the belief that West Ham was built on local players.[33] Until the mid 1950s there is nothing besides rhetoric to show that the club made a special effort to attract local youth to the side and even less evidence that anyone came to the club because they had been a supporter. There was nothing resembling peer pressure amongst local schoolboys to join West Ham and the local teachers or game masters did not direct their charges towards training at Upton Park. For a variety of reasons, these conditions changed in the mid 1950s, but those developments lie outside the scope of this essay.[34]

One of the other supposedly distinctive features of the West Ham tradition can be discussed very quickly. That is its commitment to play attacking, attractive football, even if that meant avoiding the hard play that might be necessary to ensure victory. The stylish play appears to have been created in the kinds of supporters long after the fact – another form of rewriting history. Throughout most of its twenty-five-year stay in the Second Division no one ever pointed to the distinctiveness of its play. A long-time player, Dick Walker, was eloquent on that part of the club's history. He was with the club from 1934 to 1953 and was very proud of the acclaim that his club gained. But he was insistent that no one at West Ham ever suggested that the club do anything differently or hold back from the tough approach that existed at its level of football.[35]

Walker's career is illustrative of two parts of the West Ham mythology. He was one of its most popular players, as well as a captain. He described himself as 'a good player, who did not know how to do very much with the ball', but could, 'make sure that the other fellows didn't get to do anything with it'.[36] That is scarcely the life story of a player dedicated to the finer parts of the supposedly elegant West Ham approach towards football. Much of Walker's popularity stemmed from the perception that he was the quintessential 'Hammer' and east Londoner. His success on the field appeared to validate much of the West Ham mythology. Walker was a local, born in Hackney Marshes and raised in the huge Dagenham estates. However, he had no ideas of playing professionally until he was a young man who was spotted by a West Ham scout. When he went to West Ham to train, he had never been to Upton Park, and had no idea about the club, its personnel, or its traditions. He became a 'Hammer' because they invited him and no one else had. Walker's status at West Ham grew because he established a rapport with the supporters, those in attendance and in the local community. He knew how to take a joke and banter with the crowd. During the week, he was seen around the community, whether taking the bus to training, opening local charity fêtes, or talking to people on the street.

Dick Walker enjoyed playing for West Ham and getting paid for it. But at no time did he ever regard what he was doing as amusement or a game.[37] He was on the pitch to perform attractively for the crowd *and* to do a job. That meant ensuring that everyone around him paid similar attention to their obligations. The supporters appreciated his willingness to joke with them and to see the sometimes ridiculous side of football. It was important for him to live up to the idea of the happy-go-lucky east Londoner. But the crucial thing was that the club also showed everyone that they were putting out their best effort at all times. The attribute that reigned supreme amongst the West Ham system of values was the absolute necessity to make an effort at all times. That was expected from everyone associated with the club – player, trainer, manager, and director. The one unforgivable error by anyone associated with the club was to give the impression that they did not care enough to do their best for the organisation and the communities of which it was a part.[38]

By the time the worst days of the depression hit east London, West Ham United had become an integral part of the social fabric of the region. It remained a visible symbol of the individuality of the area and the ability of one of its institutions to challenge successfully the rest of the metropolis. West Ham United could harness the emotion of local people because the club had established a special identity for itself that extended to the point of creating a self-sustaining mythology.

The 1923 season established West Ham as the most important football institution in the extended East End. There were two types of new supporters who emerged: the people who were interested in football and chose to follow West Ham United, and those whose primary interest was a local club called West Ham United. Both of those groups accepted that West Ham was distinctive. There was a need to identify what made West Ham different, aside from an accident of geography. The club consciously played upon the dual nature of its heritage: West Ham with its tough docker ('Irons') tradition, and the more affluent areas to the east of its comfortable setting on Green Street. As times got harder, the glories of 1923 became even more important as a symbol of past success. The teams that followed 1923 had a series of mediocre seasons followed by the ultimate failure of relegation in 1932. That disaster, coming in the midst of the social and economic woes, made it all the more important for the club and its supporters to have something to hang on to – the 'West Ham way' – which was a combination of ideals of loyalty, family and a certain style of play. Whether they were accurate or not was nowhere near as important as whether they were believable enough to fit the hopes of a beleaguered community.

The mythology surrounding West Ham could not substitute for the harsh realities of life, but it could give the community another way of showing that it possessed something special in its local football club. That had to be something that even the grinding poverty of the 1930s and the record twenty-five consecutive years in the Second Division could not diminish. The longer the mystique of a West Ham approach towards football and life continued, the easier it became to accept it. There was no doubt that the initial validity of the concept was provided by the events of 1923, the time in which a little-fancied club from the poorest area of London showed it could do things its way and succeed. West Ham's hold on the loyalty of its local community was partly a vindication of the public-relations skills of the club. That phrase might sound strange describing an organisation that has always been old-fashioned in its approach towards dealing with the public. In this case, 'public relations' does not mean the glitter of PR, but the embodiment and legitimising of the needs and hopes of a distinctive public whose support was crucial to the success of the club. The year 1923 provided the all-important basis on which West Ham gave a new definition to public relations and by which its public came to define success.

Notes

1 For the best study of the ethos of the traditional East End, see the brilliant book by W.J. Fishman, *East End 1888* (London, 1988).

2 For a detailed analysis of the men who controlled West Ham United, see my *West Ham United: the Making of a Football Club* (London, 1986), pp. 17–55.

3 *Board Minutes* of the West Ham United Football Club, 17 and 31 March 1919.

4 *East Ham Echo*, 27 April 1923. The article was entitled, 'West Ham and Syd King' and the lead sentence, 'Syd King is West Ham and West Ham is Syd King.'

5 *Stratford Express*, 25 April 1923 and *East Ham Echo*, 13 April 1923.

6 The club was in bad financial straits when the decision was made to sell Puddefoot to Falkirk for £65,000. *Board Minutes*, 17 July and 22 October 1922. King had talked with Chelsea and Tottenham in January 1922 about making offers for Puddefoot, *Board Minutes*, 30 January 1922. He received a bonus from the club after the sale of Puddefoot to Falkirk.

7 *East Ham Echo*, 13 and 27 April 1923. Puddefoot continued to maintain his hold on the interest of West Ham supporters. His fortunes in Scotland were reported widely in the press and there were many stories about his supposed return to West Ham. Even the Cup Final and promotion did not dim his lustre. One example is 'Sid Puddefoot coming back?' in *East Ham Echo*, 25 January 1924. He returned to West Ham at the end of his career in time to be involved with the club's unsuccessful efforts to avoid relegation.

8 *East Ham Echo*, 20 April 1923.

9 *Ibid.*, 27 April 1923.

10 *Ibid.*, 13 April 1923.

11 *Stratford Express*, 25 April 1923.

12 *Ibid.*

13 *East Ham Echo*, 27 April 1923.

14 *Stratford Express*, 2 May 1923.

15 *Ibid.*, 5 May 1923.

16 *Stratford Express*, 2 May 1923.

17 *Daily Herald*, 30 May 1923; *Stratford Express*, 2 May 1923.

18 *East Ham Echo*, 7 March 1924.

19 *Stratford Express*, 2 May 1923.

20 Report of the Annual General Meeting of the West Ham United Football Club, 25 June 1923.

21 Report of the Annual General Meeting of the West Ham United Football Club, 15 June 1914.
22 *East Ham Echo*, 14 August 1925.
23 M. Llewellyan Smith, *The New Survey of London Life and Labour* (London, 1930–35), vol. III, p. 409.
24 *Thames Ironworks Gazette*, 3 (June 1895), p. 65.
25 Smith, *The New Survey*, vol. I, pp. 206–7. Given the origin of West Ham United ('The Hammer' of the Thames Ironworks) it is ironic that the Ironworks was the last major ship-building firm on the Thames. It went into bankruptcy shortly after the end of the war, its financial problems having been accelereated by its production of a Dreadnought.
26 Korr, *West Ham United*, pp. 11–14.
27 Smith, *The New Survey*, vol. III, p. 393.
28 *Ibid.*, vol. IX, p. 6.
29 *Ibid.*, vol. I, p. 297.
30 *Ibid.*, vol. VIII, p. 36 The authors recognised that 'leisure' was so important a subject for their study, that they devoted the final volume (IX) to that single topic.
31 *Stratford Express*, 17 March 19.
32 *Stratford Express*, 24 March 1923.
33 Interviews by the author with Wally St Pier (long-time chief scout for West Ham United), Eddie Chapman (Secretary and former player), Jack Helliar (PRO for the club), Ted Fenton (Manager from 1950 to 1961). Tony Hogg and Jack Helliar, *Who's Who at West Ham 1900–1986* (London, 1986).
34 For a complete discussion of this aspect of West Ham United and the way in which the club developed local talent see my *West Ham United: the Making of a Football Club* (London, 1986), chs. 7, 9, 11, and 14.
35 Interview by the author with Dick Walker.
36 *Ibid.* and interviews with Ken Brown, Frank O'Farrell, Ernie Gregory, Noel Cantwell, and Malcolm Allison.
37 Interviews by the author with Dick Walker, Ted Fenton, Reg Pratt (Chairman of West Ham United from 1950 to 1979) and Trevor Smith (Sports Editor of the *Ilford Recorder*).
38 The crucial importance of giving the impression of trying to succeed was shown in 1936 when a director was quoted to the effect that the club might be better off near the top of the Second Division than being promoted and floundering in the bottom of the First Division. It was the worst public-relations debacle in the history of the club.

9

Stanley Matthews

Tony Mason

From India to the Argentine and Peru, Stoke-on-Trent was known through Stanley Matthews

Evening Sentinel, June 24 1946

> The greatest of all time
> Meraviglioso Matthews – Stoke
> City, Blackpool and England.
> Expressionless enchanter, weaving
> as on strings Conceptual, patterns to
> a private music, heard
> Only by him, to whose slowly
> emerging theme he rehearses
> steps, soloist in compulsions
> of a dream.

From *Stanley Matthews* by Alan Ross

One month before his forty-second birthday, Stanley Matthews became the first professional footballer to appear in the New Year's Honours List: on 2 January 1957 he became a Companion of the British Empire. The honour was not universally welcomed. A Hampshire colonel grumbled to the *Daily Telegraph* that now 'our leading cricketer Association Footballer and jockey have all received high recognition, is it too much to hope that the nation will recover a proper sense of values and reserve such honours for those whose services to it have been of greater moment than skill at games and horse-racing?'[1] But most critics of the award took the opposite tack led by a vulgar but vigorous *Daily Mirror* whose front page headline on new year's day shouted, 'A Snub for Sir Soccer. But not for Baron Stripe Pants.' The CBE was not enough. It should have been a knighthood to match those already bestowed on Donald Bradman, Len Hutton and Gordon Richards. As the *Mirror* scornfully expostulated, the CBE was 'an honour shared by the late keeper of Greek and Roman antiquities in the British Museum, the controller of the Third Programme, the managing director of a lead firm, the catering advisor to the Royal Air Force and the chairman of Aberdeen local savings committee'.[2] It was yet another upper-class slur on popular culture. The *Evening Sentinel*, serving the six towns of the Potteries from which Matthews came, took it as philosophically as it forecast the man himself would – 'his football days are not yet over, and the aura which surrounds his name will not be dimmed because he is not to become "Sir Stanley" '.

Eight years later he *had* become Sir Stanley while still a player – and at fifty years of age. Even the *Times* did not object which doubtless tells us something about changes in middle-class perceptions of the status of football, although like W.G. Grace before him – and he did not receive a knighthood – Matthews was a special case. Not only was he at the top of the game for such a long time, playing League football from 1932 to 1965, but in a physical contact professional sport he appeared to represent skill as against force. He remained the sportsman, one of nature's elusive gentlemen. He was never cautioned, let alone sent off. He was a perfect ambassador for club, region and country. The aim of this chapter is to explore the nature of the popularity which was eventually recognised by the state and, in particular, to look more closely at the relationship between the footballer and his largely working-class public.

There is no Sir Stanley Matthews archive, no collection of fan mail and no private papers. There are three volumes of autobiography and all provide passages of interest.[3] Above all there are the newspapers which chronicled his deeds, sometimes his every move, and the reaction to them for the best part of forty years. There are four occasions when these sources might reveal more about the nature of the relationship between Matthews and the football audience than in the ordinary run of events. The first was in 1938 when he asked Stoke City for a transfer. The second was in 1946 when a public testimonial was organised for him to celebrate his record forty-fourth appearance for the England national team. The third was when he *was* transferred from his home-town club of Stoke to Blackpool in May 1947. Finally there was the 1953 Cup Final when he won a winners' medal, an event both etched in the memory of a nation and preserved for future generations by television.

But first it seems necessary to look at what kind of player Matthews was. Sport ran in the family. His father was a barber who had been a professional boxer. Enthusiasm for sport, and in particular keeping the sport machine, the body, in good order, was all part of the growing-up process for Stanley Matthews. He began training with his father and older brother when he was only ten. His father coached him as a runner and on a notorious and traumatic occasion entered him for the Stoke-on-Trent sports at the age of six. By the age of eleven Matthews had become absorbed in football, like many young boys before and since. He was already a leading member of his elementary school team. Stoke boys and England schoolboys followed apparently inevitably. He trod a path to the professional game worn down by many pairs of hopeful boots. His father was an important influence. A tough, careful man, he insisted that the £10 obtained when Matthews finally signed as a professional with Stoke went straight into the savings bank and half the subsequent wage was deposited there each week. This careful attitude to money was not the least of the attributes handed down from father to son.

Matthews first played for the Stoke first eleven in a second division fixture against Bury early in 1932 when he was seventeen. The next season he appeared sixteen times in the team which won the championship of that league thus qualifying for a winners' medal. In 1933-4 he played twenty-nine games out of forty-two and finished as second highest scorer with eleven League and four Cup goals. Although occasionally playing at inside right Matthews was a right winger who quickly became noted for his dribbling skills and speed off the mark. As he was also a regular goalscorer in the 1930s he had forced his attention on the England selectors by the time he was nineteen. In the international trial at Sunderland in 1934 the Stoke newspaper thought he was brilliant but the quixotic selectors did not choose him for England. The paper went on to describe his qualities.

> There is probably no cleverer exponent of ball control in football than Matthews. Remarkable footwork and a deceptive body swerve are performed simultaneously when beating his man. There are few who can centre so accurately or hook the ball in so strongly with his right foot from the touchline. Yet when he cuts in, he scores quite a number of goals with his left foot.[4]

Shortly after that he scored four in one game against Leeds and in one of his early appearances for England, against Czechoslovakia in 1938, a left-footed hat-trick.

Although he failed to get into the England–Scotland match in 1934 he was picked for the Football League against the Irish League and according to the reporters present in Belfast, had a foot in four of the six goals. This match confirmed his status as an international player. The *Daily Mail* labelled him 'the cleverest player we have seen in the position for many a year' while the *Daily Herald* thought him the 'star of the evening'.[5] The Stoke players had been convinced of his special ability for some time and often drew the attention of their readers in their pre-match comments to the personal nature of the duel which was to take place between Matthews and a prominent opposition full-back.

It is clear that it was his skill with the ball, the trickery which enabled him to leave opponents flat-footed and foolish which amused, thrilled and titillated the crowd, especially at Stoke. In October 1934 against the Arsenal, currently Britain's most powerful club, he 'dribbled halfway across the field beating several men in the process . . . and was given an ovation'. And against Leicester in the following month he began 'brilliantly [and] twice drew a couple of defenders around him and then left both behind by superb footwork . . . his goal was masterly. He anticipated a through pass, rounded the full-back, and shot in'.[6]

Full international recognition came in September 1934 when he was chosen to play against Wales at Cardiff. He scored the third goal in a 4–0 win.[7] Matthews' selection for England was considered a great honour for the Stoke club and the whole Potteries district. This was in part because it was the first full England 'cap' to come to a Stoke player for more than thirty years. Only eleven Stoke players had ever been selected for England. It was also an exciting time for Stoke football. The team was not a one-man band but probably the best the club had ever put together. For the first time they were a real force in the First Division, an upper-ten or top-six club as the local paper enthusiastically claimed. The first four home matches of the 1934–5 season were watched by 120,000 people including a record attendance of 45,349 for that visit of Arsenal.

Matthews had quickly become a star player but in a quality team in an area perhaps starved of excitement and glamour and with a well developed feeling of separateness and independence. The Potteries, even in the 1930s, remained a relatively physically isolated area of north Staffordshire, apart from the large cities of Manchester and Liverpool in the north and the Black Country of the south of the county. Its economy was remarkably dependent on one industry as the 1911 census, for example, clearly showed. Of a total workforce of 111,806, over 47,000 were employed directly in pottery. Eighty per cent of the pottery workers in England lived within a five-mile radius of Stoke town hall.[8] Although there were ninety-eight separate occupations among skilled pottery workers, Stoke and the other five towns made up a largely inward-looking, single-industry region. It was a region in which the people were proud of their own achievements and their own people. This perception of isolation and uniqueness was probably one factor in determining the response of the public to the headlines which appeared on the front page of the *Evening Sentinel* of 8 February 1938: 'Why Stanley Matthews wishes to be transferred – Sensational Development.' This was the first episode with which we need to deal.

The dispute between Stoke City and Matthews seems to have arisen over the payment of benefit. Professional players were entitled to a benefit after five years' service. The maximum which could be paid at the time, according to League rules, was £650. The club had apparently offered Matthews £500 and at the end of the 1937–8 season he had only re-signed after an argument and the loss of three weeks wages. There had been a similar difference of opinion the year before. The club had later announced that all players' benefits would be paid at the rate of £650 in future. There were hints that Matthews did not see eye-to-eye with the manager of Stoke City, Bob McGrory, on several matters. And in February 1938, the player asked for a move. Several famous clubs were immediately said to be interested.[9] The possibility that Matthews might leave the club prompted the *Evening Sentinel* to make an editorial appeal to both club and player.

> Stoke City supporters and indeed the whole North Staffordshire community, are deeply stirred by the possibility of Stanley Matthews leaving the club. . . . Without Stanley Matthews Stoke City would not be Stoke City. He is a star of first magnitude. He cannot be replaced . . . Stanley Matthews must not be allowed to go.
> To Stanley Matthews it must be said that a vast public will be very grateful if he can seen his way to withdraw his transfer request, with firm assurances that his position shall be as happy as any player could desire.

The paper went on to note that there was no news like it since the Abdication. Even those uninterested in football were fascinated by the crisis. Meantime, a final decision about how it was to be resolved had been postponed for a week.[10] That was long enough for a public protest meeting to be organised for 14 February at the Kings Hall in Stoke. The conveners of of the meeting were not among the 'common or garden' football supporters of the district but pillars of the

Potteries' industrial world. All were prominent pottery manufacturers. The seven whose names appeared at the bottom of the letter calling the meeting were R. Lewis Johnson (Johnson Bros, Hanley), Ashley Myott (Myott, Son & Co.), E.H. Bailey (Twyfords Ltd), A.B. Jones jnr (A.B. Jones & Sons), Arthur Gaunt (Johnson Fireclay Co. Ltd), T.B. Roberts (George Howson and Sons Ltd), and Sidney H. Dodd, secretary of the British Pottery Manufacturers' Association. All claimed to be concerned because of the fame which the football club had brought to the Pottery district. T.B. Roberts went further when speaking to one journalist: 'The meeting is the outcome of requests to us by our workpeople to use all efforts to keep Matthews at Stoke. Some of our employees are so upset at the prospect of losing him that they cannot do their work.'[11]

The Kings Hall was packed an hour before the start with three thousand people inside and more than a thousand locked out. The *Sentinel* reported the meeting over four front-page columns with appropriate pictures.[12] Myott said that none of the conveners wished to take the place of the club's directors but they had felt 'it necessary for some responsible persons to take a lead in this matter, which is of such considerable interest in this district'. They were all anxious about the welfare of the club and north Staffordshire. Three English internationals in the Stoke team reflected credit on the whole of north Staffordshire. As for the principal, he was a 'good, clean, sober, enthusiastic, brilliant player [loud applause and cries of 'none better'] who might also be highly strung and super sensitive'. T.B. Roberts said he was as much an enthusiast as the small boys who gathered behind the Boothen goal and had been for forty years.

Dodd then moved the resolution that:

> we, the supporters of Stoke City F.C. present at this public meeting, being concerned for the welfare of the club and the district, earnestly urge the Directors to strive to their utmost to secure the retention of Stanley Matthews. . . .
>
> Further, that representatives of this meeting be appointed whose good offices shall be available to both parties, to bring about the result so ardently desired by the whole sporting community of North Staffordshire such representatives to be appointed by the convenors of the meeting.

One dissentient said any meeting with the directors should be held in public but the chairman quickly scotched that. He had had experience of wages agreements over many years, he said, and if those negotiations had been in public there would have been no peace in this

district. The talks must be frank and therefore confidential. In fact
the directors, doubtless seeing the way things were moving, had
already agreed to the principle of talks before the meeting began.
They turned down the transfer request – Matthews said he was very
disappointed – and the following evening Myott, Dodd and Roberts
spent two hours persuading the player to stay. It is not clear how they
did it but after meeting the directors again they were able to declare
that the problem was resolved.[13] Moreover Matthews had authorised
them to say that he was extremely glad at this happy outcome and
wished to assure everyone that he would continue to do his best for
Stoke City. Twenty-four hours later, 30,455 gathered to see him play
against Preston.[14]

It can probably be safely assumed that most of those people who
turned up for the Kings Hall meeting were typical Stoke supporters,
mainly working-class males. They appear to have been in no doubt
about keeping the club's star player. Letters to the *Sentinel* during the
week long saga provide additional evidence. From 9–16 February, the
Sentinel published thirty-five letters on the subject from members of
the public. Some had multiple signatories including one from Longton
signed by twenty-four people. All save three of the letters were
anxious that Matthews should stay. Two suggested a supporters'
ballot on the issue. Only one was in any way critical of Matthews
himself, suggesting he should think of all the happy times and the
supporters, especially those who went in all weathers, often without
their food but he agreed that Matthews and Stoke had put the
Potteries on the map: 'internationals made at Stoke. What a kick we
supporters get out of that'. One employer took a more caustic line:

> When in these days of wars and persecutions we reflect upon the difficult
> position which . . . confronts our local industry, all men with a grasp of the
> position and a true sense of proportion will ask themselves: 'Is this a
> moment to tolerate the loss of our outside right?'

But he had to agree that it was not. Only one letter suggested that
the whole issue was out of perspective and it was the last to be
printed after all had been safely gathered in:

> Trade is quiet, many operatives are on short time, and we are drifting into
> another war; but above all the strife is heard the monotonous chant,
> 'Matthews must not go!' Confronted by a similar situation in their own
> business, our captains of industry would probably realise that it is not
> business to keep an unhappy man in their employ, would reluctantly let

him go, and turn their attention to eradicating the root of the trouble. Anyway, is not the game more than the player?[15]

In the case of Stanley Matthews the supporters of Stoke found it difficult to separate the two. These events are interesting in several respects. For one thing they show workpeople and their employers sharing the same side and manifesting similar interests. It can hardly have done the public image of those pottery manufacturers involved any harm. It underlines that Matthews was a widely appreciated talent. It raises the question of whether such a demonstration of 'popularity' would have been mounted elsewhere, in Manchester or Liverpool, Nottingham or Bolton. It probably tells us as much about Stoke, and the closeness and inward-looking nature of the Potteries as about the pulling power of the footballer.

The second episode in Matthew's career to be examined took place eight years later and shows a different public attitude to the player. Matthews had remained a Stoke player but his ties to the community had been perhaps weakened by conscription into the Royal Air Force and a posting to Blackpool during the war years. He continued to play football regularly, often as a war-time guest player for Blackpool and he also produced many distinguished performances for England in their war-time meetings with Ireland, Scotland and Wales. In fact, so frequent did his appearances for England become that by the beginning of 1946 he was winning his forty-fourth 'cap' against Belgium beating the previous highest number of appearances. The FA announced that they would recognise the achievement by presenting Matthews with an illuminated address and £100 in Saving Certificates. Matthews was almost thirty-one – for a footballer this was uncomfortably close to the veteran stage. Some of this was undoubtedly in the mind of a local rugby player. Alfred Pearson, when he wrote to the *Sentinel* suggesting that the sporting public of North Staffordshire should also put their hands in their pockets in order to show a proper appreciation of the services of 'such an artist' whose like would surely never be seen again on the soccer field.[16] At a stroke, the pottery manufacturers' committee of 1938 was reborn. Sydney Dodd wrote to the papers to say that he had been approached to launch and organise the appeal and four days later the committee had its first meeting with Sir Ernest Johnson, President of the British Pottery Manufacturers Federation, in the chair. The President and Chairman of Stoke City also joined the committee as did the Mayor, Chief Constable and various other solid citizens including, this time,

Alderman Arthur Hollins, the long-serving Secretary of the Pottery Workers' Society, the leading trade union of the district. There was to be a public testimonial and it was to be called the Stanley Matthews Fund.[17]

The organisers probably had in mind the shilling funds of earlier times such as the one organised for W.G. Grace by the *Daily Telegraph* in his great year of 1895. The fund was to be officially opened on 1 February and closed on 30 March. The chairman knew that such an appeal required no justification but nonetheless pointed out why it was necessary. 'No one . . . had done more than Matthews to put Stoke-on-Trent in the forefront of the cities and towns of this country. . . . He is one of the most gentlemanly, unaffected of men' and 'whatever we do we cannot repay him for what he has done for Stoke-on-Trent and the wider sphere of North Staffordshire'.[18] Sir Ernest also had fixed ideas about the way such a fund should be put together. He was firmly opposed to street collections, whist drives and dances as forms of raising money. They lacked dignity. Subscription cards would be available for the smaller contributions with large-scale cards to be exhibited in local collieries, factories, business premises and clubs. Many people would want to join this tribute to a local sporting celebrity and a record of all subscribers would be kept. It was clear that both chairman and committee expected the testimonial to be one of the greatest moments in north Staffordshire public life, twenty thousand people were expected to subscribe and a total in excess of £5,000 would be raised. As we shall see, such forecasts proved optimistic.[19]

The organisers must have been surprised that there was opposition to the idea of a testimonial and it was important enough for them to feel the need to reply to it. A letter to the *Evening Sentinel* by Eileen C. Mattinson of Stoke, published on January 25 sparked it off. She began by saying that she had never written to a newspaper before:

> but after reading about the Stanley Matthews Fund, I feel I have to. We all know that he is a good player but so would be many other boys, had they had the same chance. But they had to serve their King and Country abroad on active service. He has been lucky to play forty-five war-time matches (sic).
>
> You sportsmen of Stoke-on-Trent are grateful to him for putting Stoke-on-Trent on the map. Yet, have you shown your gratitude in any substantial form to the women who gave their men, the mothers who gave their sons, the sporting ex-soldier who gave his limbs or eyes, to keep Stoke-on-Trent from being blasted off the map.

It could still be done in the name of Stanley Matthews. But if you feel his greatness should go down to posterity, why not make a greater effort!

Why not replan and rebuild Stoke-on-Trent entirely and make it a place fit for sporting Englishmen (not heroes please note) to live in. This could also be done in the name of Stanley Matthews.

But I don't see why the £5,000 should not be the first offering to start a Stanley Matthews fund for mothers, widows and disabled servicemen of Stoke-on-Trent. I'm sure Mr. Matthews would agree.[20]

That this letter struck a popular chord seems clear by the *Sentinel's* claim three days later to have received 'a number of letters' on the same subject. It printed selections from five, four of which largely shared the views of Eileen Mattinson. This prompted a reply from Sir Ernest Johnson. Of course he sympathised with those people who had written to the *Sentinel*. But he insisted that Matthews' achievement was worthy of recognition and those who wanted to give should do so. It was not charity, he stressed, but a free-will gift for a man we admire for services rendered to football: 'Stanley Matthews deserves well of us. We want him to have a successful testimonial, but I want it completely devoid of charity; it is a spontaneous gift for all the work he has done and the entertainment he has given us.' T.B. Roberts, another survivor from 1938, said some of them had gone to great lengths to induce Matthews to throw in his lot with Stoke and they owed him something for sticking to Stoke City.[21]

In the event it would probably be too severe to say that the result of the testimonial was disappointing. But it certainly failed to match the expectations of the organisers. After publishing the first few lists of subscribers and drawing attention not just to Johnson's thousand shillings but to the two shillings from a mother whose son was in the Navy and the two shillings from a widow who said she had boys of her own and wished Stanley Matthews every success – details of the fund largely disappeared from the local press.[22] Perhaps the organisation was not all it might have been. Whatever the explanation the appeal was extended beyond its original date and in June Matthews received a cheque for only £1,160 4s to which 5,500 people had subscribed. It could be argued that this was not bad after six years of total war and that it demonstrated the esteem in which Matthews was held by the Potteries public. But it was not 20,000 people and £5,000. The letter from Eileen Mattinson appears to have spoken for a good many – they were positive about Matthews but neither the form of the tribute nor its timing seemed right.

The third incident which might help us to understand the relation-

ship between the football star and his public took place in 1947 when
Matthews at last did leave his home-town club for Blackpool. As we
noted earlier, Matthews had been posted to Blackpool during the war
and in 1946 bought a private hotel there. He began training at
Blackpool FC and travelling to Stoke for matches. It is hardly
surprising that such a routine became less and less attractive to him
and the frustrations engendered blew up in the autumn of 1946
following his recovery from a leg injury which had kept him out of
the team.[23] In his absence, Stoke put together six consecutive
victories and the manager suggested that Matthews should have a
run out with the reserves. Matthews' response was that if he was fit
to play for the reserves he was fit to play for the first team and he
refused. The *Sentinel's* football correspondent, desperately trying to
keep in with both sides, thought his attitude perfectly comprehen-
sible bearing in mind 'the brilliant services he has rendered to the
Stoke club and his unprecedented achievements in international
football'. But Matthews asked for a transfer. Once again football
became the subject of a *Sentinel* editorial. Once again eleven letters on
the subject were published six supporting the player and five against.
It appeared that the differences had been reconciled when Matthews
withdraw his transfer request and the club agreed that he would
continue training at Blackpool. But the wish to move to the seaside
town where his business interests were located was too powerful to
be denied. Secret negotiations continued and were leaked to the press
in May 1947. The transfer was actually completed on 12 May 1947.
This time there was no protest movement and no big mail bag.
Matthews himself did say that he had received many critical letters
but most of the newspaper comment echoed the supporter who
wrote: 'Surely after fifteen seasons with the Potters we can spare
Stan, and . . . why should Stoke spectators grumble about his
departure when we have such a grand lot of local youngsters to
watch?'[24]

These two events show the effect of time on a player's importance
to club and supporters. The president of the club emphasised that
there should be no resentment: 'Whenever Stanley Matthews comes
back to Stoke, we shall always have in mind the great services he has
rendered to Stoke City by his football genius, his modesty and his
gentlemanly conduct. He has got his business interests in Blackpool
and we wish him all the very best of luck.'[25] He was, after all, thirty-
two with only a few years left as a player. It was sensible to be looking

to the future and a younger replacement. It must have seemed inevitable. The focus of his life had clearly shifted to Blackpool. Most supporters probably shared the president's good wishes. In May 1947 there was a lot more controversy generated in Stoke by the campaign on the issue of whether local cinemas should open on Sundays than the loss of their star player.[26] For Blackpool though, the signing of Matthews was undoubtedly a major reason why season ticket sales reached record levels before the 1947-8 season. On its eve, two thousand had been sold as against seven hundred and fifty the year before.[27]

Blackpool had never been a fashionable or a very successful club. But with the arrival of Matthews all that changed. Not only did they become established as one of the leading sides in the first division, but they reached the Cup Final three times in five years. On the first two occasions, in 1948 and 1951, they were beaten and the press made much of the sad story of the Great Footballer, Matthews, apparently destined never to obtained a winners' medal. The fact that he had not won a First Division championship medal either was ignored. When Blackpool and Matthews reached the Final again in 1953 this surely had to be the last chance. Matthews had turned thirty-eight earlier in the year. To be still playing at the highest level at thirty-eight was unusual. Moreover, there was a considerable body of public opinion that thought his neglect by the English selectors over the previous two years a mistake. The 1953 Cup Final also attracted publicity because it was Coronation year. It was the first final to be attended by a reigning Queen. More critically the Cup Final, already a national event, in England and Wales anyway, had been taken up by television. By 1953 many homes in Britain had one and ten million people were to watch the Matthews final. Because of this, and the dramatic nature of the game itself, the 1953 Cup Final became for that generation one of those events etched firmly in the memory of a nation, like the assassination of President Kennedy. Television coverage meant that many more people would feel that they had shared the moment.

The esteem in which Matthews was held by the football public spilled over into eulogy in the newspapers on Cup Final eve. In the *Daily Mirror*, Bob Ferrier wrote that Matthews had been for twenty years:

> the most astonishing single sight in football. And this no matter what else happens on the Wembley field, will make the Blackpool - Bolton Wanderers match today probably the most extraordinary Cup Final of them all.

From 100,000 people, the partisans included, will come a wave of sympathy for Matthews . . . such as football or any other sport has never known. . . .[28]

It may seem to you to be putting a football match and a football player on rather a higher plane, but this match will offer the greatest unspoken tribute, on the sport's greatest occasion, to a man who has graced and dignified football for two decades.

He is a legend in his own lifetime. . . . His ball control, speed, balance, personal physical fitness, all the outcome of original talent, practice, and the thing you cannot buy, experience, are merely parts of the pattern. . . . All my romanticism calls for a Blackpool victory – and all rational thought too.

The *Times* also referred to the 'sympathies of the sentimental majority' for this 'idol of the modern game' although the *Sporting Chronicle* poured scorn on such considerations. John Graydon wanted to see the better team win and felt sure it would be Bolton: 'I am pleased to admit that this sloppy sentimentality of "I hope Matthews wins a medal" has no place in my heart.'[29]

Bolton lost the match 4–3 after being 3–1 ahead with barely twenty-five minutes left. Blackpool scored twice in the last few minutes and Matthews contributed to two of their last three goals. All the press agreed that Matthews' own skill had turned the game. In the *Manchester Guardian*, for example, the headline was 'Matthews undermines Bolton' and the match report began 'a footballing genius called Stanley Matthews won the FA Cup here today for Blackpool'.[30] At the end:

he received an ovation such as seldom given at Wembley for any one man and he shared the traditional honour of the winning captain by being hoisted shoulder high and being carried from the field. Matthews and Matthews alone won the match for Blackpool. He alone remained cool, calm and purposeful throughout. He alone had the cunning and the confidence to exploit to the full those injuries, to Ball and Banks which disorganised the Wanderers' team.

But this was far short of the heights of hyperbole reached by the top peoples' *Times* on the one hand and the bottom peoples' *Daily Mirror* on the other. The man at the *Mirror* was captivated by the last twenty minutes when, 'from this multitude of 100,000 people came a surging groundswell of ecstatic incentive for this astonishing player. From all round this vast sun-drenched stadium came a murmuring tremor that became a continuous eruption of sound. Matthews himself was inspired. He screamed audibly for the ball. When Perry shot the winning goal from Matthews' pass:

people stood on their seats, waved coats, pounded each other with hysterical absent-minded abandon. These were the most emotional and dramatic moments I have ever experienced on any sporting field, and I don't mind telling you that I was close to tears for Matthews and Blackpool and Bolton.

This was the ultimate in great sport, the limit of sporting endeavours. I do not hope to see anything finer than this. . . . It was a privilege to be there.[31]

The *Times* inevitably waxed more patriotic and found Churchillian echoes appropriate for this other kind of national hero. Geoffrey Green wrote that the final would 'live largely because here in the presence of the Queen and the Duke of Edinburgh the game of football, the game of the people, was crowned with all felicity in this year of Coronation and national rejoicing'. Never had there been a more popular victory and never one more dominated by a single player. This popular sentiment and this performance embraced but a single subject – Stanley Matthews. This was his finest hour . . . a rightful consummation of a great career.' Matthews, the artist, effected the transformation in the match.[32]

There was more:

It is by the power to call souls out of the abyss into life that greatness is judged. So can Matthews be judged, for that is exactly what he achieved on this memorable Saturday. . . . Matthews is a superb artist, a football genius beyond compare. His work always has had that beautiful bloom that oils cannot give. He has it within him to turn mice into horses, and nothing into everything.

The *Times* even produced an editorial entitled 'Boys Own Player' and it was not even half humorous. Matthews was described as a 'veteran with a future' and the conclusion was inescapable: 'What a pity a player like that has ever to grow old.'

As for the top people themselves, one wrote to the *Times* and wondered if the events of Saturday afternoon, 2 May 1953 at Wembley did not symbolise football's capture from cricket of the status of Britain's national game. The *Daily Mirror*, meanwhile, claimed to have received a 'flood of letters' on Matthews. Space meant one must speak for all. That privileged writer praised Matthews as an essential a part of these islands as natural phenomena such as Loch Lomond or the cliffs of Dover. Surely a life's dedication to the national game – there was no doubt on this side of the classroom – demanded the recognition of the state which only a knighthood could bestow?[33] What we have been trying to do is explore the relationship between a star footballer and his audience. We have done this by examining four important moments in his career, moments which suggest three distinct phases. In the first, in the 1930s, Matthews becomes a local sporting hero the loss of whom to another club seems unthinkable; by 1946–7 he remains a celebrated sportsman but his importance has diminished due to the different perspective produced by the war and his own advancing years; the extraordinary length of his career then promoted the third phase in the 1950s and 1960s by which time Matthews had become a national institution.

We now need to assess in a broader sense what the Matthews phenomenon actually meant to members of the football fraternity both inside the Potteries and without. What did he mean to those who flocked to seek him for the best part of three decades? As we noted earlier to begin to understand the attraction of any football player you have to start by examining his public performance on the field. Clifford Webb, reporting on England's famous victory in Berlin in May 1938 for the *Daily Herald*, captures well the excitement that an in-form Matthews provided:

> What an artist this dapper laddie from Stoke can be. He played the perfect cat-and-mouse game with full-back Muenzenberg, impudently taking the ball right up to him, showing it, and then dancing away from under his nose with tantalising consistency.
>
> If and when there is established a Soccer college in England a description of the goal Matthews scored . . . should be a set piece in every text book.
>
> Matthews picked up a pass near the touchline, weaved a way through the whole German defence and finished with an acutely angled shot that was brilliantly placed about a foot inside the far post.[34]

Few footballers have had their style reported in such detail which in itself suggests exceptional power.

After 1940 Matthews scored very few goals and this added to his aura of mystery and fantasy. Similarly his well-known aversion against heading the ball provided another recognisable characteristic. Of course, the attraction of Matthews partly changed with the years. By 1945 he was thirty, not so far from the age when most professionals recognised the signs of declining vigour and began to prepare for life without the roar of the crowd. There is evidence that he was thinking along those lines too. But in the event he played for another eighteen years, the last appearance in an international being at the age of forty-two in 1957. He had become another kind of phenomenon. People went to see him so they could say they had done so before he finally retired. He was, as 1953 showed, something of an institution always in the public eye even when he did not want to be.[35]

His modesty and reluctance to seek the limelight must be counted part of the attraction. The successful in sport, as in other walks of life, are usually far from a retiring disposition but no one ever accused Matthews of being too big for his football boots. Even when he was the most experienced and senior player there is no evidence that he sought leadership – he was never captain – or exerted much authority. Nor did his exalted status provoke measurable resentment among his team-mates. He always insisted that it was game of eleven-a-side. Newspapers occasionally accused his colleagues both at Stoke and in the England team of deliberately starving him of the ball and at least twice prompted public denials, one an official statement from the FA. But there seems to have been little substance to the allegations. Again, although he was better off than most of the crowds who watched him and most of the players with whom he played, as team-mates and opponents, he did not flaunt his wealth. He was also a scrupulously fair player. He was neither cautioned nor sent off and never seemed to lose his temper even when roughly treated. But it has often been pointed out that he did have a ruthless streak and his ability to continually bamboozle his marker was intended to destroy his opponent psychologically.[36]

Although it is clear that Matthews became a national sporting figure he was also very much a regional possession. To the men and media of the Potteries he remained someone in whose achievements they could take a self-conscious pride. All his triumphs were celebrated in the *Evening Sentinel* and the report of Blackpool's cup final victory in 1953 was blazed across the front pages.[37] He was characterized as 'a famous son of the Potteries'. Although he had been a Blackpool player for six years by then 'the Potteries will always claim him as their own'. The great majority of his honours were gained with Stoke and he had brought 'great distinction' to the town. In his native district of North Staffordshire he became a tradition even if an invented one. Many people came to see him alone 'and it is a recognised fact that whever he is playing, his presence added thousands to the gates'.[38] An editorial emphasised his triumph as a source of pride for all local people. Letters to the press on subsequent days, one from a local councillor suggesting (again) the freedom of the city, also underlined his role as the 'finest type of Pottery lad'.[39]

So he was an outstanding player, modest and honest and in general symbolic of all that was best about sport in general and football in particular, a credit to the profession and to the Potteries community which had reared him. Are those factors enough to account for his sporting canonisation? Certainly he would hardly have captured the imagination of the football, and on occasion, even a wider public, without them. But there are at least three more factors which help explain his hold on the popular imagination and help us to penetrate nearer to the meaning of his performance for those thousands who turned out to see him, especially in that Indian summer of a career after 1945.

First, somewhat ambiguously, he did not look the part. Even the *Sentinel* could agree that 'on the field he did not cut an impressive figure' until, of course, he got the ball. Thin body, slightly hunched shoulders, receding hair and bony knees were all part of the post-war Matthews image. He did not look bigger, stronger nor more obviously physically gifted than many of those who turned up to watch. *You* could be him, with a bit of luck. You *might* have been, if things had turned out differently. He was the epitome of the ordinary bloke who became a star.

Second, people probably admired Matthews' dedication to fitness and practice. No one could ever accuse him of not keeping himself in the best of condition and not trying to make the most of his gifts. He *looked* rather like a professor and certainly worked at football like one with a commitment that was close to obsession. And the effort, as Arthur Hopcraft noted in an *Observer* profile in 1965, was etched in his face for all to see.[40] He neither smoked, nor drank (though he did once advertise Craven A) but he was 'totally engrossed in his football, and it was from that that all the propriety flowed'.

He worked at football and it is this that brings us to the third and final element in his popular significance. He was often called a master craftsman on the field and a gentleman off it. And it was these artisan qualities, the qualities of the skilled worker, that *The Field* wanted to stress when considering his social importance in 1957, long after that paper had given up football as a bad job.[41] For 'Quercus' Matthews was neither colourful nor flamboyant, which sporting stars were supposed to be. But it was efficiency and solid character which captured the respect of football watchers. The qualities of the artisan who kept his tools in good order. Matthews' tools were his body and his boots. He preferred light boots when heavier ones were fashionable and always liked new ones which most players did not because of the need to break them in. 'I liked the shine on them. You could look at the shine' – he once told a journalist – 'as you do with ordinary shoes – and it does something to you; it makes you proud; it makes you more alive'.[42] This is the voice of the skilled, respectable working man. Again, according to 'Quercus', it was the combination of a craftsman's conscientiousness and an 'unassailable common-sense' which was the foundation of Matthews' position head and shoulders above all other British footballers by the 1950s. This not unnaturally provided some comfort to the conservatively inclined. Matthews was a living demonstration to all ordinary men that such a one can be a national hero. Aristotle wrote that in the hero 'we see men better than the average man'. Perhaps we can agree that Matthews attracted identification because his achievements were within the bounds of human capacity. It would have taken a damn good 'un to emulate him nevertheless. Perhaps a Churchillian note is appropriate: rarely have so many been entertained so richly by a solitary football player.

Notes

1 *Daily Telegraph*, 4 January 1957.
2 *Daily Mirror*, 1, 2 January 1957. The *Daily Express, Daily Herald* and *Daily Mail* took a similar position.
3 *Feet First* (1948), *Feet First Again* (1952) and *Back in Touch* (1981).
4 *Evening Sentinel*, 21 March 1934.
5 Both quoted in the *Evening Sentinel*, 21 September 1934.
6 He also missed two easy chances, hitting the crossbar with the goal vacant and shooting wide of another gaping goalmouth. *Evening Sentinel*, 10 November 1934. In the Arsenal game he was also often beaten by Hapgood, his marker, in a 'masterly display of quick tackling'. *Evening Sentinel*, 6 October 1934.
7 *Evening Sentinel*, 22 September 1934.
8 R. Whipp, 'Women and the social organisation of work in the Staffordshire pottery industry 1900–1930', *Midland History*, 12 (1987).
9 *Evening Sentinel*, 8, 10 February 1938.
10 *Evening Sentinel*, 11, 12, 1938.
11 *Manchester Guardian*, 12 February 1938, *Sporting Chronicle*, 12 February 1938.
12 *Evening Sentinel*, 15 February 1938.
13 *Evening Sentinel*, 16, 17, 18 February 1938.
14 *Evening Sentinel*, 14 February 1938.
15 *Evening Sentinel*, 16 February 1938. The *Daily Herald* later claimed that

Matthews had only resigned from Stoke at the end of the season because he did not want to miss England's continental tour nor to lose his summer wages. *Daily Herald*, 6 May 1938.

16 *Evening Sentinel*, 14, 15 January 1946.

17 *Evening Sentinel*, 19 January 1946.

18 *Evening Sentinel*, 13 January 1946.

19 *Staffordshire Weekly Sentinel*, 16 January 1946.

20 *Evening Sentinel*, 25 January 1946.

21 *Evening Sentinel*, 28, 31 January 1946. It is difficuilt to know what he meant by this in the era of the maximum wage.

22 *Evening Sentinel*, 4 February 1946.

23 What follows is based on a reading of the *Evening Sentinel* and in particular the issues of 17, 18, 19 and 23 October 1946.

24 *Evening Sentinel*, 8 May 1947.

25 *Sporting Chronicle*, 12 May 1947.

26 On an 18 per cent poll, 18,341 said yes and 14,286 no. *Evening Sentinel*, 8 May 1947.

27 *Blackpool Gazette and Herald*, 13 August 1947.

28 *Daily Mirror*, 2 May 1953.

29 *Times*, 2 May 1953. *Sporting Chronicle*, 2 May 1953.

30 *Daily Mirror*, 4 May 1953. Even the *Daily Worker* published a short article by John Dixon, 'The footballer incomparable'. *Daily Worker*, 4 May 1953. John Graydon in the *Sporting Chronicle* did suggest that a continental defence, with its greater powers of concentration would not have allowed Matthews to get away with it. *Sporting Chronicle*, 4 May 1953.

32 *Times*, 4 May 1953.

33 *Times*, 6 May 1953. *Daily Mirror*, 5 May 1953.

34 *Daily Herald*, 16 May 1938.

35 Matthews' views about playing on were not consistent. In 1947 he was reported as saying he had only two or three years left. At fifty he felt he was still effective and not being carried by the other members of the team. In 1981 he told Don Taylor that he retired too early and could have played in midfield for at least three more years.

36 In books aimed at schoolboys which bore his name he always stressed sporting behaviour and the ignoring of coaches who urged players to 'get stuck in'. He also supported the idea that only players with unblemished disciplinary records should be chosen for England. But he did write that preventing a free kick from being taken quickly by standing over the ball or kicking it away was legitimate tactic of the defence. *Stanley Matthews' Football Album* (Marks & Spencer, 1949), p. 9, *Feet First* (London, 1948), pp. 57–8.

37 *Evening Sentinel*, 2 May 1953.

38 One journalist calculated he had been at least partly responsible for record crowds on eight grounds. I. Sharpe, *Forty Years in Football* (London, 1952), p. 119.

39 *Evening Sentinel*, 5, 6 May 1953. The editorial went on to suggest that, with Stoke just relegated to Division Two, the old slogan, Matthews must not go should be replaced by Matthews must come back. 'How appropriate it

would be if his closing years in football were devoted to help restoring Stoke City to a place in the sun.' Football could be the stuff which dreams are made of.

40 *The Observer*, 31 January 1965.
41 *The Field*, 2 May 1957.
42 Albert Barham in J. Arlott, *The Great Ones* (London, 1968), p. 84.

10

Shooting stars:
footballers and working-class
culture in twentieth-century Scotland

H. F. Moorhouse

The northern star

If golf is more typical of Scottish life generally, football is the sport that appeals to the masses. One has only got to be in Glasgow on International day to realise adequately how tremendous is the hold the game has on the Scottish mind. The enthusiasm of the Scot for the Association game is without parallel in any other race for any particular sport or pastime. Every village can boast of its goal posts, budding Arnotts, Campbells and Bobbie Walkers. For nine months the major portion of the male inhabitants of the land of cakes, Bibles and whisky discuss little else than the Saturday performances of their favourite clubs and players, and during the other three months of the year they indulge in extravagant speculation in regard to the team that is to wipe out England next April.[1]

Change the names and Connell's survey in 1906 still stands as a broad description of the significance of soccer in the Scottish male mind. Through the century, up to the 1980s when the Scottish branch of the Football Supporters Association implanted the 'statistic' in the media that, in Europe, Scotland stands second only to Albania in attendance per head of population, the game has remained what the *Glasgow Herald* called it in 1938 – 'The Ruling Passion'.[2]

Connell's statement also catches one element that has structured the ordering of Scottish stars through the years – their trajectories in regard to England. Yet another is caught in Muir's jaundiced comments on a Clydeside shipyard fitter at the beginning of the century:

football is his game, for no other can give the same thrill, the same fierce exhilaration, the same outlet for animal spirits which machinery has suppressed. It is intoxication by the eye. .... The players are his gods until their powers decline, and for Jakie Robertson or Big Jock wi' the Bunnett, it is roses, roses all the way. Any man is proud to call them friend, and talk is hushed when they take up the word. And yet if they are injured in the course of their trade they are considered merely as defective parts of a machine, and are despatched to Matlock for repairs.[3]

For 'John Macmillan', Muir's composite of the skilled non-radical working man, his wife and four children lived in a room and kitchen in Govan, he liked a drink and football argument, and Jacky Robertson and Jock Drummond, the last outfielder to play wearing a cap, were 'two of the greatest footballers who ever wore the Scottish jersey'[4] and both played for the Rangers. Scottish stars have also tended to stand in some relation to the two great clubs of the century – Rangers and Celtic. Their legends and stories tend to mix with those of the clubs and counterpoint each other, and, of course, behind these clubs lies a major cultural division in the Scottish working class between 'Protestant' and 'Catholic' groupings, and so, often, the star is not simply connected with one or other club but also with a perceived and much publicised 'split' within the working class. When Billy McNeill, famous ex-player now manager of Celtic, remarked: 'Well I've always felt we were the underdogs in this country . . . the bulk of the population will always be more inclined to be Rangers orientated than Celtic'[5], he was expressing thoughts that simply could not be applied to any English club.

In this chapter I do not intend to dwell on 'real' people or the 'actual' lives of great players. Rather I am concerned with some of the things footballers have meant or indicated or represented to the lower classes in Scotland through the twentieth century. For stars are not just superior athletes but emblematic figures. The chapter could be filled with the magical physical abilities great Scots are held to possess. Defying gravity is a popular one, with many a player able to 'hover in the air' or 'change direction' in mid-dive, but such super-human qualities are, presumably, an aura common to all stars of all cultures. This chapter is concerned with what stars tell about the preoccupations of a *specific* working-class culture. What are the aspects which seem to demarcate the 'Scottishness' of stars and what do they reveal about being Scottish to star-gazers?

My argument is that stars and stories about them relate to recurring themes in Scottish culture, and that they dramatise and invigorate certain cultural issues which, while they certainly change – the 'Catholicism' of many Celtic players, for example – retain a basic continuity through the century. Football stars expound experiences which pose the continuing dilemmas involved in social arrangements. The cultural clichés which stars embody are not all the same, for there are levels, sections and segments aplenty, but the true shooting star hits strings which resonate to wider cultural concerns than their ability in kicking a piece of leather or plastic around a field. While a star has to be a supreme performer, their 'lives' also articulate certain tensions, themes and myths and their flights contain compelling metaphors which help explain the earthy predicaments of the fans.

What I am attempting to outline here stands in some relation to Critcher's analysis of the cultural significance of soccer.[6] He uses developments in professional football as an index through which to gauge wider patterns of 'tradition' and 'change' in working-class life. He takes the star as one central element of the game and creates a typology of the cultural identities of stars since the war, reflecting alterations in their on- and off-the-field activity, which relate to wider changes in working-class culture. Broadly, his four-fold typology involves a sequence of change from the star with a 'traditional location' in the respectable working class, through 'transitional mobile' and 'incorporated embourgeoised' types, to a 'dislocated superstar' who has ejected from the working class and relocates culturally only by entering the world of show biz and celebrity. He specifically excludes non-English players (with the exception of the Irish George Best) on the grounds that 'other British players are the products of a distinctively different cultural environment'.[7] Even in its own terms there is much that is wrong with Critcher's typology, but here my aim is to indicate some of the 'messages' which emanate from Scottish stars and what *they* have to say about cultural identity. Such a review will cut right across the class-based nature of Critcher's reading of the meanings of stars and will also suggest, contra-Critcher, that one 'modern' type he perceives (and the reason he has to include the non-English Best) – 'the dislocated superstar' – is one which has a more constant place in the historical constellation than he seems to realise and is one whose meanings are much more troubling for the working-class fan than he seems to grasp.

The southern cross

I do not want to be made out a martyr or hero or something of the sort. If you want to know why I was prepared to make the sacrifice, as you call it, the answer is to be found at the bottom part of the English League table. It is true that I would have given my right hand to play at Wembley, but I do not think there is any doubt what my duty is.[8]

I have argued elsewhere that one recurrent aspect of British football that feeds the meanings the game generates is that, across the century, the English League and Scottish League have stood in a relation of buyer and seller.[9] Thus one complex of meaning surrounding virtually all Scottish stars arises from the constant, and largely unreciprocated, movement of top players out of Scottish football and, indeed, out of Scotland.

The first issue of the *Scottish Football Historian* in 1982,[10] one of a number of football papers, magazines, programmes, fanzines, exhibitions and videos which, among other things, re-tell the stories of stars of other days, stated its aim as being to embrace 'unashamed nostalgia'. It wanted to tell 'the history of Scottish football, the men and the teams which made it' and to provide a 'celebration of our great game of Scottish football'. This issue reprinted an article about Denis Law, the next one on Billy Liddell, the third on Billy Bremner, and so on. Yet none of these players ever played in the Scottish League and, consequently, had performed in only a handful of professional games on Scottish soil. This apparent oddity was not remarked on, it was, somehow, 'understood', but to see a lot of great stars has often required the Scottish fan to have a very powerful glass.

Few English internationals have ever made the reverse trip. One who did, Syd Puddefoot of Falkirk, revealed in his 'confessions' to the London *Evening Standard* in 1924, 'confessions' designed to expedite his return south, that his nationality had been something of a handicap north of the border:

> Frequently I have stood half-an-hour without kicking the ball. It's a bit discouraging after a game like this to read that 'the £5,000 Englishman wasn't worth 5 shillings to his side.' I invariably have to fetch the ball for myself. . . . It is the attitude of spectators that upsets me. You may find it difficult to believe this, but twice this season I have leaped over the railings after spectators who have called me names no man could endure. . . . My offence, so far as I can see, is an English accent. I assume this, because in all the abuse shrieked at me by spectators, the word English is employed as an adjective.[11]

And Puddefoot was not to be the last top-class Englishman to find his nationality a cause for discussion and debate in Scotland.

Overwhelmingly, however, traffic has been in the other direction. The first Home Scots versus Anglo-Scots international trial match was played in 1896. This exodus has called into question the national spirit of 'the Anglo' and has meant that a characteristic preoccupation for virtually all Scottish supporters has been whether their club would succumb to the lure of English silver and sell their favourites. The outflow was very pronounced between the wars. In *Athletic News* in 1926 the tide was measured quite precisely:

> in little more than a season 10 fully fledged internationalists, two inter-league players who would have had a cap if the Scotsmen could have played more than one centre-forward in a team, and a member of an international trial eleven have passed into English football.[12]

In December that year, the Scottish correspondent of the paper declared that without too much deliberation he could list more than seventy front-rank players who had moved south since the war and lots more who still had their names to make. Of course, such sales did not always pass without commotion. Fans threatened to burn down the grandstand at Airdrie when the rumour went round that Hughie Gallacher had been sold to Notts County but, amid recriminations, he was soon transferred to Newcastle. Basically, all Scots supporters – except those of Rangers and, less securely, Celtic – have had to expect any of their players who showed much ability (and many who did not) either to move south or join one of the great Glasgow clubs.

Not surprisingly, this set up a succession of issues in the Scottish football culture. To begin with there was a nagging doubt about the quality of Scottish league if, in effect, many of its professional clubs were acting as feeders of talent to England. In this sense, the weight of Rangers and Celtic, which could be seen as debilitating to the rest of the Scottish game, was most important in regard to England, its money and pretensions. Then, given a doubt about the relative quality of the Scots game, there was always another worry about whether Scottish players moving south could actually 'make it' in the English League. Many Scots moving south had their success monitored in reports on their early matches, and these and commentary around transfers, were often couched in a vocabulary of 'larger stages', 'proving oneself', etc. Frequently, as I will sketch later, a moral dimension was seen to be involved here, with the trip south fraught with peculiar temptations to character and personal balance. Conversely, English purchases were, and are, proof of the superior abilities of Scots players. In the inter-war years, even more so than today, this was seen as a testament to the ball skills of the Scot, the 'flair', which related to a contrast in predominant *style* of play between the two countries. Billy Meredith, and others, were often called to attest to the skill of the Scots game as opposed to the rush, hurry and use of the 'long ball' in England. *Athletic News* sent 'The Mystery International' to see Motherwell versus Celtic, and this report (and others) actually involved a series of contrasts between the Scots and the normal English League match:

> The slight difference in speed at which the game is played in the middle is more than made up for by the greater degree of accuracy. The spectator in Scotland gets far better sport and is much concerned with the finer arts of the game than mere speed. I can thoroughly recommend one of these League games to anybody in England whose appetite has become jaded by watching so many English league games where subtlety, artifice and football ability have become sacrificed to the insane mania for speed and nothing but more speed.[13]

So the same English purchases which threatened to dilute the indigenous game attested to the superiority of the Scot, so that the fatalism engendered in the face of apparently superior economic resources was mingled with the victim's pride that England simply could not get by without Scottish stars. This view gained in force in the 1960s as the, apparently successful, English national side were seen as masters of method, slaves to work-rate, whose mathematical approach (and luck) was likely to stifle the brilliant individualism which was, ultimately, the game's true glory. Baxter of Rangers and Johnstone of Celtic, destroyers of England and Leeds in the decade, provided clear evidence that English method would succumb to a Scottish flair which flourished off stony ground. The lad kicking a cheap ball, bundle of rags or tin can, honing exquisite skills on 'the barren rocks of Aden' of a tenement wasteland[14] or in the city street is a potent myth in the Scottish football culture, idealised apprenticeship of the true football craftsman. Moreover, such dexterity is often linked to the engineering and ship-building traditions of the west of Scotland, where 'Clydebuilt', as all the world knows, stood for precision, quality, and expertise, with rare craftsmanship passed on 'in the blood'. Thus, and oft-repeated, one Scottish myth – of the tanna' ba' player – supports another, of an engineering genius somehow frittered away.

Given such tensions it is not, therefore, surprising that the International between Scotland and England gained in significance between the wars with vast crowds and the echoing symbols of the 'Wembley wizards' and the 'Hampden roar'. The match had, traditionally, been a struggle between the two styles of football as well as the two countries, and English papers moaned that the inter-war 'march of men' south, was likely to destroy this true import of the fixture. The inter-League games, very popular in Scotland, less so in England, by convention normally involved players of the respective nationalities and became another annual test of standards and style. Many a Scottish star, especially those who rarely played in Scotland, hold their place in the heavens because of their performances and attitude (Law playing golf rather than watch England in a World Cup final) against the auld enemy. The middle-class, teetotal, suited, university-educated Alan Morton, who claimed the sailors' hornpipe at childhood dancing classes had helped him to be 'quick off the mark', scarcely stands in the normal line of Scottish stars, but his performances against England ensure that he is revered as much as a Scottish wizard as a Ranger immortal. The English journalist who told a Scots reporter: 'Alan Morton should be banned from these internationals. He upsets all England's plans; our selectors are at their wits end as to how to put the kybosh on him'[15] gave the sweetest adulation Scots like to hear, and Morton became the most popular figure in the massive biennial trip to Wembley which became an established feature of Scottish popular culture in the inter-war years.[16]

This trip, and the Scottish excitement that surrounded it, became one of the main occasions through which the Scottish football culture could review its old stars and measure their achievements. R.S. McColl, great centre forward and successful businessman, paid for the 1900 Scottish side – 'The Invincibles' – to travel down to the Wembley games in the 1920s and 1930s. Thus readers of the Scottish popular press could hear the views of Arnott, Campbell, Bobbie Walker, Drummond and others, while Jacky Robertson, who had become a sports journalist, provided his reminiscences of other days such as:

The First Football Strike: We Stood For Principle – And Half A Crown[17]

whose message about fighting for bonus payments – 'we had set an example to all true Scotsmen' – was probably well understood by working-class readers.

These Wembley supplements also tried to resolve another issue which the drain of players south created: doubts as to the strength of their 'nationalism'. For most of the century the Anglo has been treated with some suspicion in Scotland either because he is regarded as being picked in favour of better players still in Scotland or because of a suspect attitude. In 1930 'Brigadier' wrote of 'Some Famous Anglo Scots', a piece which ended, 'Fine players all, good Scots'. In 1932 it was 'Why The Anglo Scot Came'. In 1938 'A Good Word for the Anglo: He Has Saved Our Prestige' and so on. Doubts about the fervour of the Anglo have been underpinned, periodically, by the star (or their bosses) perceiving their duty to be with club rather than country, as with Gallacher's decision to miss the 1930 Wembley game in favour of aiding Newcastle. This tension was made quite overt in the early 1930s when a fracas between the English League, its clubs and the Scottish Football Association meant that, for a while, Anglos were not released to play in international matches played on Saturdays. This, and a continuing doubt about the availability of players in England, meant that some great players, Alex James for example, are much more closely aligned with their English club[s] than with Scotland[18] and that the *desire* of Anglos to play still tends to be suspect and open to test. Favourites who have returned to play against their old Scottish clubs have been roundly booed and, as a recent captain of Scotland has testified, Anglos have found they are not always popular at Hampden Park.[19] The *Daily Mail*'s moan in 1938, when 19 of the 22 players in the International were from the Football League, that some of the Anglos were of such long standing that they might as well have been in the English side, is one not entirely repudiated north of the border.

So, and not considered by Critcher, one cultural problem which the Scottish star tends to straddle is that of the complexities of a national identity: what is to be 'a Scot' and how that is to be maintained, or not, in the face of the economic riches of England and the perils of migration. This is an aspect of cultural identity which has a much wider span than that of 'class' and is a recurring theme through the entire history of professional football.

Gemini

Here is one way in which his death might bring a great gain. Those thoughtless crowds who call themselves Celtic or Rangers followers, whom both teams disown, who gather behind the goals of their respective favourites and cheer themselves hoarse when a member of the opposing team lies writhing in pain, if they can be brought to realise the brutal cruelty of their actions, John Thomson will not have given his life in vain.[20]

The only Scottish clubs who have seemed able to withstand pressure from England are Rangers and, less assuredly, Celtic. What they would not do for a long time was to pay similar transfer fees to those on offer from the south. Before Hughie Gallacher was transferred to England, and after, he let it be known that he would like to join Rangers. Twenty years later, Billy Steele, with Derby, but insisting on living in Glasgow and looking for a Scottish club, trained with Rangers, was an avowed fan, and their names were linked but, as a journalist put it during his record transfer to Dundee: 'Personally, I think it is absolutely ridiculous – and this applies to Aberdeen too – for any Scottish club to pay huge transfer fees for players. The richest of them all, Rangers, the best managed club in Scotland, would never dream of parting with £20,000 for a player.'[21]

Holding to this 'rule' for most of the century the two big Scottish clubs have not done as much as they objectively could have done to stop the drain of stars south, and so counter the wider worries and fatalism this has engendered in Scots fans. The other side of this coin is that both clubs have tried to appeal to much more than money when recruiting and retaining players. A stress on 'loyalty' and 'wanting to play for the jersey', neatly exemplified by MacAvennie, transferred from England, kissing the badge on the Celtic shirt at his first home game in 1987, has ever been what these clubs and supporters have demanded from their stars – a 'commitment' well beyond cash, a tradition which has tended to founder on harder currencies in recent times.

Rangers and Celtic because of their wider social affiliations and representation functions are powerful institutions in Glasgow, if not in Scottish, society. Not surprisingly then, both clubs have been able to ease the paths of stars when sterner duties called. Baxter claims to have served his National Service in central Scotland and to have missed only one game for Rangers in the period. In war time, both clubs, but especially Rangers, have been able to find their players work in reserved occupations rather than in the forces – another manifest advantage of being a star not, presumably, lost on the working (or fighting) man, especially when, as in the case of Patsy Gallagher, attendance at the shipyard in 1916 was intermittent enough to get him disciplined by both the munitions tribunal and the Scottish FA. Given Celtic's Irish and Catholic associations this affair caused some people to question his 'patriotism', while others regarded the double penalty as typical of Celtic's unfair treatment by authority.

The tense opposition of Rangers and Celtic, aided by the routines of mobility in the Scottish football world, so that both clubs have tended to recruit their managers internally and ex-players tend to become sports journalists, and aligned to wider ethnic divisions in Scottish society, has produced, across the century, a double set of generous but demanding fans. By 1900 the 'brake clubs' which followed the Glasgow teams, and which soon exhibited many features of 'modern' hooligan behaviour, were already well established. Their brakes were draped with banners featuring portraits of their favourite players. The names of stars encapsulate major events between the clubs – 'The Quinn Case' or 'The Cox-Tully Incident' are well known to readers of Scottish football literature. Relatedly, the 'mistakes' of the clubs around the ethnic divide are a source of some interest. The protestant Daniel Fergus McGrain being rejected by Rangers because of the connotations of his two christian names, or Dalglish's family ripping Rangers scarves and posters from the walls as Celtic officials stood at the door with signing-on forms are regularly repeated anecdotes and there are debates about exactly how many Orangemen have played for Celtic. The real icon of the opposition and what it 'means' is John Thomson, the young Celtic goalie, who died in 1931 after a collision in a game against Rangers. The accident is regularly replayed on television in Scotland, the 'Prince of Goalkeepers', and his magical abilities, are constantly honoured, his name is attached to cups, awards and is repeated in songs. His grave and his anniversaries are kept up. For example, the sermon at the head of this section formed part of the script of the play *The Celtic Story* performed in Glasgow in 1988, and its declaration from the stage provoked long applause from the packed audience.[22] There is no shortage of local intellectuals ready to present Glasgow's 'past' to its present inhabitants and Thomson's death is constantly used to show how important the relationship between the two clubs is and to feed the historic sense of what is routinely asserted in Scotland to be 'the greatest club game in the world'.

A memorial to Thomson is prominent in the foyer of Celtic Park while a painting of Alan Morton dominates the main entrance at

Ibrox. Morton was *the* Rangers star of the inter-war years, his importance caught in a famous Glaswegian novel purporting to be a slice of working-class life.[23] In fact, Morton's ball skill was somewhat at odds with the power and strength of Rangers style, but his evident respectability was not. The bowler hat and suit of 'the wee society man' was normal attire, not swapped for bunnett and muffler on the way home as other stars did. Club policy required bowlers and sharp creases and, until very recently, moustaches and long hair had to be foregone when a player joined the club. The Rangers tradition involved, too, a quite overt link to various Protestant organisations – the Orange Order holding its 'divine service' at Ibrox from the 1960s to 1987, for example.

Celtic has quite open links to Eire. Some of its greatest stars have been Irish and the Catholicism of others has never been in doubt from McGrory going on holiday to Lourdes with his manager in the 1930s to Charlie Nicholas proclaiming in the Celtic programme in 1982 that 'the person he would most like to meet' was Pope John Paul. There would be few British stars of any era who would follow Charlie Tully down this particular aisle of 1950:

> We were off to Rome for a peaceful holiday, a match with Lazio and to meet His Holiness Pope Pius XII. I've won a lot of medals and international caps since joining Glasgow Celtic, but this was the most exciting and satisfying experience of all. No prize, or honour, could ever be greater than this.[24]

Similarly, in few places in the world would a player crossing himself on the pitch cause the fuss that such action occasionally does in Scotland. For Celtic a prominent place in the hierarchy of Catholic institutions in Scotland has gone along with a preferred paternalistic management style for spectators and players alike. The 'ideal Celt' has been great player like Quinn and McGrory who were 'daft' for the club but seem to have received rather little in return. When Quinn ceased being the star centre-forward of the first years of this century he went back to being a miner in Fife. McGrory regarded himself as being an 'eternal sucker in the subject of wage negotiations' especially when he found out that while top goal scorer and coveted by English clubs, he was being paid £1 a week less than most of his team-mates in the inter-war years.[25] Celtic players and managers, who have pressed the paternalism too far have tended to find an iron fist behind the velvet tones, and such instances –

Crerand's transfer to England, McNeil's departure from his first spell as manager – are well known.

Celtic overtly claim to represent 'a community', while the, now, more covert affiliations of Rangers are also believed to find representation through the club. This notion, of the clubs and certain stars, 'representing' two 'communities' is insisted upon, not least in the numerous attempts at popular or even academic histories of Scottish football where terms like 'cultural apartheid', 'holy wars', 'tribal loyalties', 'simmering hostilities', 'two world views', 'almost racial divisions' and the like get tossed about with some abandon but with very little thought as to *exactly* how such hyperbole is supposed to apply to the totality of working-class life.[26] The intelligentsia that hangs around both clubs, but especially Celtic, find this Glasgow of myth and legend much more interesting than the rather prosaic and certainly 'untraditional' reality of the modern city. For example, one prominent analyst of the Old Firm, promoting a new book[27] on Scottish television provided this account of the 'present situation' in relation to the 'good old days':

> it's an irony that a hundred years ago Celtic were the sectarian team and it was only by not being a sectarian team, and it was only by saying that they would sign Protestants . . . it was the only way they could win games. Now, a hundred years on we've got a Celtic team – how many catholics? Nine? Ten? Uh, players playing for the jersey, that's what won Celtic the League last year, they had players who wanted to play for the green and white, who wanted to play for Celtic. Rangers? You've got a team of Thatcherites haven't you? You've got a team of people who are in it for the money. Who are there, I'm not saying they're not trying, as professionals they'll try as hard as they can, but playing to a contract and a weekly salary is a different thing from playing for the jersey. Now, I don't want to be seen, because I mean I criticised Rangers last time for their sectarianism, and it might seem a wee bit hard now to criticise them for their Thatcherism, but I think there's something a wee bit more normal in a wee bit of bigotry than judging everything by the tinkle of a cash register.[28]

A city of 'communities', 'tribal rivalries', 'potential bloodbaths' and so on is much easier, and exciting, to portray than a city of wine bars, mortgages, bureaucracy, contractual ties, office blocks, isolation, drugs and tourism.

In relation to Critcher's account we can see how stars can guide toward social groupings other than class. Moreover, Critcher does not consider exactly how the meanings of stars are marshalled. It is not often realised in the rest of Britain how *proud* the Scottish football culture is of Rangers versus Celtic as something the English have not got and cannot match, and in the popular football literature simple moralising mixtures with a parochial self-conceit which seeks to maintain a 'Glasgow', indeed a 'Scotland', of the *mind*. In these forms, the replays of the deeds and affiliations of the old stars become one way that a local culture industry reproduces an inbred, nostalgic, unreflective, ignorance within the Scottish working class, avoiding both fruitful comparisons *and* all the complexities of a world where lads who are 'Celtic daft' prefer continental clubs and Rangers 'break the rules' by importing English internationals.

Falling stars

but let Tommy Craig fail to deliver golden goals and see what happens. Fleet Street analysts will have him on the X-ray table, body and soul. Let him but side-step from the training diet – a glass of beer, a bit of a fling with the girls – and the Pharisees will train their inky arrows on him. And that's why I'm fashed for him. I'm faired he may go the way of all football flesh.[29]

Critcher includes George Best as the central figure in the emergence of the footballer as superstar, emblematic of a wider fracturing of the social and cultural relations which had structured the identity of the player and kept it in some connection with the traditional working class. For a while behaviour on the field – retaliation, arguing with referee – and off it – breaking curfews, indiscipline – is a source of tension for the star and others before they develop a new identity of 'superstar' involved in a world of show business, entertainment, personalities and publicity. Best moved towards this new identity and: 'in response lived it up with fast cars and beautiful women, while securing his future in a chain of boutiques. He lived out, part by choice, part by cultural compulsion, the newspapers dream version of the superstar's life'.[30]

The problem with this version of historical development is that it both simplifies the nature of the relations of star to the traditional working-class culture *and* overstates the shock of the 'new'. Celebrity status, 'bits on the side', personal dislocation and disgrace, problems on and off the field have long been a feature of the trail of shooting stars. Scotland in 1898 thrilled to the media furore surrounding the 'strange play' of Cowan in the International match and whether he had been 'under the influence' or not. More than one Scottish star already mentioned in this chapter committed suicide. Once this aspect of 'tradition' is accepted it is by no means too clear that Best, and many elements of his 'type', really represent anything new in the football firmament *or* that Critcher has read this type of star's portent to a working-class audience in its fullest form.

Across the century Scottish stars have certainly indicated that football could be a path to economic security:

> I remember well his first shop, not so very far from Hampden Park, where the chocolate boxes, nicely designed in the Queens Park black and white, won a ready vogue among the followers of our oldest club. Now R.S. McColl shops are to be seen in most towns in Scotland.[31]

and they still are. By the mid 1920s there were seventy-five shops and what was a family firm was valued at £275,000.[32] Morton, who shared McColl's middle-class background, also had his own business. While McPhail, from the working class, built up his own company in Glasgow.[33] Many other footballers have shown that fame could lead to the fortune of a publican's place, journalist's seat or manager's desk. But stars have dark sides too and an achilles heel in feet of clay has been the worst injury many a Scot seems to have carried.

In 1947 Glasgow Unity Theatre, a company devoted to plays about and performed by the Scottish working class, first performed G. Munro's *Gold in His Boots*, revived by another socialist company, 7:84 (Scotland) in 1982 as part of their 'Clydebuilt' season. The play, which had a successful run on both occasions, concerns Tommy Craig, son of a means-test miner, who becomes 'the uncrowned king of Scotland' through football ability. Despite the protestations of his father – 'Tommy'll stay in Scotland. We've exported enough brain to England' – the boy is transferred south, but Claverly, the friendly journalist, gives the prophetic warning quoted at the start of this section. In England things do not go well for Tommy, he strikes his oppressive manager, and the press picks on him with stories of booze, blondes and bonanzas. The star takes to drink at the injustice of it all and, though he finds redemption and a place in the Cup Final team at the end of the play, plenty of real Scots stars have not found that 'birds, booze and bets' in whatever combination, leads to a happy ending.

Hughie Gallacher's career was as tempestuous as they come. He scored goals, argued with refs, ran foul of authority with the best of them. His was a story of secret deals on rainswept nights in the mining village from which he came, of club-versus-country clashes, of walk-outs, fines and transfer rumours. Like many another star of the 'traditional era' he travelled through clouds of gossip with a trail of hangers-on.[34] He featured in adverts and even *spoke* on cigarette cards.[35] His deeds in England were chronicled in Scotland. Sent off for swearing at, and, reportedly threatening, a referee when tackled, he told the Scottish *Daily Record*: 'The referee said I had used bad language which is not true. The actual words I used to the referee were 'Lord, lumme, did you see that referee? What about it?'[36] A subsequent two month ban suggested that the Football Association scarcely believed this was the normal vernacular of Larnarkshire! Brave and intelligent, small and skilful, Gallacher was the epitome of the great Scottish footballer right down to the short fuse on his temper: 'But why on earth did the team have to wait so many minutes lined up before the match? I looked through my very good binoculars and studied Hughie Gallacher during that delay. I'd like to tell you what I thought he was muttering to his colleagues!'[37]

Gallagher was one star who fell to earth. In 1957 his headless body was found on the main Newcastle – London railway line. He had been working as a machinist in a factory and as a columnist in a local paper. He was about to appear in court to answer a summons that he had neglected, assaulted and ill-treated his youngest son. He told a journalist just before he died: 'It's no use fighting this when you know you can't win. They have got me on this one. My life is finished now. Drink has been my downfall. If I could have kept off the drink I would have been a different man'.[38]

Stars wax *and* wane, and crashes also echo in working-class culture. In the twice-shown BBC (Scotland) series of 1986, *The Story of Scottish Football*,[39] various luminaries listed the qualities of the typical Scottish footballer and the 'self-destruct button' or something close to it was often mentioned as an integral aspect of the tradition and there can be few older men *and* women who cannot perceive parallels in some stars' well-publicised stories of transient glory, failed marriages, wasted cash and sad addiction. Effeminacy may, as Critcher avers, have been subject to the ultimate condemnation in traditional working-class culture, but, which Critcher does not allow, strict adherence to the rules of masculinity was, and is, well-known to bring problems in its wake.

In recent years Baxter and Johnstone have written books which, with serialisations and interviews, have codified popular knowledge of their progress up from mining villages but then down the primrose path. Baxter, 'the next best Kirkaldy export after linoleum', immodest, pecuniary, 'gallus' in Glaswegian patois, is probably *the* post-war Scottish hero, his insolence and insouciance against England in the mid 1960s still a regular feature of Scottish football programmes. The 'Slim Jim' tag was redolent of 1960s chic and he lived a flashy style to the hilt, taking Puskas to parties where the main inconvenience was that Scottish council flats only have two bedrooms, and the like. Now the pub he once had near Ibrox, with its coterie of fans paying homage, is gone along with hundreds of thousands of pounds through gambling. Characteristically, there are, up to now, no regrets: 'And if I *was* a fool to myself I was at least my own fool. I always bought my round too. I always will, or you won't find me in the pub.' After all: 'Half measures are for little people'.⁴⁰

Johnstone with high wages frittered away, crashed business ventures and closed pub, became a lorry driver then a general labourer, trying to cope, the while, with a drink problem. He repeats an old truth of the working-class world: 'Doors into many different worlds open to boys who, like myself, come from humble backgrounds and it's easy to fall by the wayside.'⁴¹ Such figures can be counterposed, they counterpose themselves, to that other post-war hero Dalglish who has, in the main, avoided their path and been 'a credit to his profession', just as for every Gallacher there was a McGrory. Nonetheless, in Scotland at least, the tribulations of the star, especially if 'dislocated' by moving, as so many have, to England, can be read as part of an old, old story, and one which resonates in traditional working-class life, where many a family could plot a parallel path.

In the stars and in ourselves

Not every Scotsman can settle in English football. . . . Scotsmen are said to be clannish folk. This may be because many a Scotsman never really leaves home: his home is always in his heart.⁴²

The stars of the century, as I have tried to indicate, still shine in Scotland. Two, for example, who could 'make the ball sit up and beg' span the years in 'Neilly Gibson Better Than Baxter' in a recent *The Rangers Historian*,⁴³ just as the banners of the old brake clubs now adorn exhibitions, programmes and publications about the history of Scottish clubs and football. The galaxy of stars: doomed goalies, erratic geniuses, wee men with sharp tongues and big hearts, and the like, is one of the means through which the sense of Scotland being distinctive is maintained: partial and unpredictable, proud and put-upon.

I have tried to sketch three elements in the cultural impact of this continuing parade which do not accord with other readings of the place of football in working-class culture. Stars personalise structural matters and, so, what they symbolize is as complicated as the structural arrangements. Skill, masculinity, social mobility and class feelings are all to be found in the presentation but so too are the manifold tensions set up by economic inequality between regions, the persuasion of ethnic division and the dreadful stories of squandered talents and wasted lives. Both rise and fall, to and from the dizzy heights, can speak to that fatalism in working-class life where structural forces are reduced to matters of 'personality', 'temptation', and 'human nature'. Meanings mix and mingle, but there is no simple shift from a corporate collectivisim to a dislocated affluence. The stars in their courses send complex signals.

It is of some importance to stress this point as the sociology of soccer seems to be becoming obsessed with 'violence' and 'its' meaning to the disregard of all the other matters which the game has thrown light on over the years. While I have criticised Critcher's paper here, at least his is a genuine attempt to locate *many* elements of the game to a changing popular culture, and it is this kind of sweep that is being rapidly abandoned in contemporary social analysis. Scrutinising soccer only through the lens of 'violent behaviour', excluding fuller surveys of the sport's place in social and cultural life is a miserably myopic way to scan what still remains, in Scotland at least, what it has been through the century: 'The Game of the People'.[44]

Notes

1 R. Connell, 'The association game in Scotland', *Book of Football* (London, 1906), pp. 161–84.
2 *Glasgow Herald*, 13 August 1938.
3 J.H. Muir, *Glasgow in 1901* (Glasgow, 1901), p. 192.
4 *Glasgow Herald*, 25 January 1935.
5 *Football Focus*, BBC TV, 26 March 1988.
6 C. Critcher, 'Football since the war', in J. Clarke *et al.* (eds), *Working Class Culture* (London, 1979), pp. 161–84.

7 Critcher, 'Football since the war', p. 169.
8 H. Gallacher, *Daily Record*, 4 April 1930.
9 H.F. Moorhouse, 'It's goals that count? Football finance and football subcultures', *Sociology of Sport Journal*, vol. III (1986), pp. 245–60. H.F. Moorhouse, 'Scotland v England: football and popular culture', *International Journal of the History of Sport*, vol. IV (1987), pp. 189–202.
10 *The Scottish Football Historian*, I, 1 (October 1982).
11 *Evening Standard*, 12 April 1924.
12 *Athletic News*, 18 October 1926.
13 *Athletic News*, 5 December 1927.
14 Muir, *Glasgow in 1901*, p. 193.
15 *Daily Record*, 6 April 1925.
16 H.F. Moorhouse, 'Scotland v England: football and popular culture'. H.F. Moorhouse, 'We're off to Wembley!', in D. McCrone and S. Kendrick (eds), *The Making of Scotland: Nation, Culture and Change* (Edinburgh, 1989).
17 *Daily Record*, 9 April 1932.
18 J. Harding, *Alex James: Life of a Football Legend* (London, 1988).
19 G. Souness, *No Half Measures* (London, 1984), p. 15.
20 Minister at memorial service. *Daily Record*, 9 September 1931 and *Glasgow Herald*, 28 August 1981.
21 *Daily Record*, 26 August 1950.
22 'The Celtic story' ran from 2 May to 25 June 1988 with total attendance of 57, 544, being 81 per cent of capacity. Communication from Wildcat Stage Productions.
23 G. Blake, *The Shipbuilders* (London, 1935), pp. 102–6.
24 C. Tully, *Passed To You* (London, 1958), p. 40.
25 J. McGrory, *A Lifetime in Paradise* (Glasgow, 1975), pp. 15, 26.
26 For example, B. Murray, *The Old Firm* (Edinburgh, 1984).
27 B. Murray, *The Glasgow Giants: A 100 Years of the Old Firm* (Edinburgh, 1988).
28 *Scotsport*, Scottish Television, 21 August 1988.
29 G. Munro, *Gold In His Boots*, 1947. Typescript of play in Glasgow University Library.
30 Critcher, 'Football since the war', p. 166.
31 *Athletic News*, 18 July 1927.
32 *Prospectus for Issue of Shares in R.S. McColl Ltd*, 1925, Companies House, Edinburgh.
33 R. McPhail, *Legend: Sixty Years at Ibrox* (Edinburgh, 1988), p. 129.
34 McPhail, *Legend*, p. 36. H. Gallacher, *Sunday Post*, 14 June 1931.
35 D. Thompson, *Half Time: Football and the Cigarette Card* (London, 1987), p. 102.
36 *Daily Record*, 29 December 1930.
37 *Daily Record*, on Wembley international match, 16 April 1934.
38 *Glasgow Herald*, 12 and 15 June 1957.
39 *Only a Game? The Story of Scottish Football*, BBC TV (Scotland), 5 parts, April and May 1986.
40 J. Baxter, *Baxter: The Party's Over* (London, 1984), p. 2.
41 J. Johnstone, *Jinky: Now and Then* (Edinburgh, 1988), p. 109. And see *Fire In My Boots* (London, 1969).
42 A. Jackson, *Athletic News*, 11 August 1930.

43 *The Rangers Historian*, no. 6 (Glasgow, 1988).
44 *Glasgow Herald*, 14 August 1937.

11

Focal heroes:
a Welsh fighting class[1]

Dai Smith

Prize fighting is . . . popular and is carried on in public places for the amusement of the crowd. The contests seem to be arranged in the hotels of the Rhondda, and are very rarely free from personal animosity, in which case the engagements are fought out with brutal savagery, and invariably for a prize of money. . . . How comes it that in a country where Nonconformity is so strong and boasts of its strength, and the Church of England is also active, that so large a proportion of the colliers spend their leisure in questionable forms? Is it because they prefer these brutal pastimes, or are they driven to it because there is a complete absence of any form of light and harmless amusement to be found in the village after the day's work is done? . . . The ministers, as the leaders of thought in the villages and small towns of South Wales, make a great mistake by setting their faces against all forms of popular and innocent amusement. The theatre, the music hall, the social party, the dance, football . . . are rigorously excluded from the Rhondda . . . There will be little change in the morals of the Rhondda until a new crusade is started, a crusade for the promotion of rational recreation.

Rhondda Leader, 4 September 1897

I sat . . . in the bar of the public house where the town rugby team [Pontypridd] gathered strays to play for its second fifteen. Noticing my interest, the landlord pointed out an ancient browning photograph of three world champion boxers, all born and brought up within a five mile radius.
    'Champions of the World, boy!' he told me pointedly; 'not bloody Machynlleth!', attributing all the aspects of parochialism to that remote North Welsh town. This was, of course, the hub of the universe talking and the landlord . . . never let you forget it.

Alun Richards *Days of Absence 1929–1955* (1986)

It would not perhaps surprise the Englishman who wrote that short masterpiece 'The Fight' that no boxer appears in *The Oxford Companion to English Literature*. It would no doubt have delighted William Hazlitt to learn that the same cannot be said of *The Oxford Companion to the*

Literature of Wales. This is not because Welsh writers have moved to the same hypnotic rhythms that have entranced American authors, from Twain to Hemingway and on to Mailer and Joyce Carol Oates, for there is not much more than one, fine boxing novel by Ron Berry (*So Long, Hector Bebb*, 1970), a colourful, historical fiction by Aleander Cordell (*Peerless Jim*, 1984), and occasional stories and poems by Alun Richards and Leslie Norris. The literary pedigree of Welsh fighters is really attested to by the umbilical cords which once made them emblematic of their society. It would be unthinkable to omit the names of Freddie Welsh, Jim Driscoll and Jimmy Wilde from the standard histories of modern Wales. Their region (the south of Wales) became representative of the whole of Wales before 1914 through the national sporting prowess of her rugby teams, her world champion cyclists, and, above all, her boxers; for, if the Edwardian years brought grammar schools, triumphant Welsh XVs and a patina of social cohesion to a booming Welsh world, it was boxing which continued to seize the imagination of its working class. The progress was neither rational nor harmless but it was certainly triumphant.

Tom Thomas from the Rhondda won the first Lonsdale belt for a British middleweight champion in 1909; when he died of pneumonia, aged thirty-one, in 1911 his coffin was carried to the grave by fellow-members of the Labour and Progressive Club. Bill Beynon of Taibach won the British Bantamweight title in 1913; he continued work in the pit where he died under a fall in 1932, aged forty-one. Percy Jones of the Rhondda was the flyweight champion by 1914 and dead, after gassing in the war, by 1922. Countless others, more and less famous than these heroes shared the abrupt origins of their supporters whilst their meteor-like careers were obvious metaphors for a society where sudden death or misfortune, neither rational nor harmless, was all too commonplace. And all of this flashing defiance occurred, and was effectively over, in the first two decades of this century. The young Alun Richards, grammar-school educated and rugby-team trained, was, in the 1940s, already of another world but those sepia-tinted, local champions were, indeed, a focal insight into what his society had been. He knew already, that his absent father had once sparred with his fellow townsman, Freddie Welsh, and, later, would learn that the lightweight champion had once sparred with F. Scott Fitzgerald.[2] Boxers were as much the totems of modern life in 'American Wales'[3] as they were in America itself. 'Leaders of thought' may have wilfully missed the point, then and now, but the deep social significance of boxers for societies-in-flux is one that the history of modern Wales amply affirms even if it is imaginative writers rather than historians who have hitherto grasped the point.

Writers have long been attracted to fighters because of the elemental nature of fighting, the fight as ritual and ceremony or as a pattern which can be broken at any second. Conversely the emphasis on the individual, on the irruption of fate into the ring, or the uneasy concept of fighting as a sport when it is really no such thing, all this presents the *social* historian of boxing with problems not generally encountered in description and analysis of team or representative sports, of structured games, of play that serves to bond performer and audience. The boxer stands alone. His relationship to his particular society is as complex as the spectator's role is ambivalent. The risk of injury may be transmuted through a network of skill and laws until phrases like 'the noble art of self-defence' and 'the sweet science of bruising' serve as advertising copy for the administrators and admirers but the raw edge of boxing can never be completely overcome since it is this which lies at the heart of its attraction.

It was this willingness to step outside the safety of socially acceptable behaviour which, paradoxically, made boxing *the* working-class recreational activity in industrial Wales. At its highest level it became the most envied attainment. The relationship of the working class to its fighting class is, then, the first point of entry for the social historian intent on elucidating its appeal. No matter how involved other social groups may have been in staking, organising, betting on, watching, and even incorporating fighters into a wider ethos it was from *within* the working class that the energies of the conflict were to be found. Much of the emblematic character of boxing is, therefore, dependent upon the complex tension in any society or nation between the proletariat and its socialising framework. *Some* images of sport became useful or enjoy a common currency. *Others* maintain a distance which derives from their alien nature.

The intriguing fascination of rugby football within Wales is because of its uniting of such disparate factors of class and nationality to make a game universally applauded by the Welsh. 1935 was a year deeply marked by strikes, riots and demonstrations within the South Wales coalfield yet in December of that year, surveying the colliers, steelworkers, policemen, teachers and varsity men who comprised the Welsh fifteen which beat the All Blacks of New Zealand by one point, the national newspaper *Western Mail* could, truthfully, reflect:

Wales is proud of this victory: she is particularly proud of the fact that Welsh peers and Welsh labourers – with all the intervening stratas of society – were united in acclaiming and cheering the Welsh team. It was . . . a victory for Wales in a sense that 'probably' is impossible in any other sphere.[4]

Clerical denunciation of rugby had long since been muted in Wales. Boxing, however, even in the mid 1930s could still attract a withering double shotgun blast from those self-appointed keepers of the Celtic flame – nonconformist ministers and university professors. One of the latter, Professor W.J. Gruffydd, of the Welsh Department of the University College of South Wales and Monmouthshire, snarled in Welsh:

the itch to compete is such a dominating feature in Welsh social life. I remember times in the history of the nation when the pulpit and the eisteddfod gave it great scope – who was the best preacher, who had won the chair, what choir had won, which of the two lawyers was going to win the election. Today [1937] . . . in Glamorgan at least – what is of over-riding significance for us as Welshmen are the prospects of Jack Petersen or Tommy Farr, or some other Englishman born in Wales to overcome with his fists an Englishman born in England or a black man from America.[5]

Tommy Farr was actually an Irishman born in Wales, in 1914 in mid Rhondda. The Rev. Gwilym Davies, a cultural luminary in early twentieth century Wales, acknowledged Farr's Welshness and his honesty in admitting his mercenary motivation, but little else. Years ago, he informed the *Western Mail*, a few days before Farr fought Joe Louis in August 1937, it would have been unthinkable for a white to face a black man for a championship but:

Today, such has been the swing back to the primitive that the staging of a world contest is regarded as of such international importance that the BBC looks upon it as a 'national emergency'. . . . The fact that Tommy Farr, a Welshman, happens to be 'the White Hope' does not alter the principle. Nor indeed does it minimise the hideousness of the whole affair. . . . the glory is in the cash. The shame is in the lowering of the public taste that 'it revels' in commercialised brutality between black and white on a scale hitherto unknown.[6]

The Rev. Davies was singing solo where once the churches and civic leaders had been able to orchestrate a chorus of disapproval. Besides it was not 'the lowering of public taste' that was the real issue but the public display and approval of it. What gave Farr's encounter with Joe Louis in New York its contemporary resonance and, subsequently, such legendary appeal in Wales was a concatenation of sporting tradition, social circumstance and popular culture. If Tommy Farr, battered yet unbowed after fifteen rounds against one of the greatest heavyweights ever, had *not* lost on points the Welsh would have had to invent the defeat. By losing Farr remained, in a symbolic sense, integrated in his community. By surviving with such conspicuous courage he embodied the stricken coalfield. He could date film stars, cut records, and wine and dine at places only glimpsed on the cinema screen without this brush with glamour endangering any popularity. After all he was making inaccessible dreams tangible. They, too, had worked in the mines, skivvied in hotels, walked to London with holes in their shoes, sought work in the trading estate of Slough, and even scrapped in fairground boxing booths. Farr's unexpected rise to fame in 1936 and 1937 was his distinguishing feature. He remained identifiable. What he knew, as he became the first British heavyweight to challenge convincingly for a heavyweight title, and the last to do well, for decades either side of 1937, was that the fight's outcome was less important than his attitude and the reflection of that in his performance.

The kind of qualities expected of Farr were more those associated with a mission of mercy than a commercial prize fight. The point is that he reciprocated. His brother, Dick, sent a cablegram to be read by Tommy on entering the ring: 'We trust you Tommy. Win or lose our faith in you remains unshaken.'

In Court Street, Clydach Vale where he was born the homes were festooned with flags and streamers. The roving reporter from Cardiff, intent on describing the 'elaborate arrangements . . . for jollification', instead noted that an old lady 'reiterated a statement often made during the past few days – "Tommy has the spirit, we have hope" '. Such emotional investment in a boxer was, if anything, intensified by the postponement of the fight, at New York's Polo Grounds, because of heavy rain. In Tonypandy the flags – Red Dragons and Union Jacks – and the photographs in every window and the life-size cardboard cut-out of Farr stayed in place. Those with radio sets opened up their houses. Others crowded to listen to the transatlantic crackle in assembly halls up and down the valley. Fireworks, beacons and impromptu bands waited in readiness. The streets were crowded into the early hours of the morning. Some miners were allowed out early from the night shift of the Cambrian Colliery where Farr had once worked: 'Begrimed and smiling

A Welsh fighting class

through the coal dust, which made each face look blacker even than that of Joe Louis, they darted from the cage . . . and clattered down the streets, eagerly discussing the chances of their former workmate.'

Those who stayed at work underground heard snippets of the fight's progress relayed through the galleries by word of mouth. Those who actually listened did so in alternate bouts of tense, hushed silence and paroxysms of excited cheering. Five thousand people, many women with babies in their arms, stood outside the Assembly Hall at Clydach Vale; just as they would have done for news of a pit disaster: 'When at the end of the last round – the round in which Farr, according to the commentary did so well – it was announced that Louis had won, there were groans and hisses and boos from many in the crowd, but after this disappointment they joined together in singing *Land of My Fathers*.'

The fighter was more in tune with those singers than the bemused newspaperman who wrote the name of the Welsh national anthem in English. It was reassurance they required, and received, from Farr. Before the contest *he* had sent a cable: 'Please assure all they have genuine trier. Have backed myself. . . .. Will not let them down.' And, immediately afterwards, on the air there was no braggadocio or disappointment in his voice only the familial tone of 'a genuine trier' uniting self and community: 'Hello Tonypandy. . . . I done my best. . . . We, I, showed 'em I got plenty of guts. You know, the old Tommy Farr of old.'[8]

Tommy Farr had laid down a template. Other Welsh boxers would adhere to the pattern in the decades to follow. Gallant, or unfortunate or even doomed challengers whose progress was as littered with sporting clichés as South Wales was burdened with the stereotypes imposed on it by the 1930s. Even Howard Winstone's brief tenure of a world title in the 1960s seemed little more than a consolation prize. Farr had become the epitome of the hungry fighter. The legend outlasted the pub and gym fighters of the inter-war years to make boxing an outcrop of the experience of unemployment and a hard, industrial society. The reality was that Farr, himself, was at a pivotal stage in the relationship of the fighting class to the working class in South Wales. He was more the heir to a declining tradition than the begetter of a new one. When he entered the ring on that starry night over fifty years ago he wore 'a yellow dressing gown with the Welsh Dragon emblazoned on the back'. It had been worn in New York before – 'by another great Welsh fighter, Freddie Welsh'.[9] Farr's homage was real but it was not, ever, the gallantry of defeat that Freddie Welsh's career symbolised but rather the arrogant glitter of expected success.

The image of boxing by the mid 1930s was an amalgam of virtuous characteristics now fit for public consumption if not for universal imitation. Wales' national newspaper in an editorial eulogy to Farr's 'skill and courage, unfailing pluck and resource, in a clean fight . . . never . . . marred by the faintest suspicion of a foul' hastened to assert that 'not only Tonypandy but all Britain has every reason to be proud of his achievement'.[10] Yet, fourteen years earlier, in 1923, when Jimmy Wilde, then aged thirty-one and Britain's only world title holder, had been knocked out in the seventh round in New York, the report was a bare, uncommunicative paragraph. Wilde was, in 1923, an unhappy reminder of the combination of popular culture and political unrest which had made South Wales so zestful and unstable a region for the first two decades of this century. The world champions produced then could be patronised by grandees but were, in a strict sense, as uncontrollable as their groundling supporters. Farr's crouching pugnaciousness was the ferocity of a cornered yet cunning animal; Jimmy Wilde, at half his weight, was all style, speed and confidence. Those were not the trinity the Welsh working class were required to possess or applaud by the end of the 1930s. The day after Farr's epic encounter the *Western Mail* printed a cartoon entitled *The Doctor's Dilemma*. The smiling, frock-coated doctor was a caricature of the Minister of Labour, Ernest Brown, then on a visit to South Wales. News pictures showed him sun-tanned and plump after a holiday. In the cartoon he stands, amused but puzzled over the seated, shirtless figure of a pasty-faced, emaciated middle-aged man on whose arms body and chest are tattooed the names of Farr's opponents, two boxing figures called Tommy and a grizzled head of the hero himself. The legend underneath it all read: 'What the Minister of Labour may expect to find in the course of his examination of the unemployment conditions in Wales.'

If boxing could be so purposefully used at the end of the 1930s, it still remained difficult to *absorb* earlier phases of its history. Acute readers of the contemporary press might have drawn this conclusion after reading a local obituary notice in 1938.[11] The dead man was one George Jones, ex-collier from the Cynon Valley, aged sixty-seven. His more familiar name was 'Georgie Punch', a nickname attributed to a fearsome right hand which he had wielded effectively in two hundred and fifty contests. He had been an early beneficiary of the late Victorian cult of muscular Christianity since it was an Anglican curate at St Margaret's Church, Aberaman, who had introduced the choir-boy to 'the noble art'. He proceeded, via a body-building trade as blacksmith's striker, to graduate in the late 1880s as a formidable mountain-fighter at a time when the mountainous plateaux between Merthyr and Aberdare and the Rhondda, those epicentres of the iron and coal industries of Victorian Wales, were covered with so-called 'bloody spots' where local champions and their numerous backers slugged it out, bare-knuckled and often ill-matched, for round after round. A round ended when exhaustion intervened. Stake money, side bets and honour were at issue. The fights were, by the 1880s, illegal, and occasionally raided by the police. They competed, by the turn of the century, with the travelling booths of semi-professionals who moved, regularly, with and without the accompaniement of fairs all over the coalfield. George Jones fought in the booths as, later, did Jim Driscoll of Cardiff, Jimmy Wilde and Tommy Farr, but Georgie Punch's fighting itinerary was chiefly in this twilight world of fights not designed for press or publicity.

The latter could not always be avoided. One of Punch's contemporaries 'Young' Dai Rees was fatally injured by falling and hitting his head in an arranged fight at the old slaughter house in Aberdare. The other fighter involved, Twm Edwards, was arrested and later acquitted of manslaughter. Twm went on to win money against professionals in Jack Scarrot's booth at the famous Neath Fair. His brother, Wil, moved from Aberaman pit to Ruskin College and successfully moved, in 1917, at the South Wales Miners' rules conference in Cardiff, that the Federation's second object should be 'the abolition of capitalism'.[12] If capitalism staggered on into the 1930s, so did mountain-fighting or, at least, a whiff of it. Certainly Georgie Punch was still challenging an old grudge opponent from the Rhondda for £100 a side with 'the knucks' when he was sixty-four, and, failing to elicit a response, widened it to take in *any* sixty-five year-old man in the country under nine stones. There was no response. Clearly his reputation preceded him: such encounters as thirty-nine rounds and seventy-two rounds at the Finger Post Quarry or even over four at the Horse and Crown, Pontypridd or maybe his victory over fourteen rounds in the old 'Bonky', Fforchneol Field, Cwmaman with 4-oz gloves with the fingers cut off, were not forgotten. Nor were the names of the Aberdare champion Dai St John or Tom 'The Bum' James, Ezer Thomas or 'Rothwell the Fighting Barber'.[13] Gloved contests and Queensberry rules with timed rounds did not make these parochial battles anachronistic in South Wales, but an insatiable demand for spectacle as a product that could be consumed by a wider public in an accessible way did soon provide the alternative of bouts staged in pavilions and theatres.

The opposition was stern and multi-faceted. The geography could be as confusing as the simultaneous existence of mass chapel attendance and equally popular pursuits. The *Aberdare Times* in 1885:

> A more disgusting thing than prize fighting it is hardly possible to conceive. . . . That it should happen in our midst is an outrage to decency, and the brutes who take part in it . . . should be punished severely. We cannot look upon such people as anything better than beasts. One would think, by reading of such things that we were in some savage country, and not in civilised England.[14]

Twenty-three years later, and despite the manslaughter case in between, the Trecynon Nonconformist League was demanding the 'suppression of pugilism'.[15] Neither England nor civilisation had yet encroached upon Aberdare. Nor, it seems, had it reached Cardiff in 1910 when Jim Driscoll's return from a triumphant tour of America where he had established himself, in fact if not in title, as the world's best featherweight, was rapturously greeted by a crowd which thronged the city streets from station to hotel. At the end of that year the fight-mania reached fever pitch when a long-awaited bout between Driscoll and Freddie Welsh was arranged in Cardiff. The fight proceeded to a backdrop of one petition to the Lord Mayor from Cardiff citizens, headed by the Bishop of Llandaff and the President of the Cardiff Free Church Council, which protested 'that it would have a degrading effect upon the people' and, another, from local Wesleyans demanding that steps be taken 'to prevent such exhibitions in future'.[16]

Jimmy Wilde was then eighteen and set to work for one more year underground in the pits at Ferndale. He was already fighting in the booths but his early training came from the man with whom he worked underground, a mountain-fighter called Dai Davies. They sparred in food breaks and in the crowded bedroom of Dai Davies' house. All was done semi-secretly because Dai's wife was a strict chapel-goer and strongly disapproved of fighting as did his daughter, 'Lisbeth, whom Wilde courted and married when she was sixteen and he was eighteen. His determination to box almost wrecked their young marriage. What saved it was a strike which 'finally healed the breach':

> Not only was the money I had saved out of fighting supplying us with food where other families were lacking it, but I was able to earn more money when 'off work' than I had during full time at the pit.[17]

By then, 1911–12, Freddie Welsh at lightweight, Jim Driscoll at featherweight and Tom Thomas of the Rhondda at middleweight had all won national fame by claiming the belts that Lord Lonsdale presented for championship fights at Covent Garden's National Sporting Club. Wilde himself would become British and European flyweight champion and Lonsdale belt holder by beating Tancy Lee there in 1916. The club provided a dinner-jacketed seal of approval for certain fighters. Nothing could have been further from the boxing cradles in which those men had been raised. Jimmy Wilde, more than anyone, seems to have been bedazzled by the acceptance offered by high society. In 1921, after much chicanery behind the scenes, he still insisted on fighting the great American bantamweight, Pete Herman, rather than disappoint the Prince of Wales who was in the audience. He was soundly beaten. Wilde's autobiography, written in 1938 by a ghostwriter so inept that he makes Jimmy Wilde sound like Noel Coward, ends with Wilde, already semi-destitute, proudly chatting with the same prince at a charity function in South Wales.

Yet the bathos of incorporation can be overdone. The popularity of the pre-1920 champions from Wales depended more on their incomparable style than on rooted tradition and as much on their overall carelessness in life as on their risks within the ring. Tommy Farr made £36,000 out of the Joe Louis fight alone, and, as he put it himself, stored his money like a squirrel does his nuts. Wilde, Welsh and Driscoll all died in relative poverty.

Jimmy Wilde lived on until 1969. The money he had made, £70,000 on retirement was considerable for its time, had been dissipated by the late 1920s in hare-brained investments in London musicals, Welsh cinemas and valley houses and a starting-price business that went wrong. He readily boxed in 1921 in a charity exhibition for the miners then locked out and five years after Pancho Villa ended his reign with a foul blow and another beating in New York, he could be found acting as referee in another charity show to raise money for a once-promising Merthyr bantamweight who'd been accidentally blinded when sparring with Driscoll. The bantamweight's name was Billy Eynon. He had been army and navy champion in 1916 when he fought in a natural bowl at Salonika before some two hundred thousand service men. From the early 1920s one-eyed Billy Eynon fought to raise money for the soup kitchens now required by the two hundred and fifty thousand miners and their families in South Wales.[18] It was an effortless change of direction. Frank Moody, who had been a dazzling success in the States, returned to Pontypridd in the mid 1920s to a hero's welcome and, like the hero he was, boxed for nothing in 1932 to raise funds for the local cottage hospital. The town clerk, surveying the economic ruin of his town, claimed that the mines would re-open and prosperity soon return. The insistent juxtaposition he added was 'Freddie Welsh's Pontypridd is still the capital of Welsh boxing'.[19]

Charity was *expected* of these men. None gave more freely than Jim Driscoll who actually refused a return bout in 1910 with the world featherweight champion, Abe Attell – whom he had decisively beaten in an earlier 'No Decision' contest – because he had promised to box in a charity function for Nazareth House, the Catholic orphanage in his native Cardiff, and for which he worked steadily in the early 1920s. A picture of 'Our Jim' still hangs there. Letters to the press to this day testify to the human impact of the man. His funeral cortege in January 1925 was followed through the streets to the Catholic cemetery at Cathays by over a hundred thousand people. In a sense they mourned themselves because no one would be able to act in South Wales with the dangerous freedom of a Driscoll for decades to come. He was forty-five when he died of pneumonia: toothless, greying, tortured by the stomach ulcers he had incurred in keeping his weight below nine stone, and quite impoverished. His legacy as a boxer was just as useless and just as precious to the South Wales he left.

The last major fight he had was against Charles Ledoux, aged twenty-seven. The year was 1919, and Driscoll, already in ill-health, was thirty-nine. The fight was made, at weight, 8 stone 12 lb, over twenty rounds. Driscoll out-boxed, out-thought and bamboozled Ledoux for fourteen rounds. Then he ran out of steam. Ledoux caught him and punched him at will. Photographs show an emaciated Driscoll, face drawn and bewildered, but his gloves up staggering to the ring's centre for the sixteenth round while Ledoux, anxious and arms outstretched, moves towards him, aware, as was everyone other than Jim, that his corner had thrown in the towel. In Driscoll's case survival was not the issue, though he was only stopped this once in his career. He was an artist inside the ropes not an honest journeyman. Those who had seen him knew they had been part of a golden age when boxing not only 'took form' but was also assessed aesthetically.[20]

Jim Driscoll had been born in Newtown, Cardiff's Irish community, in 1880 into a large family.[21] He worked as a printer's devil but found that he preferred fighting with old newspapers wrapped around his hands. He was already a seasoned booth fighter when the gentlemen of the National Sporting Club took him up in 1903. His upright stance and classical left lead then wrote him into the annals of boxing fame: to British and European championships and world renown. Driscoll's life to 1914 had gone hand-in-glove with the development of South Wales from a raw, frontier industrial society to one of the focal points of a coal-based British Empire. His own city had swollen in size three-fold in his own lifetime. It had been the second fastest-growing city in Britain for two decades. The population of Wales had rocketed from one-and-a-half million in 1871 to two-and-a-half million by 1911. Two out of every three people in Wales lived in the industrial southern belt by 1914. Driscoll saw from 1890 to 1910 shanty-town Cardiff build merchant houses, mercantile banks, imitation Venetian-palazzos, baroque French hotels and elaborately embellished arcades. To the north the coal valleys were sucking in even more people to work in pits whose produce made Cardiff the greatest coal-exporting port the world had ever seen.

This was a confident, self-aggrandising world; in some ways the last burst of the British industrial revolution. Only here industrialisation, of a basic kind, was accompanied by the consumer and spectator society made available in Britain, on a wide scale, from the late nineteenth century. Music hall, sheet music, rugby and soccer, coffee shops, grandiose public halls, ready-made clothes and cheaper travel were the other side of the same coin on which was written high wages, intermittent employment, strikes, collective politics, and trade unions. It was a society of sudden shifts of individual and communal fortune which moved through much that was novel and uncertain, and enticing.

Between the 1890s and 1910 the population of Wales grew at a rate only exceeded, in percentage terms, by the United States. The Rhondda novelist Gwyn Thomas (born in 1913 of a family whose grandfather had re-migrated from America to South Wales) wrote that in school he sat next to the sons and daughters of Somerset, Devon, Gloucester, Scotland, and Ireland, Yorkshire and London. The Rhondda, he asserted, was a part of America that hadn't got to the boat. Jim Driscoll, of course, certainly caught it. He outclassed all the American featherweights he met in the so-called 'no decision' contests which state laws about boxing enforced in the USA, i.e. only a knock-out could take a title away. Bets were decided by newspaper comment, decidedly hard for a British boxer to influence favourably. It was not hard for Driscoll. The *New York World*'s sportswriter, after seeing Driscoll turn Johnny Marto inside-out, told his readers that Driscoll was the kind of fighter who *deserved* to have refreshing champagne poured over his locks – a common practice between rounds then – because, he wrote, Driscoll went faster than anything he'd ever seen other than a $20 bill. When he returned he was, understandably called by the press 'Prince of Wales' but the nickname that stuck to him, 'Peerless Jim' was handed out in New York by Bat Masterson, the gun-toting deputy of Wyatt Earp who'd turned sportswriter.

Driscoll, however, did not *need* American approbation. For an illusory moment both he, *and* his world, *were* the significant other. He did not chase Abe Attell for his title in the way that Benny Leonard would pursue and, finally, knock out Freddie Welsh in a 'no decision' contest that went wrong for Welsh in 1917. That, too, was in Manhattan where Benjamin Leiner was a 'part' in Irving Howe's words 'of that trying on of roles, that delight in assuming new identities, which Jews began to experience after emigration from eastern Europe. Benny Leonard said Howe was proving that a Jew could be the champion lightweight boxer.'[22] 'Peerless Jim' from Cardiff's 'Little Ireland' became the 'Prince of Wales' *in* 'American Wales'. That was identity enough. And fame. In the summer of 1912 after he knocked out a formidable French fighter, Jean Poesy, in round twelve, *Boxing* magazine's reporter crowed:

> One has seen Jim the Master in so many dressing-rooms noisy with laughter of the victorious that to-night was no change. It was the same old merry Driscoll with a laugh for everybody. . . . All the excited Welshmen and Irishmen who crowded the room were laughing and chattering at the same time, and the most merry of all was, as usual, James Driscoll.[23]

A year later, already retired and blown up, he returns to London and toys with the idea of a scrap for 'a record purse' with Kid Lewis:

Jim arrived in town – well, perhaps not exactly bearded like the pard, but anyway wearing a pair of mustachios which any pirate might envy. At the first assault . . . Jim asserted that he was through with the game, that he scaled 11 stone if he scaled an ounce, and that the time had arrived when the other boys might well be allowed a fair chance . . . [yet] . . . the Peerless Prince [was convinced] . . . that life has few joys to offer which can compare with those of the magic square. He was also incidentally reminded that it has few martyrdoms so dire and tragic as those of the training camp to a man who has sampled the bright lights of Broadway, Piccadilly or St Mary Street – for at all events more years than he cares to count.[24]

Driscoll might strut abroad but his true stage was at home. For a time the local had become universal and St Mary Street Cardiff, Broadway New York. Within two decades in South Wales there would only be the memory of a style and the sentimental fixative of a world glued into dyspeptic nostalgia. The politics of Wales would seek collective exits, reforming and pragmatic, or revolutionary and idealistic, but the popular culture that had been vibrant and exciting would lurch into a communal necrophilia of stage Welshness or stutter towards a rootless imitation. It is for this reason that *the most* focal of individual boxing heroes is, paradoxically, the one who took the extremes of American Wales to one of its logical conclusions.

Freddie Welsh was an athlete whose driven personality caused him, literally, to re-make and re-name himself. He became a totem of that modernity which his fostering society craved, and almost attained. If to be modern is constantly to give up that which you become then Freddie Welsh lived on the knife-edge of that quintessential modern experience. The fact that it was through boxing that his cubist personality was revealed to others only underlines the importance of understanding such appeal to those Welsh who were not, yet, in the early 1900s, socialised by schooling or limited by the boundaries of tradition. Tommy Farr inherited the cumbersome paraphernalia of a made world. Freddie Welsh drew his own maps. Maybe it was the splintering of any assured personal identity that makes him so profoundly reflective of an unsure, cocksure, fragmented Welsh identity.

He was born in Pontypridd in 1886 on the fringe of the coalfield.[25] It was a new town in a new world even if what was to become the Welsh National anthem by the twentieth century had been composed there thirty years before his birth. The town had been called Newbridge. *His* real name was Frederick Hall Thomas. His father was fairly well-to-do, an auctioneer and a member of families who farmed in and around the market town *before* it became a commercial and rail hub for the surrounding, mushrooming colliery townships. His mother's name was Fannie Brahma perhaps, herself, one of the in-migrants to booming South Wales. Frederick was sent away to school in Bristol. This was no hungry collier boy even if he did become the idol of those who were, like Jimmy Wilde. The boy's father died. His mother remarried and Freddie's home was now the Bridge Inn, Pontypridd. An aunt kept the Bunch of Grapes. Maybe he was now caught up, to an extent, with the sporting world of Pontypridd and even the likes of Georgie Punch. There's no evidence that he did likewise and, certainly, when he ran away aged sixteen he left no reputation behind. He went to Canada. He travelled the rails, like Hemingway's Nick Adams in that early boxing story. 'The Battler', until he reached Philadelphia. Maybe he came via Scranton where, in the USA's thirty-seventh largest city,[26] the largest transatlantic contingent of the Welsh had settled to work the mines, damn the Irish and join the Republican Party. He became interested in physical culture and combined it with boxing. It was now that he left his name behind, and, in America, became Freddie Welsh. He practised assiduously. His self-confidence, his self-esteem almost, were fanatical. It was time to go home. It was there that *he* had to prove himself first.

Freddie Welsh was, at first, treated with some contempt in his home town. He was, in 1907, aged twenty introduced to a Cardiff manager, Harry Marks, who later recalled how: 'Welsh on our first introduction was a spectacle indeed. Attired in a large black sombrero hat with a long, clerical-looking coat, he seemed a typical foreigner. I took him in hand, however, and I soon found that he was full of British grit.'[27]

As virtually an unknown, Welsh made a successful debut at the National Sporting Club. This was the gentleman turned pro with a vengeance, and Eugene Corri, a famous referee who handled Welsh's title victory against the American Willie Ritchie in London in 1914, remembered him as a 'dandy-loking Welshman . . . an ardent student of John Ruskin . . . all his leisure was spent in reading the best English authors'.[28] Neither this, nor his Americanised accent nor, even less, his American style of fighting endeared him to his home town patrons. In Pontypridd, they were merely aggravated when on 17 April 1907 he knocked out, all on the same day, Evan Evans in one round, Charlie Weber in two and, with a symmetry he made his hallmark, Gomer Morgan in three. In September the gentlemen of the town put up a purse privately arranged (and this two years after Evans Roberts' religious revival, allegedly the apogee of nonconformist Wales) and Welsh fought Joe White, Canadian-born but resident in Cardiff and a rated welterweight, for the purse and £100 stakes a side. A loft in a warehouse was provided by a local industrialist for a select, invited audience: 'there was no secret about the fact that, although in his native town, South Wales sportsmen were longingly hoping that in White they had found one "to burst the bubble that was Freddie Welsh" '.

Freddie had aped everything American as a result of his sojourn 'over the ditch': in manner and speech; in fact, in every way he had become truly Yankee. His cockiness and his methods, revolutionary in their conception, had rather offended the conservative susceptibilities of the 'sports' of Pontypridd, and they did not conceal their hope that he would get a lacing. White was a tall, lean lad with a long reach and an expert in ringcraft and generalship – and having most of his fights in America it would appear as if Freddie would be "hoist with his own petard".[29]

Welsh knocked him out in the sixteenth. From then on the conservative 'sports' were neither here nor there. He *packed* crowds in. In 1909 at Mountain Ash Pavilion some fifteen thousand – the biggest fight crowd assembled to that date in Wales – he beat the Frenchman Henri Piet. Welsh used 'booster techniques' familiar in the States. He charged for his sparring sessions. He took a percentage of the gate. His defence was immaculate but his speciality was infighting and chopping blows on to his opponents' kidneys. When he beat Young Joseph in this way the kidney punch was made illegal by the National Sporting Club. He was British lightweight champion by 1910 and pursued Willie Ritchie across Canada and America until given a chance to challenge him for the world crown. That was in 1914 when Freddie enticed Ritchie into fighting by receiving, himself, no more than his training expenses.

His ring career had run on parallel lines to that of Driscoll. It was inevitable that they meet. The two had become friendly, dandies-about-town, Cardiff town; Welsh lived with and, in 1913, married a waitress he'd earlier met in a Cardiff restaurant. A rare surviving photograph shows Driscoll and Welsh together, straw-boatered, bespoke suited, watch fobbed and grinning. It seems they had no wish to fight each other. The prospect for others was tantalising. Over months, in 1910, a whispering campaign and wrangles over money turned the clash into a grudge match. The parallel lines were being forced to converge. The result was a fight at a time and a venue and with consequences richly symbolic. Alexander Cordell in his colourful novel *Peerless Jim* rightly makes subtle use of it as a centre piece. It was the real fight of the century so far as Wales is concerned. After it the lines diverged.

Welsh and Driscoll met at the American Roller rink in Cardiff for a purse of £2,500 on 20 December 1910. Twelve miles away troops were stationed in Pontypridd to guard the magistrate's court where the leaders of the Cambrian coal strike were being tried for their part in the Tonypandy riots the previous month. Observers commented that the atmosphere was subdued but there was electric undercurrent amongst the 10,000 assembled:

> The waiting moments were beguiled by a band which played national tunes; but, whereas Rugby crowds amuse themselves, in similar circumstances by bursting into song, there was no vocalism last night, and for once even the familar *Land of My Fathers* failed to inspire the musical soul of the Principality.[30]

As for the fight, Welsh was quicker and cleverer than many had suspected. He also enraged Driscoll by holding, boring and kidney punching. Driscoll slowly forced his way back into the contest where the two styles were not proving harmonious when, in the tenth round of the twenty rounds scheduled, to the dislike of contemporaries but the delight of the historian in need of an image, Driscoll, goaded beyond sense, butted Welsh under his chin and across the ring, over and over. The fight was immediately awarded to Welsh on a foul.

Freddie Welsh was the first to bring a legitimated world championship back to Wales. When he did so, – in July 1914 at Olympia before thousands of his fellow countrymen, both miners and mineowners – he immediately returned for a triumphal procession in the valleys of South Wales. His message was patriotic achievement, his meaning was global conquest:

> When I think of the size of . . . our little country, and then think again how small that portion of it is that we call South Wales, I am lost in wonderment and filled with pride at the recollection of the things that have been done by the men of our race. . . .
> Boxing is . . . the sport which fits in with the Welsh temperament. It

calls for quick thinking, for ready hands, and nimble feet . . . hardy bodies and high courage. I know that Welshmen have all of these things. I am looking forward to the time when we shall hold a 'straight-flush from fly to heavy of British boxing championships. Even then the limits of ambition will not have been reached for there will be the world's titles to strive for'.[31]

The champion promptly left for America. A short time before Benny Leonard deprived him of that crown in New York City, Welsh had written to the Governor of New York to offer his services in running boxing shows 'at which I will meet contenders for my title and turn the receipts . . . over to a fund to equip a [sportsmen's] regiment' for overseas service. He added:

> If the regiment is organised I am, of course, ready to serve in any capacity. The United States is my adopted country. I have lived here for 15 years; my wife and two children are American, and I feel that the entrance of America into the war is the call to arms for every man who, like myself, has been given an opportunity to earn a living in this great country.[32]

The Americanisation of Freddie, and his own 'late' entry into the fray, was reported sardonically by the Welsh Press. His popular support remained undiminished.

Nevertheless, Freddie Welsh had become the focal 'American' which the localised Jim Driscoll could not be. Scott Fitzgerald, in 1926, caught the essence of this phenomenon, and its doomed solipsistic heroism, when he created the late Victorian, James Gatz who becomes Jay Gatsby of the American century by a regimen of fanatical self-improvement through physical exercise and study. All given reality by fate:

> James Gatz [of north Dakota] – that was really, or at least legally, his name. He had changed it at the age of 17 and at the specific moment that witnessed the beginning of his career . . . I suppose he'd had the name ready for a long time even then. His parents were . . . unsuccessful . . . his imagination had never really accepted them as his parents at all. The truth was that Jay Gatsby of . . . Long Island, sprang from his Platonic conception of himself. . . . So he invented just the sort of Jay Gatsby that a 17 year old boy would be likely to invent, and to this conception he was faithful to the end.[33]

Fitzgerald's friend, the sports journalist and short-story writer, Ring Lardner, who knew Welsh well and placed references to him in his work, taught the great novelist to see the lineaments of modernity in physical competition and in its mass consumption. The connection is as teasingly tenuous in the 'real' world as it is insistently tenable for all who would truly imagine it. The boxer who once read, and mixed with, the best authors *may* have read Fitzgerald's masterpiece before he died, aged forty-one, in a downtown New York hotel room in 1927 and he *may*, indeed, have once requested that his ashes be scattered over Broadway, but there can be no imaginative doubt that he really meant Broadway, Pontypridd.

Notes

1 I should like to thank the following for invaluable advice, and some specific information: Harold Alderman (boxing historian extraordinaire); Mike and Kitty Flynn for telling me about Jim Driscoll and serving some wonderful beer which Alan Bush helped to drink; Neil Evans, Chris Williams, Alun Richards, and Eddie Thomas.
2 See D.S. Lister (former British Amateur Heavyweight Champion), *How to Box* (London, 1952), who recalled how E.M. Richards, his 'old opponent' had learned his devastating left-hook from Freddie Welsh; this, and other information, from Welsh's relative, Alun Richards.
3 The phrase was applied to South Wales in the early 1920s by Alfred Zimmern in *My Impressions of Wales* (1921).
4 See David Smith and Gareth Williams, *Fields of Praise* (Cardiff, 1980), p. 292.
5 W.J. Gruffydd, *The Years of the Locust*, in translation (Llandysul, 1976), p. 175.
6 Letter in *Western Mail*, 28 August 1937.
7 See the *Western Mail*, 25 August and for the preceding quotes, *ibid.*, 27 and 31 August 1937.
8 Recording of Farr in author's possession.
9 *Western Mail*, 31 August 1937.
10 *Ibid.*, 1 September 1937.
11 *Glamorgan County Times*, 28 May 1938.
12 W.J. Edwards, *From the Valley I Came* (London, 1956), p. 163.
13 *Glamorgan County Times*, 28 May 1938.
14 *Aberdare Times*, 26 December 1885.
15 This and the preceding reference are from Martin Barclay 'Class and community: Aberdare 1880-1920', unpublished MA thesis, University of Wales, Cardiff, 1985.
16 *Western Mail*, 21 December 1910.
17 J. Wilde, *Fighting Was My Business* (London, 1938), pp. 30, 44.
18 Interview with my father's late friend, Billy Eynon of Merthyr.
19 From the programme in possession of Glen Moody (one of the 'fighting Moody brothers' of Pontypridd).
20 E. Michael, 'Famous boxers under the searchlight', in *Welsh Boxing Board of Control Handbook* (1931).

21 Information on Driscoll has been assembled from my reading of the contemporary press and various boxing guides.
22 I. Howe, *The Immigrant Jews of New York* (London, 1976), p. 473.
23 *Boxing*, 8 June 1912.
24 *Ibid.*, 29 November 1913.
25 Information on Freddie Welsh from contemporary press and guides.
26 See W.D. Jones, 'Wales and America: Scranton and the Welsh', unpublished PhD thesis, University of Wales, Cardiff, 1988.
27 *Western Mail*, 29 July 1927.
28 Eugene Corri, *Gloves and the Man* (London, 1927).
29 WBBC Handbook, 1931.
30 *Western Mail*, 21 December 1910.
31 *South Wales Daily News*, 13 July 1914.
32 The letter, obviously made public, was reported in the *Glamorgan Free Press*, 10 May 1917. Freddie Welsh became an American citizen and served, as a captain, in a rehabilitation hospital in Washington, DC.
33 Scott Fitzgerald, *The Great Gatsby* (London, 1963), pp. 104–5.

Index